USING HEALTH ᴇᴄᴏɴᴏᴍɪᴄs
IN HEALTH SERVɪᴄᴇs

STATE OF HEALTH SERIES

Edited by Chris Ham, Professor of Health Policy and
Management at the University of Birmingham and Director of the
Strategy Unit at the Department of Health

Current and forthcoming titles

Primary Care
Noel Boaden
The Global Challenge of Health Care Rationing
Angela Coulter and Chris Ham (eds)
Health Care Reform
Chris Ham (ed.)
Managing Scarcity
Rudolf Klein, Patricia Day and Sharon Redmayne
The Purchasing of Health Care by Primary Care Organizations
Nicholas Mays, Sally Wyke, Gill Malbon and Nick Goodwin (eds)
Using Health Economics in Health Services
Ruth McDonald
Evaluating the NHS
Martin A. Powell
Managed Health Care
Ray Robinson and Andrea Steiner
Demanding Patients?
Anne Rogers, Karen Hassell and Gerry Nicolaas
The Incompetent Doctor
Marilynn M. Rosenthal
Planned Markets and Public Competition
Richard B. Saltman and Casten von Otter
Implementing Planned Markets in Health Care
Richard B. Saltman and Casten von Otter
Critical Challenges for Health Care Reform in Europe
Richard B. Saltman, Josep Figueras and Constantino Sakellarides (eds)
Public and Private Roles in Health Care Systems
Claudia Scott
Accreditation
Ellie Scrivens
Reforming Markets in Health Care
Peter C. Smith (ed.)
Regulating Health Care
Kieran Walshe
Understanding the NHS Reforms
Peter A. West
Whose Standards?
Charlotte Williamson
Patient Power?
Bruce Wood

USING HEALTH ECONOMICS IN HEALTH SERVICES

Rationing Rationally?

Ruth McDonald

Open University Press
Buckingham · Philadelphia

Open University Press
Celtic Court
22 Ballmoor
Buckingham
MK18 1XW

e-mail: enquiries@openup.co.uk
world wide web: www.openup.co.uk

and
325 Chestnut Street
Philadelphia, PA 19106, USA

First Published 2002

A catalogue record of this book is available from the British Library

ISBN   0 335 20983 1 (pb)   0 335 20984 X (hb)

Library of Congress Cataloging-in-Publication Data
McDonald, Ruth, 1960-
    Using health economics in health services : rationing rationally?/Ruth
McDonald.
        p. cm. – (State of health series)
    Includes bibliographical references and index.
    ISBN 0-335-20984-X – ISBN 0-335-20983-1 (pbk.)
    1. Medical economics – Great Britain.   2. Health services
administration – Great Britain.   3. National Health Service (Great
Britain)   4. Health care – Rationing – Great Britain.
I. Title. II. Series.

RA410.55.G7 M377 2002
338.4′33621′0941–dc21   2001059112

Typeset by Type Study, Scarborough
Printed in Great Britain by St Edmundsbury Press,
Bury St Edmunds, Suffolk

To Jane, Jean, Paul and the three little pigs

CONTENTS

List of tables   viii
Series editor's introduction   ix
List of abbreviations   xi
Acknowledgements   xiii

1 Introduction and methods   1

2 Rational decision-making and health economies   8

3 The HA context: an overview   41

4 Case study I: a cost-effectiveness analysis of
   cholesterol-lowering drugs   77

5 Case study II: system-wide modelling of CHD services in
   Poppleton HA   94

6 Case study III: statins, heart failure and chest pain
   in Baxby   122

7 Towards understanding   152

References   170
Index   179

LIST OF TABLES

Table 2.1 Harrison's typology of decision-making theories 11
Table 2.2 Health economic studies at local level in the
NHS PBMA exercises 27
Table 2.3 Studies assessing the impact and relevance of
health economic analyses in practice at
purchaser level 28
Table 3.1 Revenue budget percentage split for
Poppleton HA 1999/2000 43
Table 3.2 Cardiovascular-related non-elective activity
Poppleton Hospital Trust (1996/97) 69
Table 5.1 CHD initiatives in and around Poppleton HA
– proactive 96
Table 5.2 CHD initiatives in and around Poppleton HA
– reactive 97
Table 5.3 A brief guide to the main procedures provided
for patients with CHD at the tertiary centre trust 98

SERIES EDITOR'S INTRODUCTION

Health services in many developed countries have come under critical scrutiny in recent years. In part this is because of increasing expenditure, much of it funded from public sources, and the pressure this has put on governments seeking to control public spending. Also important has been the perception that resources allocated to health services are not always deployed in an optimal fashion. Thus, at a time when the scope for increasing expenditure is extremely limited, there is a need to search for ways of using existing budgets more efficiently. A further concern has been the desire to ensure access to health care of various groups on an equitable basis. In some countries this has been linked to a wish to enhance patient choice and to make service providers more responsive to patients as 'consumers'.

Underlying these specific concerns are a number of more fundamental developments which have a significant bearing on the performance of health services. Three are worth highlighting. First, there are demographic changes, including the ageing population and the decline in the proportion of the population of working age. These changes will both increase the demand for health care and at the same time limit the ability of health services to respond to this demand.

Second, advances in medical science will also give rise to new demands within the health services. These advances cover a range of possibilities, including innovations in surgery, drug therapy, screening and diagnosis. The pace of innovation quickened as the end of the century approached, with significant implications for the funding and provision of services.

Third, public expectations of health services are rising as those who use services demand higher standards of care. In part, this is stimulated by developments within the health service, including the availability of new technology. More fundamentally, it stems from the emergence of a more educated and informed population, in which people are accustomed to being treated as consumers rather than patients.

Against this background, policymakers in a number of countries are reviewing the future of health services. Those countries which have traditionally relied on a market in health care are making greater use of regulation and planning. Equally, those countries which have traditionally relied on regulation and planning are moving towards a more competitive approach. In no country is there complete satisfaction with existing methods of financing and delivery, and everywhere there is a search for new policy instruments.

The aim of this series is to contribute to debate about the future of health services through an analysis of major issues in health policy. These issues have been chosen because they are both of current interest and of enduring importance. The series is intended to be accessible to students and informed lay readers as well as to specialists working in this field. The aim is to go beyond a textbook approach to health policy analysis and to encourage authors to move debate about their issue forward. In this sense, each book presents a summary of current research and thinking, and an exploration of future policy directions.

Chris Ham
Professor of Health Policy and Management at the
University of Birmingham and Director of the
Strategy Unit at the Department of Health

LIST OF ABBREVIATIONS

A and E	Accident and emergency
ACE	Angiotensin-converting enzyme
AF	Atrial fibrillation
AMI	acute myocardial infarction
BCS	British Cardiac Society
CABG	coronary artery bypass graft
CARE	Cholesterol and Recurrent Events
CD	contracts director
CE	Chief executive
CHD	Coronary heart disease
CHI	Commission for Health Improvement
DPH	Director of public health
ECR	Extra contractual referral
FD	finance director
GMC	General Medical Council
GMS	General Medical Services
GP	General practitioner
HA	Health Authority
HAZ	Health Action Zone
HCHS	Hospital and Community Health Services
HESG	Health Economists Study Group
MA	Marginal analysis
MD	medical director
MI	Myocardial infarction
NHS	National Health Service
NHSE	NHS Executive
NICE	National Institute for Clinical Excellence
NNT	Number needed to treat

NSF	National service framework
PA	Pharmaceutical adviser
PBMA	programme budgeting and marginal analysis
PCG	Primary Care Group
PCT	Primary Care Trust
PM	Project manager
PTCA	percutaneous transluminal coronary angioplasty
R and D	Research and development
RCT	Randomized controlled trial
SMAC	Standing Medical Advisory Committee

ACKNOWLEDGEMENTS

This research could not have been undertaken without the assistance and co-operation of the staff of Poppleton Health Authority, to whom I am eternally grateful. I particularly want to thank the Contracts Director and the Medical Director and his team. They made me so welcome during my stay that when I left, facing the prospect of writing up the results felt like being cast adrift in an open boat with no sign of land!

In desperation I rang Steve Harrison, whom I'd never met, but whose many books and articles I had encountered in my review of the NHS policy-making literature. Steve responded to my mayday call with an offer of immediate and ongoing assistance. My debts to Steve are enormous. Without his help the process of writing the book would certainly have been a lot more tortuous and protracted. My open boat would be closer to the Yangtze than the Mersey by now and my hair would be greyer as a result!

I am also grateful to Adrian Bagust for allowing me to use his system-wide model for coronary heart disease and for his role in facilitating the modelling work. Adrian's advice and assistance which ranged from visits to Poppleton to guidance and support with the technical aspects of the modelling have been invaluable.

Thanks are due to the NHS Executive (North West) whose financial contribution towards the McDonald household budget allowed me to work on my thesis and feed my family at the same time.

I want to thank my friends and colleagues at Liverpool University and the Nuffield Institute for Health for putting up with me and providing moral support and advice during the whole thesis process.

Finally, despite my monotonous conversation, total neglect and the demands made on them by my unsociable working hours, my friends and family have continued to provide support to me throughout the whole process. Although I never tell them, since I have mostly taken it for granted, I am very grateful. That they haven't given up on me long ago, now that I reflect on it, is a source of amazement.

1

INTRODUCTION AND METHODS

For 11 years I worked as an accountant in the National Health Service (NHS). I joined the service in 1984 when the Griffiths reforms were ushering in general management and sweeping away the old-style consensus way of running things. The recruitment rhetoric at the time was aimed at attracting finance managers for the future who would be 'proactive lateral thinkers', 'facilitators', and people who would be interested in health and see money as a means to improving health, rather than as an end in itself. Slowly, it dawned on me that 'health' is such a complex and daunting subject and balancing health-service books such an all-consuming task, that accountants in the health service spend very little of their time engaging with issues of health at all. Financial scandals in the NHS, which attracted criticism from government watchdogs, helped swing the pendulum back towards probity and financial regularity and away from innovation and initiative in the NHS finance function in the 1990s. Even the regional finance staff recruitment process was amended to place greater emphasis on candidates with 'relevant' degrees (accountancy, business studies) and those with irrelevant degrees (like myself, a politics graduate) were to be looked on less favourably.

In 1995 I left the health service to study for a MSc in Health Economics at York University. I was motivated by a desire to be more closely involved in making the most of our limited resources, as opposed to questions of how we balance the books and get more sick people through the system year on year. I was encouraged by colleagues at the Health Authority (HA) who would comment in service review meetings that 'what we really need is a health economist' and buoyed up at the prospect of learning about health and economics for a whole year. Despite my best attempts to resist the brainwashing of finance training over many years, however, I had acquired aspects to my personality which are essential components of the hard-nosed finance manager. Pathologically risk averse, cautious in my responses to even the best of news, I had become downright cynical at the mention of anything touted as 'the answer' to the problems facing NHS managers. I approached the MSc with some scepticism, particularly since I was conscious that in all my time in the NHS, I had never seen health economics impacting on decision-making.

During my time at York, I learned much that was interesting and potentially useful. However, I was conscious, along with classmates who had worked in health services in the UK and overseas, that health economics was taught, largely, in a political vacuum. Similarly, when I attended meetings of the Health Economists Study Group (HESG) in York and later in Brunel University I was struck by the failure of health economists to engage with real world decision-makers. Health economists appeared to hold a rather high opinion of the discipline, but this was based, it seemed to me, on the opinion of other health economists present at study-group meetings, rather than on some tangible evidence of benefits.

Back in Liverpool, I was approached by NHS colleagues who were keen to establish an NHS health economics user group, for success stories to present at the inaugural meeting. Along with health economists based in Lancashire and Yorkshire, I struggled unsuccessfully to identify somebody, somewhere – anywhere – to give a talk on their practical experiences of using health economics to make a difference in the real world. Although there were thousands of publications reporting the results of economic evaluations, the literature relating to the use of health economics in practice was sparse.

I wrestled with a number of questions, the answers to which I could only guess at.

- How could I reconcile the rave reviews given to papers presented at the HESG, with the lack of evidence about health economics in practice?
- How could I account for the views of HA colleagues who clearly saw health economists as being 'the answer', when my experience of NHS decision-making suggested that most of the time we weren't even clear on the question to be answered?
- Was my experience of NHS decision-making (at regional, HA and hospital level, pre- and post-reforms) somehow untypical?

- Could it be that the lack of success stories was down to a failure to apply health economic principles and practices, rather than the failure of health economics as a practical aid to decision-making?

In 1997 when Poppleton HA approached the Prescribing Research Group at Liverpool University in search of a health economist to work with them for 2 years, I welcomed the chance to put health economics to the test. How, if at all, could we reconcile rational health economic decision-making tools with the real world of political fudges and constraints and all within the domain of public accountability?

This book is the outcome of over 2 years' fieldwork in the HA aimed at shedding some light on this issue. It asks 'What happens when we attempt to use health economics at local level in the NHS?'

THE STUDY AND ITS METHOD

Researching decision-making is a difficult business. If policy-making is a black box, then the best way to understand the process is to look inside the box. Since what people say they do may be different from what they think they do which may be different again from what they actually do, methods which rely on questionnaires and interviews may be limited in their ability to provide a reliable picture of events and processes within the black box. The published studies which focus on the impact of health economics at local level in the NHS have used questionnaires, interviews or focus groups to gather research data. These studies identified *potential* benefits or *perceived* barriers, based on the views of the researcher or views expressed by HA decision-makers. A major limitation of this approach, however, is that it often relies largely on eliciting respondents' views in reply to (often narrow) questions and sheds little light on how people behave in practice. Although survey data raise issues for consideration, there are often limited opportunities for following up these issues in any depth.

For this study, I was based within the HA on a full-time basis for a 2-year period. My role as a health economist working closely with Poppleton HA gave me a rare opportunity to observe the decision-making process and the contributions of key actors to that process, at close quarters and over time. During the course of the research, Primary Care Groups (PCGs) were created which involved all general practitioners (GPs) in an area together with community nurses taking responsibility for commissioning services in the local community (Department of Health 1997). This study combined participant observation and documentary evidence to explore and analyse the decision-making process around health economics support to the coronary heart disease (CHD) strategy within the HA and one PCG.

When I arrived at Poppleton HA, I had had no formal training in observational methods, but I had learned from all the texts I had read on participant observation the importance of keeping a research diary. I briefly considered, but then dismissed, thoughts of taping events since I felt that this would be too obtrusive a means of collecting data. Instead I scribbled notes during meetings and conversations, adding in details as soon as was possible after the event.

There were occasions on which I refrained from note-taking, in one-to-one conversations for example, because it didn't feel right. The sight of me scribbling would, I felt, in more intense situations serve to inhibit the behaviour of those I observed. In these cases I wrote up notes later that same day wherever possible. Whenever I talked to the members of my immediate team, however, I scribbled since I had frequent conversations on a one-to-one basis with these individuals who appeared to feel at ease with the scratch of biro on paper. This may be because often such conversations were a mixture of task-based discussion ('What shall we do next regarding problem X?'),which required that I make notes anyway, and collegial conversation.

At other times my involvement in proceedings hampered my ability to both observe and participate and my notes were constructed from memory shortly after the event. I tried to make notes in a non-selective way, rather than focusing on the events around the economics input and this proved useful when writing up. What at the time appeared to be mundane events or insignificant comments helped in my recall of scenes and contexts, and at times proved to be very significant indeed. When I started working in the HA, I spent long periods with little to occupy my time so that I got quickly into the habit of reflecting on events and commenting on my own perceptions of what I was observing. These journals provide the bulk of the material for the book.

Much has been written on the central importance of the observer in observational research (Murphy *et al.* 1998). Gold (1958) identified four roles which may be adopted by the observer from complete participant, through participant as observer, observer as participant to complete observer. During my field work at the HA, I adopted all of these roles, apart from 'complete observer' at different points in the study period, since Gold's complete observer role entirely removes a field worker from social interaction with informants. The complete participant role involves covert observation. Whilst my research was overt, insofar as the key actors knew of my dual role as health economist and researcher, I attended many meetings at the invitation of the Medical Director (MD) where I was introduced simply as 'our health economist' or not introduced at all. Since it was easier not to embark on a long and elaborate explanation of the nature and method of my research I chose, on many of these occasions, to stay silent about my research role.

In Gold's view, the selection of roles should be made on the basis of the focus of the study and the role best suited to studying this, but Gold's rather rigid categorizations fail to capture the more subtle process of shifting between roles, according to the setting and the researcher's positioning in it (Schatzman and Strauss 1973). During my time at Poppleton HA, I consciously shifted between roles, partly on the basis of the role which best suited my area of interest, but partly in response to the extent to which I was required or felt obliged to actively participate in policy processes. For most of the time I straddled observation and participation falling into Gold's middle categories. However, on occasions I lurched into complete participation, going through the motions of observation but questioning my own abilities to be both observer and participant at one and the same time because of the extent of my immersion in the issues of interest.

I can take some comfort from the writings of Herbert Gans (1982), who suggests that only by complete immersion can one really confront the incentives and pressures that influence the behaviour of those under scrutiny. Gans also acknowledges the difficulties of this approach, however, writing that for the researcher whose strategy is total immersion 'It is almost impossible for him to be both a total participant and an observer of himself and other people. Sometimes, one can be a total participant for a short time, and thus obtain empathy into the situations and for the people under study in a direct fashion' (1982: 54).

Participant observational studies differ in the degree to which observational researchers participate in the day-to-day activities of those being observed. Whilst maintaining a distance between researcher and researched may allow the observer to take a detached view of proceedings, the danger with this approach is that policy actors may modify behaviour as a result of a heightened awareness of the observer (the problem of 'reactivity') (Becker and Geer 1960). Too close an involvement, however, will impair the researcher's ability to observe events with sufficient detachment. The maintenance of the research diary and the process of reflection and analysis associated with this helped guard against 'going native' during the fieldwork element of the study. The field notes were coded and cross-referenced with documentary evidence from official publications and internal papers. An iterative process of data analysis was undertaken which involved reading and rereading field notes during the data-gathering phase (Becker *et al.* 1961). This helped place subsequent events within some context and assisted in the identification and refinement of emergent themes. In addition, this approach reflected practical considerations in relation to the analysis of a large volume of data gathered over 2 years.

The selection of the HA was governed entirely by the ability to gain access. Since it was anticipated that the use of health economics to inform resource-allocation processes would be less than simple, the preference was for working in a supportive environment in order to give the techniques a 'fighting chance'.

The HA was chosen largely because it had expressed an immediate need for health economics advice and offered a supportive and accessible environment.

It is worth mentioning that although the term 'health economics' covers a wide spectrum of research and analysis (for example health sector reform, and supply and demand of health care) the health economic methods used in this study relate solely to economic evaluation. This aspect of health economics is concerned with the assessment of costs and benefits of health-care technologies and is far and away the largest area of research for the health economics community.

PLAN OF THE BOOK

What follows is an examination of decision-making at local level in the NHS. It begins, in Chapter 2, by looking at the existing literature on decision-making and on the use of health economics in practice in the NHS. Chapter 3, describes the general HA context in terms of the role and accountability relationships of HAs. This chapter describes the research setting and the key actors in the process. These descriptions are brief, and intentionally so, given the need to preserve the anonymity of the organization and individuals involved.

The next three chapters outline attempts to use health economics in practice in Poppleton. Chapter 4 describes the events surrounding the economic modelling of cholesterol-lowering drugs, and examines reasons why the results of the exercise were not incorporated into policy. The subject of Chapter 5 is the use of a system-wide modelling approach, which includes all CHD services in the HA. Chapter 6 is concerned with decision-making in a PCG. The final chapter presents the conclusions of the study and considers the prospects for health economic analysis in the brave new world of Primary Care Trusts (PCTs).

This study focuses on a single HA which may cause some readers to question the extent to which conclusions can be drawn from this single case. Harry Wolcott describes how this was an issue in relation to his proposal to study what being a principal at a village school entailed. Although there was a literature telling principals what they ought to do, what they actually did had received little attention. Wolcott's proposal was to follow a principal through a year of his professional activities.

> Heralding the study as 'ethnographic' immediately raised questions – in those days non-quantifiable procedure was suspect in educational research ... For all the concern about method ... it may be of interest to note that I was never pressed for the content of what I expected to find, only for the generalizability of my findings: 'What can we learn from a study of just one principal?' (It took two decades for me to recognize the obvious answer: All we can!)
>
> (Wolcott 1995: 107)

This book looks at what happened when I provided economic advice in one HA. To those who ask what we can learn from one HA, I would answer 'All we can', but I will return to what can be learned in the concluding chapter.

2

RATIONAL DECISION-MAKING AND HEALTH ECONOMICS

The research which forms the subject of this book was prompted partly by a desire to examine how, if at all, the 'rational' approach underpinning health economic analyses could be reconciled with my earlier experiences of real-world NHS decision-making, which did not appear to conform to this rational model. At this point it is worth pausing to consider what is meant by 'rational', as rationality may be largely in the eye of the beholder.

RATIONALITY AND DECISION-MAKING

Chambers Dictionary defines 'rational' as 'endowed with reason . . . sane, intelligent, judicious', yet the use of the word in relation to policy-making is ambiguous since various writers have used the term 'rational' in a number of ways. For some it means individuals maximizing satisfaction, others conceive of it as a choice process without regard to how successful a person is in achieving goals, and others see rationality as broadly synonymous with intelligent and purposeful behaviour (Levine *et al.* 1975).

For Carley, however, despite these multiple perspectives on rationality:

> there is much in common among authors when one considers the working definitions in use. All relate to two very similar ideal types of the 'rational man'. First, in economic thought, to be rational is to select from a group of alternative courses of action that course which maximizes output for a given input, or minimizes input for a given output. Secondly, . . . to be rational

is to select a course of action, from a group of possible courses of action, which has a given set of predicted consequences in terms of some welfare function which, in turn, ranks each set of consequences in order of preference . . . rationality refers to consistent value-maximizing choice given certain constraints.

(Carley 1981: 10)

Here, then, is the essence of economic rationality. This rational (sometimes referred to as 'rational comprehensive') model of decision-making implies a complete knowledge of the decision-making environment and the maximization of a value based on this information. The model emphasizes intellectual aspects in a process designed to link means to ends. An occasion for choice is taken as given and value consensus is established before the decision (often by treating the organization as one person) (Olsen 1976). In short, the rational model assumes the existence of 'purposive choice of consistent actors' (Allison 1971). It also assumes that each decision for the economically rational man is programmable (Jabes 1978), but the model does allow for change since the rational organization is a learning organization, adapting to and incorporating new information into its analytical framework.

This model has been criticized for its failure to both explain the empirical reality of decision processes and acknowledge the limitations and boundaries of rationality in human decision-making. It has been suggested that the rational approach, although flawless in its axioms, does not tell us much of practical value about rationality and its application to real behaviour (Churchman 1958). Additionally, rational models are seen as too rigid in drawing sharp distinctions between ends and means, values and decisions, and facts and values. What counts as 'fact' is notoriously subject to the interests and values of the parties involved (Smith and May 1980).

Max Weber's writings on bureaucracy and rationality bring out some of these tensions. On the one hand, the administration of the modern capitalist state is vast and complex and requires a bureaucratic machine based on rule-following to allow for its smooth running.

The fully developed bureaucratic apparatus compares with other organizations exactly as does the machine with non-mechanical modes of production . . . 'Objective' discharge of business primarily means a discharge of business according to *calculable rules* and 'without regard for persons' . . . Bureaucracy develops the more perfectly, the more it is 'dehumanized', the more completely it succeeds in eliminating from official business love, hatred and all purely personal, irrational, and emotional elements which escape calculation. This is appraised as its special virtue by capitalism.

(Weber 1978: 973–5, original emphasis)

The growth of bureaucratic or 'formal' rationality, in which decision-making is the product of universally applied rules and regulations, is seen as essential to the development of modern capitalism. However, such formal or rule-based rationality may come into conflict with value-driven or what Weber terms 'substantive' rationality. The latter is concerned with values and 'cannot be measured in terms of formal calculation alone, but also involves a relation to the . . . content of the particular given ends to which it is oriented' (Weber 1947: 185). Given that formal rationality, is indifferent to the social values which are central to substantive rationality, the potential for the two to come into conflict is clear.

RATIONALITY AND IMPLEMENTATION

The notion of purposive behaviour, of selecting a course of action to achieve specified ends, is central to the concept of rationality. Implicit in this model is the idea that, having identified a course of action, decision-makers have the power to implement policy in pursuit of their goals. This in turn implies a view of implementation which assumes a series of logical steps progressing from intention through decision to action. This view sees 'policy' and 'implementation' as separate and distinct elements, with implementation following on from decision-making. But there are alternative decision-making models which conceptualize the policy process and the place of implementation within that process in rather different ways.

Harrison's typology of decision-making theories serves as a useful device in this respect (Harrison 1985). This typology classifies theories according to two dimensions. The first is the distinction between those categories which focus on rationality at the macro level of the organization and those which assume rationality can be seen at the micro level amongst groups, occupations and individuals. Second, the theories are categorized according to the extent to which actors' behaviours are assumed to be maximizing and proactive, as opposed to satisficing and reactive.

Table 2.1 Harrison's typology of decision-making theories

	Rationality at macro level	*Rationality at micro level*
Maximizing/Proactive	Unitary models	Pluralistic models
Satisficing/Reactive	External control models	Bounded rational models

Source: Harrison (1985)

UNITARY MODELS

These models are labelled 'unitary' because of their conceptualiz-ation of decision-making in terms of unified organizational objectives, but they can be seen as embodying the principles of the rational model outlined above. Unitary models with their exacting requirement for rationality at the organizational level within the context of maximizing, proactive behaviour represent an ideal type, something to aspire to rather than having any basis in reality. Implementation in these models is 'top down' and is regarded as a matter of communication and control systems, 'implementation-as-control'. Implementation failure is therefore a problem of control.

BOUNDED RATIONAL MODELS

The focus of rationality in these models is at the individual or group, as opposed to the organizational level. There is no assump-tion here of maximizing proactive behaviour, but at the core is the notion of actors responding to problems as opposed to proactively pursuing objectives.

Herbert Simon's writings on 'bounded rationality' reflect the cognitive limitations of human beings to consider fully the conse-quences of all alternative courses of action (Simon 1945). Instead, the decision-maker chooses an alternative which is good enough ('satisficing'), rather than one which is designed to maximize his or her values. Decision-making is simplified by the acceptance that not all possibilities will be examined, but this runs the risk that import-ant options and consequences may be ignored. The decision-maker may exclude options which conflict with other more deep-seated values, interests and goals. Behaviour is reactive in the sense that the organizational environment frames the process of choice. Simon's tendency is to offer rules for *the* decision-maker, but this ignores the complex and collective nature of the process (Hill 1997).

Incremental models acknowledge the collective nature of decision-making and depict the process as one of moving slowly, taking small step-by-step changes at the margins. Here, the test of a good policy is that various analysts find themselves directly agreeing, whereas in Simon's rationality, the test is that it can be shown to be the most appropriate means of meeting a specified end. Muddling through tackles immediate problems incrementally, by considering alternatives which differ only marginally from existing policies (that is by successive, limited comparisons) rather than focusing on some distant goal. Again, this model is reactive, responding to problems rather than proactively goal seeking (Lindblom 1959).

Later variants of this model (Braybrooke and Lindblom 1963) describe a process of 'disjointed incrementalism'. Decision-making is disjointed as it is undertaken in a fragmented fashion by different agencies. Decisions are not subject to an overall plan, but emerge from a trial-and-error approach. Such coordination as there is emerges from what Lindblom calls 'partisan mutual adjustment' rather than attempts at central planning (Lindblom 1979). This adjustment is the process whereby individual decision-makers coordinate their behaviours and the decision-making process is one of adjustment and compromise which facilitates agreement. The outcome of this:

> may be a great deal more intelligent and even more democratic than is normally achieved through hierarchical co-ordination of efforts, in the sense that a great diversity of considerations often are brought to bear, and in the sense that no one set of participants can readily dominate others.
>   (Lindblom and Woodhouse 1993: 68)

Allison's 'organizational process' model is another variant of the incremental approach. Decisions here are viewed less as deliberate choices and more as '*outputs* of large organizations functioning according to standard patterns of behaviour' (Allison 1971: 67, original emphasis). Routines and standard operating procedures are emphasized here. Organizational change occurs only slowly and is influenced by existing organizational capabilities and procedures.

Bounded rational theories should not be seen as 'rationality' minus a bit. These theories are incompatible with the rational model of decision-making, since here the decision processes do not draw on proactive or systematic enquiry. Instead, bounded rational theories suggest reactive behaviour, a drive to action regardless of whether it impacts on the problem, and a focus on means rather than ends. They are characterized by a vagueness of stated intent to allow post hoc rationalization about their success. The test of implementation is not then the extent to which formal objectives have been achieved. Indeed, those who agree policy may have lost interest long before implementation so instead the question should be ' "has the policy made things better than they otherwise would have been?" and if so "better for whom?" '(Harrison 1985: 118).

PLURALISTIC MODELS

Schmitter defines pluralism as:

> a system of interest representation in which the constituent units are organized into an unspecified number of multiple, voluntary, competitive, nonhierarchically ordered and self-determined ... categories which are not specially licensed, recognized or subsidized, created or otherwise controlled by the state.
>
> (1974: 934)

Pluralist models focus on decision-making in the context of a plurality of views and conflict or bargaining processes. The focus of rationality within these models is at group or individual, as opposed to organizational, level. Differences in group or individual objectives are mediated through the exercise of power. The result is either a compromise or, where differences in power are great, domination by one individual or group. Allison's analysis of decision-making in the US context depicts a 'political model' comprising 'players who make decisions not by a single, rational choice but by the pulling and hauling that is politics ... what moves the chess pieces is ... the power and skill of proponents and opponents of the action in question' (Allison 1971: 144).

The notion of mutual adjustment and compromise features heavily in those pluralist models which assume that power is widely distributed in society. Other variants of the model see the process as much less about resolution via compromises and much more about the domination of policy processes by powerful groups or individuals. For example, public choice theories view individual bureaucrats as wielding and abusing power with the bureaucrat portrayed as a utility-maximizing individual who equates budgetary and bureau growth with the maximization of self-interest (Niskanen 1971). Certainly, such thinking influenced policymakers in the UK. The drive for efficiency and dilution of bureaucratic powers by separating purchasers of care from providers were central planks of the 1989 White Paper *Working for Patients* (Department of Health 1989). Within the HA context, budgets are allocated to service providers with only a small amount remaining for central headquarters expenditure. The squeeze on management costs in HAs has served to further limit the amount available to potentially self-seeking bureaucrats. Proponents of public choice theory might argue that the failure to find evidence which supports their view is due to the success of reforms designed to curb bureaucratic power. However, such theories fail to account for factors such as altruism or a public service ethic in the motivational make-up of HA decision-makers.

Neo-elitist theories of organization in relation to health policy have focused on the power of professional groups in shaping policy and implementation. Harrison and colleagues cite the influence of the British Medical Association and the Royal Colleges: 'no organization representing patients enjoys anything like this degree of influence' (Harrison *et al.* 1990). More recent observers have commented on the shift in power away from professionals to managers and administrators, both at operational and national level (Harrop 1992; Smith 1993).

Success or failure of implementation is largely a relative notion, determined by one's position in the process (Elmore 1978). Considerations of implementation from the perspective of pluralist theories emphasize bargaining and compromise. The question to ask here is 'What kind of policy will be implementable?', reflecting the fact that the potential for implementation actually determines policy choices in the first place (Harrison 1985).

EXTERNAL CONTROL MODELS

The focus of rationality in these models is at the level of the whole organization. Organizational behaviour is determined primarily by the need for organizational survival in the face of threats from the external environment. Marxist theories view events within organizations as a microcosm of events in society. Such approaches to policy point to the influence of economic interests on political action and see the state as maintaining the dominance of particular social classes.

Public sector organizations such as the NHS are seen as engaging in the reproduction and legitimation of capitalist social relations and attempting to reconcile competing demands (Offe 1984). For Salaman (1978) internal organizational negotiations and struggles must be seen in terms of extra-organizational positions and resources of the participants – their class membership. Organizational survival is predicated on the contribution made to the bourgeois control of society.

New Marxist theories view the state as maintaining order through the promotion of capitalism and securing legitimacy through the allocation of resources. State agencies and their policies reflect constant struggles between contradictory ideologies of citizenship, social need or individualism and of competitive individualism, commodification and productive efficiency (Cawson and Saunders 1983).

Pfeffer and Salancik's resource dependence model is another example of external control theory. Its premise is that organizations, as social systems, require a continuing provision of resources and a continuing cycle of transactions with the environment from which the resources are derived (Pfeffer and Salancik 1978: 148). Survival is dependent on meeting the demands of external agencies which control the flow of resources to the organization. Organizations are involved in an ongoing struggle for autonomy and discretion, confronted with constraint and external control.

Organizations are 'coalitions of varying interests'. Participants frequently have incompatible preferences and goals. Decision-making here can be evaluated by asking whose interests are being served. Since power organizes around critical and scarce resources, participants who furnish resources that are more critical and scarce, obtain more control over the organization. The determination of what is critical and scarce is itself open to change and definition (Pfeffer and Salancik 1978).

The 'symbolic role of management' is an important feature of this model. Here the manager is a symbol of the organization and its success or failure. As a symbol of control, managers can be rewarded when things run smoothly and used as scapegoats when things turn out badly. The 'responsive role of management' within this model sees decision-making less as a process focusing on choice and more as an information-gathering exercise. Once information about the environment and possible consequences of alternative courses of action is amassed, the choice is usually obvious. This role emphasizes the importance of processing and responding to the organization's context. The critical factor is that constraints are imposed on the actor (Pfeffer and Salancik 1978).

Implementation failures within the external control framework are attributed to the fact that either non-implementation carries insufficient threat of loss or that the organization has underestimated the likelihood or magnitude of such loss.

FROM ORDER TO AMBIGUITY: THE 'GARBAGE CAN' MODEL

These models differ in the way they view group or organizational activity, but share a conception of decision-making as discerning and affecting a coherent world. Underlying them is what March has defined as three concepts of order in decision-making. The first is reality, in terms of one objective world which can be perceived. 'An object either exists or it does not. An event either has happened or it has not. . . . History is real' (March 1994: 176).

The second idea is causality, the notion that reality and history are structured by chains of causes and effects. Choices are intended to affect outcomes, and decisions are means to desired ends. Experience and causal inferences about that experience provide a basis for informing future actions. The third idea is intentionality, the notion that decisions are the product of purposive individual preferences.

An appreciation of ambiguity and the willingness to challenge reality, causality and intentionality as core concepts are at the heart of 'garbage can' decision processes (Cohen *et al.* 1972). The garbage can model is the antithesis of 'rational' decision-making. Whilst rational, satisficing, political bargaining and external control models are characterized by the ideas of order which March describes, the garbage can model is characterized by a lack of clarity or inconsistency in reality, causality or intentionality. Whereas rational and conflict/bargaining approaches view the organization as a vehicle for producing decisions, in the garbage can model, outcomes are seen as unintended products of certain processes having dynamics of their own (Olsen 1976).

The central characteristic of the garbage can model is ambiguity and this ambiguity extends to purpose, processes, outcomes and histories. Ambiguity is distinct from uncertainty in that the latter implies limitations to knowledge which will be reduced by seeking information over time. When a situation is described as 'ambiguous', a decision-maker is 'less confident that any one thing is true, or that the world can be partitioned into mutually exhaustive and exclusive states, or that information will resolve the lack of clarity' (March 1994: 179).

Key features of this approach are as follows.

- Problematic preferences: Problems, alternatives, goals and solutions are ill-defined. Ambiguity characterizes all aspects of the process.
- Ambiguous technology: Cause and effect relationships are uncertain or unknown.
- Fluid participation: Involvement of individuals varies from one time to another, resulting in fluid boundaries in relation to the shape of the organization and the audience and decision-makers for any particular choice.

Problems and solutions are not connected as decisions, but are the outputs of independent streams of events within the organization. The process has been described as follows:

Suppose we view a choice opportunity as a garbage can into which various problems and solutions are dumped by participants. The mix of garbage in a single can depends partly on the labels attached to the alternative cans; but it also depends on what garbage is being produced at the moment, on the mix of cans available, and on the speed with which garbage is being collected and removed from the scene.

(March and Olsen 1976: 26)

Four streams of garbage can decision-making can be identified:

1 problems, which derive from a gap between current and desired performance;
2 solutions, which exist independently of problems;
3 participants, who come and go and participate to varying degrees; and
4 choice opportunities, when an organization is expected to produce behaviour that can be called a decision.

In the garbage can model, solutions are proposed even when problems do not exist, choices are made without necessarily solving problems, problems may persist without being solved so that participants may feel they are working on the same problems over long periods of time. The view of independent 'streams' in the policy process which are linked at critical junctures has been used to develop thinking on the way in which policies get on to agendas in the first place and why it should be that problems remain unresolved, or simply fade from prominence (Kingdon 1994).

Kingdon, in his analysis of US government policy, adapted the garbage can model developed by Cohen and colleagues. In the Kingdon variant a decision is the outcome of three streams: problem recognition, policy proposals and political processes.

Problem recognition reflects the ways in which one issue rather than another captures the attention of groups and individuals in and around government. A change in a quantitative indicator ('It helps for problems to be countable', 1994: 93) or a focusing event or crisis may be the stimulus for 'recognition'. Problems sometimes need a push.

Policy proposals are not necessarily developed in response to specific problems. Policies may be developed in 'policy communities' where ideas float around gaining prominence and then in many cases fading. Third, there are political processes such as changes of office holder, public opinion and pressure group lobbying.

In essence Kingdon's theory suggests that an issue is only likely to reach a decision agenda where the three streams of problems, policy and politics are joined. The joining of these streams is likely to take place during the appearance of a 'policy window' and such windows open infrequently and do not stay open long.

USING THE MODELS – DESCRIPTIONS, NOT PRESCRIPTIONS

Unitary models make unrealistic claims with regard to organizational unity of purpose and instrumental rationality. The assumptions of these models are at odds with empirical observation of life in the health service. However, such models are worthy of scrutiny, since many decision-makers believe that they act rationally or at least aspire to the rational ideal. Additionally, government reforms of the NHS have been aimed at increasing rationality in the service (Hunter 1980). Unitary models embody the assumptions of rationality which underpin health economic analysis. It is, therefore, important to contrast events in the field with the prescriptions of rational choice in order to understand why solutions generated by health economic analyses are not always compatible with the needs of policymakers. In neoclassical economics, rationality embodies the notions of maximizing proactive and purposive behaviour at the level of the individual 'rational economic man' (Gravelle and Rees 1992: 6–8). In what Harrison calls 'unitary' models these assumptions are held to apply at the organizational level, but given the strong assumptions about unity of purpose which these models embody, the organizations involved are treated as effectively acting as single agents. To avoid confusion, the term 'rational model' will be used throughout the remainder of the book to reflect a process wherein decision-making is characterized by proactive maximizing behaviour encompassing the following steps: at the outset values are defined, then objectives compatible with those values are identified, next all relevant options for achieving the desired objectives are specified, the consequences of each option are calculated and compared and finally, the option which maximizes the values defined at the start of the process is chosen as the preferred solution.

It is not difficult to see that bounded rational models, which stress the limits to human cognitive abilities, have some application in the health-care context. This context is characterized by vague and complex objectives and processes which allow front line health-care workers to define service objectives implicitly in their day-to-day work (Lipsky 1980). Certainly the NHS is no stranger to symbolic action, which is a key feature of bounded rational models.

Within the bounded rational typology, incremental models have been used by a number of writers to describe decision-making processes in the NHS (Hunter 1991, Harrison *et al.* 1992). In terms of resource allocation in particular, HAs do not undertake zero-based budgeting exercises to appraise all service investments from scratch, but adjust resources at the margins over time. The allocation of funds from the NHS Executive (NHSE) moves HAs towards funding targets using a phased process of small steps, in recognition of the fact that realignments of expenditure will most easily be achieved via a process of gradual adjustments (NHSE 1998a).

Incrementalism has been used by many writers to describe policy processes in the NHS and its recognition of conflict and diversity, alongside small changes at the margins, provides a more appealing tool from which to analyse events at Poppleton HA. However, an examination of health economics in practice will require analysis of *how* decisions are made and *why*. It is not clear that incrementalism as a theory is sufficiently detailed to provide answers to both these questions. Only by examining organizational politics is it possible to explain *why* some processes are more incremental than others.

Pluralist theories potentially illuminate the 'why' as well as the 'what' of decision-making by seeking to explain relationships of power and influence in NHS policy arenas. Although the application of such models to the NHS is by no means a new phenomenon, the number of studies which focus in detail at the HA level is disappointingly small. Additionally, although doctors may at the same time be HA managers, much of the literature which examines power relationships in health tends to pit doctors against managers in the struggle for power or relegates managers to some off-stage mopping up or conciliator role. Often medical power refers to hospital-based doctors with scant attention being paid to GPs who are both purchasers and providers of health care and increasingly are being given responsibility for balancing budgets, assessing health needs and commissioning care.

External control models, which emphasize the interdependence of complex public service sectors, have some resonance in the context of the NHS. Power accrues, within this model, to those actors who provide a critical resource for the organization and who cannot readily be replaced in that function (Pfeffer 1981) and the NHS as an employer is highly dependent on professional associations for the supply and quality of personnel (Harrison 1981). Another factor influencing the environment in which NHS bodies operate is the increased emphasis on patient and public opinion in government policy documents, together with the involvement of patient groups in litigation.

The garbage can model offers another analytical approach. By acknowledging the importance of individual actors as well as structures and the symbolic nature of participation, the model provides a lens from which to view processes, structures and actors. The garbage can approach places ambiguity, that is ambiguity of purpose, of power, of process and even of the past, at the centre of the analysis.

Hunter's study of decision-making in two Scottish Health Boards saw the adherence to routines partly as the result of 'puzzlement' about what should be done. Hunter cites Heclo who maintains that social politics should not be characterized predominantly in terms of conflict or power play. This is because 'the issues faced in social politics are so complex, the major difficulty may not be the exercise of political will, but the determination of what that will is, or ought to be' (1980: 43). The model, therefore, provides a means of assessing the extent to which puzzlement and ambiguity explain why events happened as they did.

A review of the literature on decision-making reveals how the process becomes more complicated than the picture painted in the rational model. The concept of multiple actors with competing preferences and the notion of alliances constructed to exert undue influence over the decision-making process may provide some understanding of the context of decision-making in practice. However, they serve to undermine the notions of systematic and unified purposive action which characterize the rational (health economics) paradigm.

DECISIONS AND POWER

Decision-making in organizations or groups involves multiple actors, often with conflicting interests and aspirations. When preferences between individuals or groups conflict, efforts may be made to proclaim a common objective or shared identity ('We all have the patients' best interests at heart'), but as a device for removing conflict this method may have little success in practice. When the decision-making context is one of inconsistency of interests and identities, the decision process will be characterized by some degree of struggle between competing interests.

Steven Lukes (1974) in presenting a conceptual analysis of power outlines three 'conceptual maps' which reveal the distinguishing features of three views of power. The 'one-dimensional' view of power, based on the writings of Robert Dahl, involves a focus on behaviour and observable conflict of interests: '*A* has power over *B* to the extent that he can get *B* to do something that *B* would not otherwise do' (Dahl 1957: 202–3). Bachrach and Baratz go beyond this definition, explaining that understanding 'power' entails more than examining key decisions and actual behaviour.

> Power is also exercised when A devotes his energies to creating or reinforcing social and political values and institutional practices that limit the scope of the political process to public consideration of only those issues which are comparatively innocuous to A.
>
> (Bachrach and Baratz 1970: 7)

In other words, power can include non-decision-making, the practice of limiting the scope of actual decision-making to ' "safe" issues by manipulating the dominant community values, myths and political institutions and procedures' (Bachrach and Baratz 1963: 642). Lukes sees this 'two-dimensional view' of power as an improvement on the one-dimensional view, but points out that '*A* also exercises power over [*B*] by influencing, shaping or determining his very wants' (Lukes 1974: 21). This allows for consideration of social forces and institutional practices as well as individuals' decisions in keeping potential issues out of the process. This dimension encompasses the 'supreme and most insidious exercise of power to prevent people ... from having grievances by shaping their perceptions, cognitions and preferences in such a way that they accept their role in the existing order of things'(Lukes 1974: 24). The problem for the researcher is in identifying the existence of power and conflict if these are unobservable.

RATIONALITY AND POWER

The concepts of power and rationality and the dynamic relationship between the two are examined by Flyvbjerg in his study of democracy in a Danish town. As he notes, the Enlightenment tradition views rationality as a well-defined, context-independent concept. Flyvbjerg is critical of '[m]odernity's elevation of rationality as an ideal [which] seems to result in, or at least coexist with, an ignorance of the real rationalities at work in everyday politics, administration and planning'(Flyvbjerg 1998: 2–3). He quotes Machiavelli's dictum that 'a man who neglects what is actually done for what should be done learns the way to self-destruction' to argue for 'a reorientation towards "what is actually done" '. Flyvbjerg, in his study of what actually happens (as opposed to what the normative rational planning model dictates *should* happen) in the planning of a new bus station concludes that

> Power concerns itself with defining reality rather than discovering what reality 'really' is ... power defines what counts as rationality and knowledge and thereby what counts as reality ... Power does not limit itself, however, to simply defining a given interpretation or view of reality, nor does power entail only the power to render a given reality authoritative. Rather, power defines, and creates, concrete physical, economic, ecological and social realities.
>
> (Flyvbjerg 1998: 227)

In Flyvbjerg's interpretation, 'rationalization presented as rationality is a principal strategy in the exercise of power'. Such rationalizations are difficult to detect since they are presented as rationality and only by deconstructing ostensibly rational arguments can we detect whether it is a rationalization. Flyvbjerg points out that actors may be unwilling to do this for fear of destabilizing the decision-making process or incurring negative sanctions.

If Flyvbjerg is correct, the results of 'rational' health economic analyses will be ignored or distorted (as rationalizations) when they do not provide results in accordance with the views of powerful policymakers. Health economists would argue that their 'rationality', which draws on the neoclassical economics in the Enlightenment tradition, is not context dependent. Indeed, the use of explicit criteria, which are open to scrutiny, is intended to guard against the sorts of abuses of power of which Flyvbjerg writes. He himself acknowledges that '[i]n a democratic society, rational argument is one of the few forms of power the powerless still possess. This may explain the enormous appeal of the Enlightenment project to those outside power.' However, he goes on to quote Machiavelli again, who places little trust in rational persuasion: ' "We must distinguish" he says in *The Prince* "between . . . those who to achieve their purpose can force the issue and those who must use persuasion. In the second case, they always come to grief" ' (Flyvbjerg 1998: 37).

Such a view of the relationship between power and rationality may explain why there is so little literature on the application of health economics in practice at local level in the NHS. It may also explain why, on occasion, HA decision-makers do attempt to use health economic approaches. If the policymakers at the HA are not powerful, then their recourse to 'rational' processes may be understood in terms of the appeal of rational argument to those outside power. In this scenario, rational approaches may be used to fill the legitimacy gap which inhibits action on the part of HA decision-makers. This legitimacy gap is not an issue for clinicians. Harrison and colleagues, in their review of medical power in the NHS prior to the Griffiths reforms note how doctors rely on 'manipulation of "common-sense" or "traditional" ideas that complete [Lukes'] . . . third dimension of power' (Harrison *et al.* 1992: 19). Variations in clinical practice are well documented, but these are usually explained in terms of the exercise of clinical freedom, which is itself a statement of power, rather than an appeal to rationality, or 'my patients are different', rather than by means of 'rational' argument or documentation (Evans 1990). Even in today's climate of evidence-based medicine, many clinician arguments for funding are based on emotional appeals, rather than well-constructed business cases. Chapter 3 notes how the tertiary trust research and development (R and D) manager feels that his ability to produce relatively good-quality research and documentation weakens their position relative to other hospitals, where in the absence of data, appeals for funding are made without recourse to 'rational' argument. The existence of good-quality information allows for the possibility of deconstruction to expose ostensible rationality as rationalization.

Whilst Flyvbjerg's model provides a useful reference point against which to compare NHS decision-making, it assumes that those who possess power have a clear purpose in mind when they exercise that power. The literature on public-sector organizations presents a less ordered picture, with unclear and competing objectives seen as characterizing the decision-making context (Ranade 1997). A more useful model might combine Flyvbjerg's ideas on the dynamic relationship between power and rationality with a decision-maker who is much less purposive, invoking the garbage can's concept of ambiguity. Such a model would provide a basis for understanding why it should be that relatively powerful decision-makers are, at times, attracted to 'rational' techniques such as health economics. Where genuine ambiguity prevails, the solution can be generated from the economic analysis to be rolled out in its original form. If the decision-maker is genuinely uncertain and finds the results acceptable they can then impose it on others, or in some manipulated form (rationalization presented as rationality), if the analysis has helped persuade the decision-maker that some other course of events is preferred.

A further refinement to Flyvbjerg's model might help explain recourse to health economic tools on the part of powerful decision-makers. In his study actors are characterized as either powerful or powerless. This may be appropriate for the narrow context in which his actors are operating, but at the HA level power is not a binary variable. There are degrees of power and domains of power. Whilst a HA director may have a high level of control in terms of his or her immediate domain (over his or her subordinates), he or she may have little power over fellow HA directors and still less outside of the HA over independent GP contractors. The fragmentation of decision-making in the NHS means that HA directors are unable to exert direct control over stakeholders outside of the HA (see Chapter 3). All this makes life complicated for HA staff who are expected to know just how much power they can wield within any domain at any one time and be able to adjust their actions accordingly. Alternatively, one might expect to see individuals who attempt to create reality, in the way Flyvbjerg describes but fail miserably, because they apply a constant idea of their own power, based on their immediate domain, to actions in contexts where their power is severely limited.

Similarly, whilst GPs are independent of the HA, a representation of them as omnipotent clinicians presents too crude a picture. Lipsky's work on 'street-level bureaucrats' may have some resonance here. These front line care workers enjoy wide discretion in their day-to-day working environment and relative autonomy from organizational authority. They 'socialize citizens to expectations of government services and a place in the political community. They determine the eligibility of citizens for government benefits . . . In short they hold the keys to a dimension of citizenship' (1980: 4). However, these actions reflect an 'attempt to do a good job in some way. [T]he job, however, is, in a sense, impossible to do in ideal terms'. Lipsky asks 'how is the job to be accomplished with inadequate resources, few controls, indeterminate objectives and discouraging circumstances?' One tactic is to 'modify their concept of their jobs, so as to lower or otherwise restrict their objectives and thus reduce the gap between available resources and achieving objectives' (1980: 82). So although these workers enjoy considerable autonomy in the allocation of resources to clients, the way in which they perform their duties is itself a response to an inability to secure sufficient resources for their service.

Lipsky's work focuses on those involved in direct client contact, but this modification process is faced by HA decision-makers on an almost constant basis. In Lipsky's analysis 'any recognition that performance is less than adequate is likely to make these bureaucrats seek and find the explanation someplace other than in their own inadequacy' (1980: 82). Street-level bureaucrats are interested in processing work consistent with their own preferences, whereas managers are interested in achieving results consistent with agency objectives. However, this is to assume a constancy, clarity and consistency of objectives which appears to be lacking in HAs. The notion that some HA managers are like Lipsky's street-level workers struggling to do the best they can, defined in terms of their own preferences may be helpful in understanding the realities of HA life. If this is the case, then attempts to use health economic solutions predicated on some notion of certainty and rationality will do little to change the outcome of decision processes. They will serve merely to make decision-makers more uncomfortable and more aware of the gap between their service ideal and reality.

HEALTH ECONOMICS IN PRACTICE AT A LOCAL LEVEL

In contrast to the huge volume of literature relating to decision-making and the very many studies published each year reporting the results of health economic evaluations, there are few case studies of health economics in practice at a local level in the NHS. A paper commissioned for the 25th anniversary of the Health Economists Study Group at the University of York outlined examples of the impact of health economics on policy (Hurst 1998). These stretched over 25 years, were all at national level and based on a rather loose definition of 'impact'. In addition, health policy was defined as 'statements of intent and plans of action developed by the Department of Health in relation to health and health services' (1998: S47). Although the NHS is a national body, resources are allocated between service providers and between clinical specialities or programme areas on a local basis. From the paper it is not possible to assess the impact on HAs of central policy directives, or more specifically, of health economic evaluations.

Tables 2.2 and 2.3 indicate the scope and methods of 17 studies, which focus on the use of health economic analyses at local (HA/Board) level. Table 2.2 summarizes those that present accounts of programme budgeting and marginal analysis (PBMA) priority-setting exercises. PBMA involves examining the existing allocation of resources to a 'programme' and examining alternative (usually resource-neutral) ways of allocating those resources (Donaldson 1995).

A programme can be based on a disease (such as CHD), client group (for example the elderly) or a service (such as maternity services). The emphasis is on including a variety of stakeholders to obtain a shared understanding and to promote ownership of the final recommendations, with the aim being to consider competing candidates for investment according to a clear and explicit framework. However, the process is data hungry and time consuming.

Those studies which have addressed the issue of applying health economics in the real world identify various barriers to the use of health economics. From the range of reasons highlighted across

Table 2.2 Health economic studies at local level in the NHS PBMA exercises

Author(s) and publication date	Study setting	Study focus	Outcomes/outputs in terms of policy process reported
Donaldson and Farrar (1993)	One Scottish Health Board	Dementia services	No information provided
Cohen (1994) Cohen (1995)	One Welsh HA	Multi-programme approach initially; main focus on maternal and early child health services	Yes, agreement to incorporate findings into strategy documents and contracts
Lockett et al. (1995)	One English HA	Macro approach to include all health services	Yes, agreement to incorporate into strategy documents for future; no agreement on areas for disinvestment
Twaddle and Walker (1995)	One Scottish Health Board	Gynaecology services	Yes, agreement to incorporate findings into contracts
Craig et al. (1995)	One English HA	Macro approach to include all health services.	No, work ongoing
Brambleby (1995)	Two localities within one English HA	All health services	Yes, in terms of communicating and informing No, in terms of changes implemented
Madden et al. (1995)	Zonal agency, covering four HAs in England	Two programmes: heart disease and mental health	No information provided
Street et al. (1995)	One English HA	Dementia services	Yes, expert group withdrew and the process was halted
Ratcliffe et al. (1996)	One Scottish Health Board	Maternity services	No information provided
Ruta et al. (1996)	One Scottish Health Board	Child health services	Yes, recommendations from PBMA exercise incorporated into policy
Scott et al. (1998)	One Scottish Total Fundholding Pilot Site	Diabetes care	No information provided
Henderson and Scott (2001)	One Scottish Total Purchasing Pilot Site	Stroke care	No information provided

Table 2.3 Studies assessing the impact and relevance of health economic analyses in practice at purchaser level

Author(s) and Publication date	Scale and scope	Research focus	Methods and sources
McNamee and Godber (1995)	Evaluation of 'purchaser intelligence pilot', which provided health economic input into decision-making, primarily in two English HAs	Factors contributing to success (where 'success' is not defined explicitly)	Researchers' personal experiences and impressions gained as those involved in the provision of 'intelligence'
Harrison (1996)	Evaluation of 'purchaser intelligence pilot' (see above)	Outputs in terms of policy relevance/implementability Outcomes in terms of changing contract patterns and less tangible spin-offs	Interviews, documents, correspondence, expert opinion
Drummond et al. (1996) Drummond et al. (1997) Walley et al. (1997)	Survey of all prescribing advisers and directors of public health at commissioner level in England, Scotland and Wales (hospital pharmacists also surveyed)	Investigation of perceived barriers to the use of economic evaluation in relation to drug therapy	Questionnaires
Miller and Vale (1997)	Key decision-makers in one English HA ($n = 12$) and one Scottish Health Board ($n = 17$)	Purchaser attitudes to the use of PBMA	Interviews
Green (1998) (unpublished SCHARR report)	Observations and findings from the development of marginal analysis in one HA	Barriers contributing to the failure to develop a full marginal analysis process	Observation
Duthie et al. (1999)	Sample of decision makers ($n = 34$, HA staff = 6) from all over England (included GPs and hospital staff)	Relevance of health economic studies to decision-makers	Interviews
Hoffman and von der Schulenburg (2000)	Large-scale European survey of decision-makers in nine European countries, which included 22 UK NHS staff	Influence on decision-making	Focus groups and interviews
Stoykova et al. (2000)	Decision-makers in two HAs	Usefulness of economic evaluations contained on NHS economic evaluation database	Focus groups

different studies, the obstacles can be categorized in terms of departures from the rational model.

First, there are barriers arising from the lack of information and the scale of uncertainty, in the process. The rational model is cognitively too demanding. Second, the rational model has little to say about implementation, or at least naively assumes that decision-makers either have the power to secure compliance or those involved in implementation share common values. Third, the rational approach is not concerned with the relationship between 'rationality' and power. Indeed, it has little to say about larger-scale power relationships or about questions of legitimacy in relation to decision-makers and their values.

Rationality is too cognitively demanding

In order to conduct health economic evaluations at a local level, information is often needed on local costs, effectiveness of treatment alternatives and disease prevalence and incidence. Since performance monitoring of contracted activity is on the basis of completed episodes of care and providers are paid according to the level of patient episodes completed, a large amount of effort is put into collecting this information. In contrast, epidemiological data is more difficult to obtain. Identifying disease prevalence is difficult, as some individuals, although 'ill' in terms of suffering from a disease, do not come into contact with the health services, or at least do so only infrequently. Furthermore, most patient contacts are within general practice, and historically there have been few incentives in the system for GPs to collect this type of data (Scobie *et al.* 1995).

Data on the clinical effectiveness and costs of procedures obtained from trials may prove difficult to adapt to local circumstances. Clinical trials measure 'efficacy', within a strictly controlled environment, which is often limited to a narrow focus on the type of patient treated. HAs commissioning care for populations, which include a broad range of patients, often with comorbidities, need information on effectiveness of treatment outside the rarefied trial environment. Published trials may not reflect the local setting in terms of service configuration, delivery or cost. Since the range of costs varies widely across the country, the presentation of standard or study-specific costs will be of little help to commissioners in assessing the likely local financial consequences of service changes.

There are also problems in obtaining accurate and relevant local cost information. Even where procedure costs are available, untangling these average costs, which relate to a given volume, to identify marginal costs, in an attempt to apply these to a varying volume, may well prove difficult.

These problems are a recurring theme in the PBMA studies reviewed. Twaddle and Walker (1995: 101) identified 'making assumptions about changes in patient outcomes' and 'applying flawed cost figures to activity data' as two of the deficiencies of their approach. They are not hopeful that such problems can easily be resolved. Departure from the rational ideal of perfect information will be necessary in order to make progress, but decisions about 'what counts as evidence' will require choices to be made about whose decision will count in this process. This has implications, both for policy formulation and implementation which are discussed in more detail below.

One respondent in a study of HA decision-makers describes the cognitive problems encountered, saying 'We cannot be sure we are reviewing the right areas of service ... we are a long way from knowledge-based purchasing and still rely on historical trends' (Miller and Vale 1997: 8). So the complexities are not restricted to obtaining relevant evidence, but extend to selecting candidates for scrutiny in the first place. Decision-makers may lack the knowledge to decide in advance which areas to tackle first, in order to maximize the benefits from potentially resource-intensive economic evaluation exercises.

In the survey conducted by Drummond and colleagues, lack of information was less of an issue, perhaps understandably, because comments on existing studies (as opposed to conducting new studies) were elicited. However, 'personal difficulty in interpreting the studies' was cited as fifth most important in a list of 13 obstacles to the use of cost-effectiveness studies. This was despite the fact that 40 per cent of respondents had received training in health economics. The obstacle 'health authorities as a whole don't really understand the process' was ranked eighth in the list (Walley *et al.* 1997).

Health service provision is characterized by complex, dynamic systems in which cause and effect relationships are not easily delineated. Posnett and Street argue that PBMA's 'essentially static [budget matrix] ... offers no insight into the way in which services relate directly to the flow of patients through the system, or to the alternatives available at decision points in the flow' (Posnett and Street 1996: 149). They argue against using expert opinion to generate options for change in favour of evaluation 'based on objective principles, and not on arbitrary judgement' (1996: 151). In advocating the construction of a decision tree in which '*all* relevant options are identified prior to evaluation' (1996: 152, emphasis in original), they place huge requirements on the information-gathering and information-processing capabilities of individuals involved and they move away from the pragmatism which advocates of PBMA see as one of its major strengths. In reality, the construction of such a model is likely to be an extremely difficult and time-consuming process. Any modelling process will entail a decision on what is included and what is not included within the model, so it may be difficult to avoid the sort of arbitrary decisions which they attack. Additionally, by ignoring certain parameters which are key determinants of health, the modelling process may provide spuriously scientific, but essentially flawed, analyses.

Complexity in relation to cause and effect and the dynamic nature of health systems does not feature widely in the studies of health economics in practice. This may be because the PBMA studies were conducted by health economists who were, in the main, in favour of this 'essentially static' process. The implication is that dynamic, complex relationships were not acknowledged by these economists, or were seen as too difficult to handle, and so ignored. Alternatively, this failure to examine ripple effects may reflect the *ceteris paribus* assumption of 'all else remaining equal' which underlies neoclassical economic theory.

The *ceteris paribus* assumption is also a feature of economic evaluation in general. Despite aspirations to take the broadest possible (societal) perspective, economic evaluations often consider only a narrow range of costs and benefits due to a combination of pressure to meet sponsors' agendas, the difficulties in placing monetary values on items which do not have market prices and the problems of identifying wider effects, due to complexity of the cause and effect relationships of changes in health services.

This is a problem with rationality generally, as there are many situations (such as choosing a job) where satisficing is the only practical approach. Health economic analyses, by aspiring to the rational ideal fail to acknowledge also the 'irrationality' of exhaustive searches which produce the same response as satisficing may have done with much less time and effort.

RATIONALITY AND IMPLEMENTATION

Just as the rational model has little to say about policy implementation or assumes that implementation will follow from rational analysis and unity of purpose, most of the PBMA literature reviewed gives only brief consideration to implementation or ignores the issue altogether.

Only four of the studies go beyond the production of results, reporting the incorporation of PBMA proposals into contracts or strategy documents. Lockett and colleagues reported the failure to identify options for disinvestment, indicating that implementation would rely on the receipt of any growth money (Lockett *et al*. 1995). None of the PBMA studies shed any light on how findings were (or were not) implemented.

The fact that PBMA entails the involvement of different stakeholders working towards a consensus is an acknowledgement that reconciling conflicting interests and objectives is essential if PBMA is to have any hopes of success at the implementation stage. Unfortunately, although consensus at the planning stage may be required for successful implementation, too many studies by ignoring implementation appear to give the impression that this is both a necessary and sufficient condition for success.

Green's experiences of attempting to use marginal analysis (MA) in Rotherham HA suggest that the unity of purpose assumed by the rational approach is unrealistic. He lists a whole series of barriers to the application of MA, including differing priorities within the HA, with the top-level support not shared throughout the organization, and resistance to change. Even where clinical teams were in agreement with the process, there was 'acceptance but no action' and 'provider protectionism' was also seen as an obstacle. Green notes that the process was 'out of synchronization' with the purchaser's timescales and that the HA was unable to commit fully since other short-term objectives were given priority (Green 1998).

Harrison's 1996 study also highlighted problems in relation to implementation. The process was characterized by differences in perspective in relation to what constitutes 'effectiveness', 'evidence' and 'costs' with clinicians conceiving causality and probability in a different way from epidemiologists, health service researchers and economists (Harrison 1996). The report acknowledges that assumptions made at the start of the project about the extent of direct purchaser control over services and the availability of clear evidence were erroneous. The reality revealed a situation that was much less straightforward.

Several studies remark on the fact that HAs do not have direct control over providers. Brambleby describes 'the sort of futile conversation' which has characterized discussions with providers and results in 'stalemate . . . frustration all round' (Brambleby 1995: 136). He attributes the uncertainty, change and risk which characterizes purchaser planning to fluctuations and delays in the resource-allocation process to the inability to control external factors such as high-cost cases which represent inescapable obligations and the devolution of former regional specialties with high-cost low-volume cases to HA level, increasing variability and risk locally.

This 'devolution' is part of a wider trend towards a fragmentation of service responsibilities in the public sector between a variety of public, private and voluntary providers (Ranade 1997). The changes from line bureaucracies to fragmented service agencies have produced a system of 'governance' (as opposed to government), which involves getting things done through other organizations. Rhodes describes the consequences of this institutional differentiation which include complexity and confusion, opaque accountability and a diminished capacity to steer (Rhodes 1997). This 'hollowing out of the state', as Rhodes calls it, is discussed further in Chapter 3, but it has important implications in terms of the rational model's assumptions about unity of purpose and the power of the decision-maker to effect implementation.

This process of working through other agencies is very different from the sort of 'top-down' approach described in Gunn's model of perfect implementation which requires that there is a single implementing agency or at least if other agencies must be involved, that dependency relationships are minimal (Gunn 1978).

Craig and colleagues (1995) suggest that economic advice has made little progress because in practice resources are allocated by purchasers, hospital managers and doctors pursuing conflicting objectives which differ and which may not even be defined in the same terms. Changing clinical practice is difficult enough (Poses *et al.* 1995), even when there is broad agreement on the benefits of doing so. Implementation problems will be exacerbated if clinicians are unhappy with the choice of outcome or cost parameters in economic evaluation.

In Harrison's study, criticism in relation to the MA of magnetic resonance imaging in the diagnosis of acoustic neuroma focused on the failure of the analysis to acknowledge the value to the patient of a true negative result (Harrison 1996). A US study by Detsky and colleagues, which examined physician attitudes to decision analytical models, found that clinicians may value information even if it does not specifically change patient management ('pure' information). They suggest that models that do not consider the value of 'pure' information may lack face validity for clinicians whilst patients may place a lower value on such information. A clinician may value pure information because he or she wishes to know what the future may hold even if it cannot affect what happens to the patient, while patients may be concerned only with getting well with minimum discomfort. If there is indeed a discrepancy in objectives, prescriptive models may yield different recommendations for clinicians and patients (Detsky *et al.* 1987), which again raises the question of whose values are to count in deciding what goes into the process of economic evaluation.

The desire to reduce uncertainty (at a potentially high cost) revealed in Detsky and colleagues' study may reflect the fact that clinicians are unwilling to follow evidence-based medicine's abandonment of linear certainty in clinical determination, in favour of a stochastically founded probabilistic approach (Tanenbaum 1994). The implications for implementation are enormous. Although clinicians are influenced by elements of both models, '*in the last analysis* it is the traditional model that predominates in medical decision-making' (Harrison 1998a: 25, original emphasis).

Duthie and colleagues' study of NHS decision-makers to health economic inputs to decision-making found that GPs were more concerned with patient satisfaction and quality of life issues, whereas HA personnel preferred 'to see hard data on efficacy and cost' (Duthie *et al.* 1999). When participants were asked to comment on 44 health outcome sentences in terms of relevance, only in 'a few cases' was universal agreement reached. Fifteen sentences were rejected by the majority of respondents either because they were not deemed worthwhile (these included sentences on marginal costs and benefits and patient preference data), they were not understood (for example statements encompassing Quality Adjusted Life Year – QALY – or number needed to treat concepts), or because the fundamental premise was challenged (such as a willingness to pay and trade-off between length and quality of life data).

Health economists are constantly striving to improve their methods and continue to research areas such as eliciting utility or health state preference values, calculating rates of time preference for discounting future costs and benefits and modelling utility functions for individuals. Interestingly, the methodological issues which preoccupy and often divide health economists do not feature as major concerns from the perspective of NHS policymakers in the PBMA studies reviewed. This lack of concern with methodological shortcomings may reflect partisan reporting by commentators who seek to minimize the drawbacks of economic evaluation techniques. It may be that by incorporating the values of stakeholders in the evaluation process and making the methodology and its assumptions explicit, PBMA will reduce the extent of criticism related to methodology. However, a more pessimistic interpretation is that as policymakers do not use economic evaluations, they do not understand the limitations of the techniques employed in constructing such information. If major reservations around methodology were reported by local policymakers, this may indicate, at least, that economic analyses were being 'used' in some sense.

The inflexibility of the NHS financial regime is seen as a barrier to the implementation of health economic 'solutions' at local level (Drummond *et al.* 1996; Hoffman and von der Schulenberg 2000). The regime's rigidity is twofold. First, finances are fixed and allocated annually. There is no provision for carrying forward resources from one year to the next and HAs are required to balance their budgets every year so that borrowing against future resources is not permitted. Under such a regime, it is likely that local decision-makers will adopt a short-term perspective. Since PCGs face similar restrictions, it seems likely that this short-termism will continue.

Second, resources are allocated in separate budgets and, for HAs, transfers between budget heads were, until recently, not permissible (from 1999/2000 this is no longer the case). This means that additional expenditure on drugs, which was compensated for by reduced hospital costs could not be funded from savings in the hospital budget. Even with the abolition, from 1999/2000 (Department of Health 1997), of the divisions between various parts of the budget, there are practical problems in releasing resources from hospitals (Ferguson and Baker 1997). This is due, in part, to the fact that marginal changes in activity are unlikely to release significant savings. Small reductions in ward occupancy rates rarely free up sufficient resources to allow ward closures and due to the pressure on beds, capacity will be taken up by other patients in the system. For example, a study conducted in Tayside identified increased day surgery as a priority, but later found that resources released from such a strategy would be minimal (Ruta *et al.* 1996). This issue is raised in several of the other PBMA studies reviewed. Studies which identify 'savings' in hospitals may have little impact, because such savings are notional and not cash releasing. Over 42 per cent of respondents to one survey thought the fact that 'savings' identified in cost effectiveness analyses of drug therapy were 'not real' was an important obstacle to applying them in practice (Drummond *et al.* 1996).

Amongst HA pharmaceutical advisers surveyed by Walley and colleagues, 'savings elsewhere in the NHS' was fifth in a list of five key economic issues and 'acquisition costs of drug' was first (Walley *et al.* 1997). This may be because of the financial regime operating at the time. The fact that the most important obstacle to the use of pharmacoeonomic evaluation in Drummond and colleagues' study was the inability to move resources from secondary care provides some support for this proposition (Drummond *et al.* 1996). With a change in the financial regime removing this barrier, decision-makers may now have more of an incentive to take a wider focus when reading economic evaluations. However, this will depend on a number of factors, including the extent to which they share common values and objectives.

Economic evaluations ignore the policy context within which decision-makers operate (both the foreground and the background) because they consider only the costs and benefits of particular health technologies. They aim, like published clinical trials, to make research findings public, but questions of implementation are not considered. PBMA studies, on the other hand, involve working with multidisciplinary groups to develop locally sensitive proposals. Although, disappointingly, these studies reveal little about implementation, it is likely that by carrying out the work at local level issues of implementation will be raised.

Miller and Vale's study of decision-maker attitudes to PBMA highlights reluctance on the part of commissioners to engage in such explicit prioritization exercises. This lends support to the idea that 'muddling through' is seen as the preferred option (Miller and Vale 1997). However, this does not explain why purchasers in some cases choose to undertake local priority setting in a more explicit manner. The perceived lack of legitimacy on the part of HA managers which has been identified as a barrier to engaging in explicit prioritization exercises may, paradoxically, explain why it is that some HAs have engaged in more explicit activities. As Klein and colleagues write, 'health authorities – precisely because of their uncertainty about their legitimacy – have made much greater efforts to open up the processes by which they reach their decision' (1996: 127). This would explain the attraction of PBMA to HAs, as it may be seen as legitimizing the process by the inclusion of stakeholders and the opening up of discussion. It is not clear, however, that health economists view things in this light.

Posnett and Street's advocacy of refining the methodology in order to curb discussion and involvement suggests a more secretive, or at least less inclusive 'black box' approach to the process. No doubt their experiences at West Pennine HA, where the stakeholder group chose not to cooperate further after the initial workshop, has influenced their views in the matter (Posnett and Street 1996). Cohen writes of the need to 'not expose the values of the group to the general public'. 'This is important because many people who may be happy to make value judgements behind closed doors may be less enthusiastic (to say the least) about having these valuations exposed publicly' (Cohen 1995: 152). The free reign of value judgements 'behind closed doors' is hardly conducive to the sort of legitimizing process described by Klein and colleagues.

Miller and Vale's study which examines purchaser resistance to engaging in PBMA-type exercises highlights the 'reactive' nature of management as a barrier to proactive priority-setting (Miller and Vale 1997). Reactive management is not confined to the NHS or even the public sector, so it is too simplistic to attribute this entirely to large-scale medical power relationships. However, concerns around legitimacy, puzzlement stemming from uncertainty (Hunter 1980) and the importance of providing symbolic reassurance to the public in accordance with the wishes of central government, along with medical power and authority in the NHS provide some explanation of why it is that managers might be reluctant to act. Miller and Vale perhaps fail to appreciate this when they recommend that '[p]urchasers only do what they are told to do, so let's tell them to adopt a PBMA approach'. Apart from the lack of understanding of the limitations placed on HA decision-makers which this statement displays, the authors do not consider the possibility that it may be in the interests of the centre, which does the 'telling', for HAs to refrain from explicit processes which threaten to undermine public confidence.

ISSUES ARISING FROM THE LITERATURE REVIEW

The small number of studies which report attempts to use or attitudes of decision-makers towards health economic techniques in practice present a picture which is at odds with the rational model of decision-making. For the most part, these studies focus on the 'foreground' of the decision process in terms of the cognitive demands it places on decision-makers and the absence of a sole unifying purpose shared by those involved. There are statements within these studies which hint at the wider context, but only rarely are these pursued explicitly.

A reading of the wider literature on decision-making provides a framework within which to read the health economic findings. For example, Cohen cites 'dealing with dominant personalities' as a key issue for consideration in relation to PBMA exercises. However, this suggests that if the 'dominant personality' was a HA chief executive, then this individual might be able to impose his or her views on the group in the same way as any other dominant personality might. The literature on medical power suggests that there are reasons why clinicians rather than other stakeholders may dominate such groups. Indeed, in Cohen's example, the dominant personality was indeed a 'powerful and articulate consultant' (Cohen 1995). Brambleby, himself a doctor, reports how discussions with the hospital clinical director ended in deadlock as the trust clinician refused to fund developments out of 'efficiency savings' within the directorate or from elsewhere in the trust. Despite this, Brambleby sees PBMA as part of the ' necessary groundwork to move discussions on to a more constructive footing' (1995: 136). This assumption appears to be based rather more on blind faith than evidence and ignores completely the wider context, in terms of clinician motivation and legitimacy, in which this exchange is taking place. The question of why it should be that a HA clinician can exert so little influence over his hospital counterpart is not elaborated upon.

Coupled with the failure to consider the wider context is the absence from the health economic studies of any attempt at conveying the local context facing HA commissioners. This is understandable as the PBMA research focus is largely confined to a description of methodology and its application, intended to inform those considering the use of PBMA rather than a detailed consideration of context-specific issues. Similarly in the case of surveys or interviews, respondents cover a number of sites, so that results are expressed in broad terms. Additionally, these studies describe expressed opinions, but cast little light on what is done in practice. For example, Drummond and colleagues (1996) found that HA respondents reported having read and acted upon economic evaluations of drug therapy. The fact that these analyses were either fictitious or not yet in the public domain raises questions about the reliability of data collected in such studies and the motives of respondents.

In other words, the question of what has happened in practice when attempts have been made to try to use health economics at the local level remains largely unanswered. This is not to suggest that there is one answer to this question as events will reflect organizational structures and individual preferences together with the methods used and reasons for engaging in the process. However, the hints given in the comments made by Green and by Harrison suggest that the subject merits further investigation.

The question of medical power and how this relates to the use of health economics has not been the subject of empirical research, so one can only speculate on the relationship between the two. The tendency in the literature to ascribe actions and intentions to 'the medical profession' or 'medical power' is to suggest a degree of cohesion and uniformity of belief and purpose which may be inadequate for the analysis of policy at the micro level. Doctors, despite the impression given in the literature on NHS management, are not all based in hospital trusts, but work within the NHS in HAs and in primary care. Whilst some writers recognize that doctors may be at one and the same time medics and managers in trusts, this role in HAs is largely ignored in the literature. Similarly, GPs perform roles as purchasers and providers of care since, regardless of who holds the budget, for elective care it is the GP who makes the decision to commit resources. Whilst the general and rather vague statement that attempts to use health economics are thwarted by the exercise of medical power may have a superficial appeal, it is merely a tentative hypothesis and does not explain how in practice such attempts are thwarted at the micro level. The question of why it should be that doctors working in the HA are unable or unwilling to exercise sufficient power to tackle their hospital counterparts is also a matter for investigation.

Finally, Hunter's observations around 'puzzlement' and Heclo's phrase the 'unwinnable dilemmas of social policy' have a prima facie appeal given the ambiguous and uncertain environment in which clinicians work. Hunter in one of the few in-depth studies of resource allocation within the NHS at local level, placed great emphasis on the idea that 'the issues faced in social politics are so complex, the major difficulty may not be the exercise of political will, but the determination of what that will is, or ought to be' (Hunter 1980: 43).

This idea suggests that rational and other purposive (means-ends) models of decision-making are at best less than complete in terms of explaining decision-making processes in HAs. This has important implications for health economic analyses predicated on the rational approach. The notion of puzzlement and the garbage can model allow for the incorporation of uncertainty and ambiguity, on a large scale, which is seen to typify the complex nature of health-care systems and medicine itself. Additionally, drawing on Kingdon's work on agenda setting, the use of this model as one of the lenses through which to view policy-making might help to provide an explanation of why particular policy items are considered for economic appraisal and others are not.

In an environment characterized by uncertainty and ambiguity, the extent to which decision-making can be understood in terms of puzzlement and organized anarchy (the garbage can model for example) rather than unity of purpose is worthy of further consideration.

3

THE HA CONTEXT: AN OVERVIEW

INTRODUCTION

The White Paper *Working for Patients* (Department of Health 1989) and subsequent legislation (NHS Community Care Act 1990) created a quasi-market for health care within the NHS. The aim of this was to replace monopolistic state providers with competitive ones, free of direct HA control. The old system, wherein District HAs accountable to Regional HAs managed health services, was replaced by a system of contracting for health care between different purchasers and providers.

The reforms created two types of purchaser: HAs and GP fund-holders. Each of these was required to assess need and purchase health care to meet that need within a fixed budget. Health-care purchasing, in theory, centres around a process of 'rational' decision-making, incorporating health needs assessment (Stevens and Gillam 1998), target-setting and planning, implementation of policies (translated into health-care contracts) and monitoring of progress (Department of Health 1989). Economists were quick to seize on the reforms as potentially increasing the demand for economic appraisal (Henshall and Drummond 1992).

HEALTH ECONOMICS AND HEALTH COMMISSIONING

The health economic approach relies heavily on evidence-based medicine (Sackett *et al.* 1996) to demonstrate efficacy and/or effectiveness of treatment. If costs and benefits arising from interventions are to be calculated, then some reliable measure of benefits must be used. 'Evidence' ideally (for proponents of evidence-based medicine the randomized controlled trial is seen as the gold standard) is gleaned from large randomized controlled trials of sufficient rigour and objectivity to provide reliable results on which to base policy decisions. The commitment to evidence-based medicine is reflected in the government's financial support for bodies such as the Centre for Reviews and Dissemination at York University and the Cochrane Collaboration, the role of which is to collect and disseminate evidence on health-care treatments. However, there is still a long way to go on the issue of quality of life data. A recent review of clinical studies on the Cochrane Controlled Trials Register found that only 4.2 per cent of studies reported endpoints which included some sort of quality of life measure (Sanders *et al.* 1998). This is hardly surprising since the measurement of quality of life or 'utility' is more problematic than that of other endpoints such as mortality or myocardial infarction (heart attack).

For health economists, having obtained the required evidence of effectiveness, the next step is to apply the test of cost-effectiveness to the various competing candidates for scarce health-care resources and to prioritize resource allocation in order to secure maximum 'health gain' from a fixed health-care budget (Maynard 1996).

The appeal of health economics is that priorities are generated 'rationally' via a systematic process of calculation and analysis. The appeal for the government, is that rationing in this manner may be presented not as a decision to deny treatment taken by selfish or uncaring individuals, but as the product of a scientific process which encompasses the principle of clinical need and combines with this the concept of value for money. An 'independent' review approach to priority-setting allows responsibility for decisions based thereon to be deflected from the individual policymakers to the process itself.

THE RESEARCH CONTEXT: POPPLETON HA

In addition to the HA chairman and other non-executive members, each HA had a chief executive, a director of public health (DPH) and a finance director (FD) as required by law. Poppleton HA had other directors at the start of the project, including the medical director

Table 3.1   Revenue budget percentage split for Poppleton HA 1999/2000

Budget heading	Allocation (%)
Hospital and Community Health Services	80
General Medical Services	3
Prescribing	17

(MD), who formed part of the HA management team. All of these directors were directly accountable to the chief executive (CE).

The MD, a former GP, had responsibility for, among other things, prescribing and CHD. For the duration of the research, I was based within the medical directorate which comprised a number of pharmacists, secretarial support and a project manager for the CHD strategy. The MD worked closely with the contracts director (CD), whose duties related to the negotiation of contracts with local providers of health care.

Poppleton HA received an annual budget for the purchase of health care. Prior to 1999/2000, there were separate budgets for different expenditure heads. The Hospital and Community Health Services' (HCHS) budget covered all hospital and community services health care for the HA's resident population. This allocation was based on a formula designed to reflect health need (Carr-Hill *et al.* 1994). The HA also received an annual cash limited budget for expenditure in primary care covering such items as contributions to practice staff salaries, computers and premises-related costs in general practice. This was known as the General Medical Services (GMS) cash limited budget. These budgets were allocated annually and HAs were not normally allowed to borrow against future allocations or carry forward large sums for future years. In addition to these two funding streams, the HA received an annual prescribing budget to cover the cost of drugs prescribed in general practice. This prescribing budget represented an indicative budget and was not cash limited in the same way as the other resources, yet HAs were expected to contain expenditure within budget. The percentage of total budget allocated to each of these areas is illustrated in Table 3.1.

Within Poppleton HA the distribution of the primary care (GP) prescribing budget between individual practices was the responsibility of the MD and his staff. Practice prescribing budgets were usually allocated on the basis of historical expenditure rather than on any needs-based formula. Prescribing was seen as being on the fringes of HA business, largely because the focus of HA activity was on the commissioning and monitoring of hospital and community health services, for which resources were cash limited.

Just as HAs were not permitted to save or borrow across financial years, virement of funds across budget heads was not permitted previously. In 1999/2000 a unified budget was introduced which removed this division between budget heads. Poppleton HA had, historically, experienced difficulty in containing prescribing expenditure within budget, although other budget heads had generally remained in balance.

Following the creation of GP fundholding in 1991, certain groups of GPs opted to become budget holders (GP fundholders) with responsibility for prescribing and certain aspects of elective health care. For these GPs, health-care budgets were allocated under three headings: prescribing, HCHS and GMS, but virement across budgets was permitted and the resources were effectively treated as a single budget. Underspending GPs were permitted to carry forward any unspent resources for use in future years. GP fundholding was abolished with effect from April 1999.

HA ACCOUNTABILITY FRAMEWORK AT THE TIME OF THE RESEARCH

HAs were accountable to the NHSE which was responsible for advising ministers and for formulating and ensuring implementation of policy on health care. It had a strategic rather than operational role. The NHSE had specific responsibility for advising the Secretary of State on:

- setting and maintaining a strategic framework for the NHS;
- securing and allocating resources for the NHS; and
- developing policy for services delivered by the NHS (Department of Health 1995).

Prior to 1994, HAs were accountable to Regional HAs which performed the regulatory role undertaken by the NHSE. Although this move has been seen as a tightening of central control over HAs (Klein 1995), the potential for detailed scrutiny of HA activities was reduced due to the small numbers of staff involved in the monitoring process at the NHSE regional offices.

Other factors contribute to this reduction in the ability of the centre to control the outputs from what are large, fragmented and complex systems. Privatization and the creation of new agencies and quangos in the public sector have led to a fragmentation of service responsibilities between a variety of public, private and voluntary providers (Ranade 1997). This 'hollowing out of the state' has reduced the ability of the government to coordinate and steer complex sets of organizations and has prompted a tightening of control over financial resources and a strengthening of central regulation and monitoring. However, such hands-on controls may not provide sufficient leverage for the centre to steer the networks (Rhodes 1995, 1999).

These changes have produced a system of 'governance' (as opposed to government), which involves 'getting things done through other organizations' (Metcalfe and Richards 1990: 220). The notion of 'governance' in which hierarchies are replaced by networks is important for understanding the context within which HAs operated. Although they were accountable for health services provided to their populations, HAs did not have direct control over the organizations and individuals supplying those services. Getting things done through other organizations was a key feature of HA business, but HAs often lacked the leverage to do this. Pressure to contain 'management costs' at HAs meant that a small number of staff were responsible for commissioning a wide range of health services with the result that they were placed at a disadvantage when dealing with hospital consultants who are expert in their field.

HAs faced incentives to portray their performance in as favourable a light as possible to the NHSE and the asymmetry of information, with the latter having little detailed knowledge of events of local level, made this an easy option. The HA had clear lines of accountability to the NHSE and the need to meet central directives dominated the policy agenda at the HA. However, the HA had a high level of discretion in many areas, with the result that in certain realms of activity its accountabilities were ill defined or non-existent.

If the centre is seen as intrusive in its forms of control, unreasonable in its requests and remote in terms of its understanding of local events, a view that was expressed often at Poppleton HA, its legitimacy may be questioned at local level. This would create the potential for HA managers to pursue courses of action based on their own view of what would be best for the service or for patients. Those economists who advocate central directives to impose programme-budgeting exercises on reluctant HAs (Miller and Vale

1997) might wish to consider the advisability of such action within the wider context of HA decision-making and accountability.

In April 2002 the existing 95 HAs were replaced by 30 Strategic HAs, the role of which is to lead the strategic development of the local health service and performance manage PCTs and NHS trusts. Revenue allocations are now made directly to PCTs and regional offices have been abolished.

GPs, HAs and accountability – a case of insufficient leverage?

Klein has written that 'one of the paradoxes of the NHS since its creation has been that it exercises least control over those who, in theory at least, exercise the greatest influence in determining the demands for health care: general practitioners' (Klein, 2000: 183).

GPs are providers of care and act as agents for their patients, directing them on to other health-care professionals. The GP performs a gatekeeper role in determining who is referred and to where, filtering access to hospital care. Thus, the GP has a major role in influencing demand for hospital services, but GPs had hitherto successfully resisted attempts to bring them into the mainstream NHS, preferring instead to retain their independent contractor status. This meant that although the HA was responsible for balancing budgets, resource use was influenced, in large part, by the activities of GPs, over whom the HA had little control. In addition to the impact on prescribing expenditure and elective care referrals, the GP's actions, in terms of the standard of care provided in primary care also impacted on emergency admissions.

Whilst the HA's role was to secure care for its population, which meant balancing needs and denying effective care on the grounds of resource scarcity, the GP deals with individual patients and may be less inclined to take a population perspective. The creation of PCGs and PCTs, which seek to align clinical and financial responsibility, may have some impact on GP perspectives. The pharmaceutical advisers at Poppleton HA complained regularly that their attempts to contain prescribing costs were resisted on the grounds that GPs were concerned to do the best for their patients, rather than consider the needs of the population as a whole. In order to reduce variations in care and promote good practice, the HA had issued various guidelines to GPs, but there was no obligation for GPs to follow these guidelines and the extent of variation in relation to prescribing and referral patterns would suggest that guideline implementation was patchy at best.

HA managers found the lack of control over GPs frustrating, but the GPs' independent contractor status has been part of the NHS since its inception. The introduction of the quasi market in 1991 and the move towards 'getting things done' through networks created new problems for those responsible for the health care of local populations. Opinions differ as to the desirability or otherwise of networks and network forms of organization (Flynn *et al.* 1996). It seems likely, however, that networks will function more efficiently under circumstances of high-trust relationships, as if trust is low, it may be necessary to bring in third parties, codify rules and spell out relations in greater detail. At this point, the relationship starts to look more like a traditional hierarchy or a market than a network (Fukayama 1995).

Low-trust and high-trust relationships in a low-accountability environment

The concept of trust has been defined in many ways. Neoclassical economic ideas on the subject incorporate the calculative actions of a utility-maximizing individual (Gambetta 1988). The assumption here is that individuals consciously assess the probable gains and losses from entering into relationships with others in a rational manner.

Others reject the 'atomistic' theories of neoclassical economics which view individuals as existing in some kind of Hobbesian state of nature, free from social relationships and institutional context. Granovetter, sees attempts at purposive action as 'embedded in concrete, ongoing systems of social relations' (1985: 487). This argument stresses the role of personal relations and networks of relations in 'generating trust and discouraging malfeasance'. However, the trust created in these personal relations, presents by its very existence, enhanced opportunities for malfeasance. For example, embezzlement is only possible because the perpetrator has built up enough trust for opportunities to manipulate accounts to be made available to him or her.

The trust in these abstract systems is an impersonal trust, which Giddens views as different from 'basic' trust. With reference to the latter, which is concerned with 'a strong psychological need to find others to trust', Giddens writes that:

> Trust on a personal level becomes a project, to be 'worked at' by the parties involved, and demands the *opening out of the*

individual to the other. Where it cannot be controlled by fixed normative codes, trust has to be won, and the means of doing this is demonstrable warmth and openness . . . trust is not pre-given but worked upon, and where the work involved means *a mutual process of self-disclosure.*

(Giddens 1991: 121, original emphasis)

Regardless of the way individual behaviour and perceptions are portrayed in alternative theories on the subject, some awareness of risk is central to the notion of trust. If we did not have to place our confidence in individuals, if their actions and motives were entirely visible, then we would not have to 'trust', but merely observe them. The separation of the roles of purchasing and providing health care increases the need for trust between the two parties because of the limited opportunities of commissioners to observe, at first hand, the services provided by the hospital trust.

Expertise and information are concentrated in the provider, and the complex nature of the 'product' being purchased means that commissioners are reliant on the maintenance and reproduction of trust in their relationships with local hospital staff if the business of contracting for health care is to run smoothly.

Fox (1974) distinguishes between high- and low-trust relationships. In the former, participants share values or objectives and a diffuse sense of long-term obligations to each other. They offer spontaneous support in a way which is free from the narrow calculativeness contained in neoclassical economic views of trust. Communication is free and honest, participants are ready to place their fortunes in each other's hands and give each other the benefit of any doubt arising regarding goodwill or motivation.

In low-trust relationships, by contrast, actors have divergent goals and explicit expectations which have to be reciprocated through precisely balanced exchange in the short term. The relationship involves calculation of costs and benefits likely to arise from any concessions and communication is secretive. Participants seek to minimize their dependence on each other's discretion and sanctions are likely to be applied against ill will or failure to meet obligations.

Fox laments the replacement of fellowship by 'calculative specificity', which is a product of market and contractual relationships permeating every sphere of social life. In the market place, labour is a commodity to be bought and sold, subject to specific definition and reward. Although high discretion is necessary for the

performance of many work activities, this 'keen calculative specificity of reciprocation' is seen as a contradiction in terms to high-
discretion relations. 'Any attempt to substitute such specificity for
the relatively diffuse commitment among members of the high-
trust fraternity would soon bring the modern work organization
grinding to a halt' (Fox 1974: 374).

So whilst high discretion may be necessary for hospital clinicians
working in complex environments, this requires that purchasers in
HAs or PCGs place high levels of trust in these same clinicians in
order to avoid the sort of extinguishing of diffuse commitment to
which Fox refers. This would suggest, therefore, that purchasers
avoid attempts to prescribe or codify provider behaviour, encouraging instead the development and maintenance of a diffuse sense
of long-term obligations. Paradoxically, however, as Granovetter
observed, the trust created in these personal relations, presents by
its very existence, enhanced opportunities for malfeasance (Granovetter 1985).

This tension between the positive and negative potential of high-
trust relationships explains, in part, why contracting relationships
between Poppleton HA and its providers may be seen more as
varying between low- and high-trust relations. The process is
characterized by asymmetry of information and is one in which providers have little incentive to furnish HAs with details which may
be used against them in the future. In their study of HA contracting
processes Flynn and colleagues (1996) write of an oscillation in
styles with purchasers moving between adversarial and collaborative modes of negotiation at different times and over different
issues. Purchaser efforts to secure more control over provider service delivery were seen as threatening by providers. The effect of
such approaches was often to corrode rather than nurture common
values and commitments, to create an atmosphere of mistrust and
to exacerbate inherent problems of uncertainty in the contract
process.

This lack of trust was apparent at Poppleton HA in relation to
tertiary cardiology services. Underperformance on contracts led
the contracts manager to accuse the provider of 'ripping off' the
HA. Representatives of the HA were aggrieved at what they saw as
service developments based on the wishes of the trust medical staff
and not in accordance with HA priorities. The HA MD accused
trust contracts staff of focusing on private-patient income to the
detriment of NHS patients and of siphoning off HA funds to
resource experimental 'high-tech' procedures. Unsurprisingly, such

comments did not result in the development of a collaborative approach and the contract negotiations remained deadlocked for some weeks. However, both HA and trust representatives reported to the civil servant responsible for performance appraisal that contracts had been agreed. Failure to agree contracts by the required date was seen as detrimental to the career prospects of the individuals involved and likely to encourage closer scrutiny of affairs on the part of the centre, whose staff were seen by both parties as having little detailed knowledge of the issues involved.

In order to build good relationships with key clinicians the MD and CD at Poppleton HA established a series of lunchtime meetings at a nearby hotel ('neutral' territory) to discuss service issues away from the cut and thrust of the contract negotiating cycle. These meetings focused on shared objectives and the initial focus for discussions was the winter pressure problems in 1996/97 which all present were keen to ensure were not repeated the following year. By meeting regularly as a group over time the aim was to encourage the sort of relationships which Fox describes in terms of a diffuse sense of long-term obligations to each other and spontaneous support in a way which is free from narrow calculativeness. The meetings were not minuted and discussions were held in an informal manner, with only a loose agenda. These attempts can be seen in terms of aiming for the free and honest communication which characterizes Fox's high-trust model. None of the clinicians from the tertiary centre attended, however, and relations with this unit remained at the same low-trust level throughout the project.

After attending one of these meetings, I was struck by the way in which the HA team congratulated itself on its achievements from the meeting. As the staff chatted in the car park afterwards, agreeing that it had all gone very well, I wondered why the meeting might not have gone well. The clinicians, who were given lunch and an opportunity to beat the drum for resources, were unlikely to prove difficult, particularly when these resources were agreed to by the HA staff. Why at subsequent meetings did the HA managers continue to speak of their achievements, when very little in the way of concrete and visible outcomes had been achieved? If the aim of the meetings was to distribute resources, then this could have been undertaken as part of the contracting process. However, if one considers outcomes in more intangible or diffuse forms, the sense of achievement can be more easily understood.

The meetings were seen as useful in terms of building links and creating trust, but the consequence was that resources were allocated to the pet schemes of individuals because they were 'trusted' members of this elite luncheon club. The clinical director of the local trust proposed at one meeting that his scheme for additional senior medical staff aimed at reducing emergency admissions be funded and his suggestion was accepted by the CD and MD. When I questioned the wisdom of this move, pointing to the potential for these staff to become just another pair of (expensive) hands in the accident and emergency (A and E) department and asking how it would be evaluated, I was told by the CD that even if it were not successful in reducing admissions it would be buying 'goodwill' with the hospital trust. Similarly, in the spring, the luncheon club members were asked their opinion on which of the investments designed to reduce emergency admissions had been successful in order to prioritize developments for the coming winter. Members gave their opinion based largely on gut feeling and without reference to any data.

If one views trust more in terms of Giddens' 'strong psychological need to find others to trust', where 'trust on a personal level becomes a project, to be "worked at" by the parties involved, and demands the *opening out of the individual to the other* . . . where the work involved means *a mutual process of self-disclosure*' (Giddens 1991: 121, original emphasis), then the value of these high-trust relations becomes more apparent. If the HA staff need to find others to trust, then contractual relations as they operate at formal contract meetings, characterized in the case of the tertiary centre by the MD's attempts at prescription and the trust's resistance and secrecy, will not fulfil the need for what Giddens calls 'basic' trust. As life at the HA is characterized by divisions and rivalries, it would be wrong to assume that HA managers can rely on in-house relationships to fulfil the need for 'basic' trust.

In an environment of uncertainty, measuring progress is difficult. The HA and hospital staff are forced to compromise on service delivery, but cling to what remains of the service ethic which drives them. In their day-to-day transactions, they often appear to be on opposite sides of the fence, so that leaving the office at the end of the day they may feel worn down by attempts to pursue common goals via an adversarial system. The appeal of these informal meetings can be understood in terms of the opportunity for those involved to engage in the kind of cooperative environment which reminds them of their common aims[1] and makes the day-to-day struggles and crises bearable. The regular informal meetings and the oscillation in the contracting process between low- and high-trust relations can be understood as attempts to contain the inherent ambivalence present when those who profess to share common goals act in a way which is perceived as being contrary to the common goals.

Low-trust relationships and a monitoring framework in which accountability flows upwards, but not downwards, promote secrecy in decision-making, and encourage stakeholders to present fictional accounts to those charged with monitoring their performance. This is problematic for studies assessing attitudes of HA decision-makers to the use of health economics since it suggests that there are incentives to respond to surveys in a less than honest fashion. Health economists who ignore the HA's need to present a public face which may differ markedly from the internal realities of the working environment risk drawing erroneous conclusions. For example, the efficiency index features prominently as a barrier to change and innovation in the health economics literature (see 'Measuring performance' below), but in 1997 when I arrived at Poppleton HA the contracts manager was dismissive of this suggestion. 'We just fiddle it', he told me. After years of living with the index, purchasers and providers had become expert at 'optimizing' patient number calculations to be declared to the centre and were happy to collude in this process. Some observers have identified a trend towards increasing secrecy of decision-making in the NHS combined with unequal access to information (Audit Commission 1994). It may be tempting, therefore, to view providers as dominating the purchasing agenda and purchasers as powerless to curb the desires of hospital clinicians, whose actions may be detrimental to the service as a whole. It was precisely the desire to reduce the perceived extent of clinician dominance which influenced the market reforms contained in *Working for Patients* (Department of Health 1989). Paradoxically, however, the reforms are seen as largely contributing to this trend of secrecy. Experiences at Poppleton HA would suggest that this crude explanation would benefit from a little refinement.

The problem with this view is that in suggesting that trusts or individual clinicians constrain the flow of information to purchasers, limiting the HA's potential for scrutiny and attempts at control, it attributes providers with an omniscience which they do not possess. Much of the effort at the acute hospitals is focused on dealing with a variable emergency workload. The relationships between the supply of and demand for health care are complex and the trust is often in the position of responding to whatever comes through the door. Since the introduction of the internal market, information systems have been geared towards producing patient minimum data sets for contract monitoring purposes. More exacting requirements, which involve the tracking of patients through complex patterns of care, may be beyond the capabilities of these systems. The information system in the A and E department of the local acute trust, for example, was not linked to the inpatient data system, making tracking of patients difficult and identifying outpatient activity for CHD patients problematic due to the way in which information was recorded.

If the acute trust were not a 'black box', the HA would, in theory, have an opportunity to use data to influence service provision. However, this raises the question of how such information would be used and the extent to which the trust is able to control activity flows to the hospital.

MEASURING PERFORMANCE IN HAs

The efficiency index

The role of the HA was broadly to assess health needs and commission and plan services to meet these needs, whilst balancing income and expenditure. In addition to meeting strict financial targets, HAs were required to demonstrate that resources were being used 'efficiently'.

HA performance, prior to 1998/9, was assessed by means of an 'efficiency index' which measured the volume of patients in the system from one year to the next alongside the resources available. The concept underlying the NHS efficiency index was loosely one of technical efficiency. HAs were required to purchase increasing activity, year on year, from a fixed resource or demonstrate disproportionate increases in activity from any real increases in funding (Raftery *et al.* 1996). Process measures of activity such as 'finished consultant episodes' or 'community contacts' were used in order to calculate the changes in volume from one year to the next. However, no attempt was required (or made) to demonstrate the extent to which the balance of funds between health programmes (such as mental health, cancers and CHD) represented a cost-effective allocation of resources. No assessment of health outcomes was made in the context of resources investment. In industrial processes which generate uniform or identical products, output measurement is easier and assessment of productivity from a fixed resource more meaningful than in a health-care context where outcomes are not easy to assess and process measures are anything but uniform.

The efficiency index was criticized heavily as creating perverse incentives (Donaldson *et al.* 1994). The need to count as many patients as possible created incentives to discharge patients as early as possible, increasing the risk that they would be readmitted in the future. Preventive medicine is less likely to be seen as a priority, it has been argued, because anything which reduces inpatient activity worsens the efficiency index position. Too crude a reading of this situation might lead one to the conclusion that the abolition of the efficiency index would resolve many problems for NHS purchasers and providers.

In practice, pressure on hospital beds meant that the local trusts were attempting to limit the amount of time that a patient spends in a bed in order to create space for the new arrivals. The consultant cardiologist explained his dilemma as follows:

> We keep people with chest pain in long enough to rule out MI,[2] but that doesn't mean that we've sorted them out. We'd like to do more for them, but we don't have the beds and . . . we know that sooner or later they'll come straight back in again with chest pain.

It would be easy to blame the monitoring arrangements for creating perverse incentives to discharge people prematurely. The hospital activity figures show that for 1995/6, 1996/7 and 1997/8, the modal length of stay for 'chest pain' patients who are not having a heart attack is 2 days, or just long enough to rule out a heart attack. The comments by the cardiologist above, and repeated by other clinicians at neighbouring trusts, indicate that there are incentives in the system to provide sub-optimal care, not because of performance-monitoring mechanisms, but in order to admit other urgent cases.

Similarly, there is nothing to indicate that HAs were more certain about the effectiveness of preventive strategies or less restricted in terms of their ability to free up resources for such schemes in 1999, following the abolition of the efficiency index than they were before. An overemphasis on the efficiency index assumes that HAs would have the power to do things differently under an alternative performance-measurement system. This view of the HA is at odds with experiences at Poppleton HA, where the HA appears almost powerless in the face of rising emergency medical admissions and uncertainty and ambiguity in relation to what is being aimed for and how to achieve it.

Other measures of HA performance

The monitoring of HA performance encompassed a range of measures reflecting Department of Health concerns, such as the management of emergency medical admissions at hospitals within their boundaries, waiting-list management and the percentage of generic drugs prescribed by GPs. In addition, progress towards meeting national targets around major disease areas were examined (Department of Health 1998a). However, it is widely acknowledged that the contribution of health services to health is small and that the NHS has very little influence over the major determinants of health (factors such as income and housing, for example). This led to a paradoxical situation in which, although HAs were charged with assessing health needs and commissioning care to meet those needs, the NHSE had yet to develop a means of measuring the performance of the HA in relation to those objectives. HAs were not required to demonstrate to the NHSE that they were actively engaged in the process of needs assessment; and, in any case, needs assessment is only of use if it is linked to the commissioning of health care to meet those needs.

In practice, HAs were required to agree contracts (subsequently 'long-term service agreements') for care with providers within set deadlines, meet waiting lists targets for elective care and manage winter pressures on emergency admissions within available resources. In other words, the emphasis was on maintaining stability, or at least maintaining the image of stability, to reassure the general public, and on minimizing the potential for adverse publicity which would attract critical scrutiny from the executive and the electorate alike.

A failure to meet waiting list targets was seen as likely to produce strongly worded phone calls or even personal visits from the NHSE. The HA staff were very aware of the need to meet waiting list targets. They resented the imposition of these targets which they saw as yet another example of a remote top-down edict distorting local priorities, but there was an acceptance that this was not negotiable and considerable effort was expended on planning, commissioning and monitoring waiting list performance. The failure to meet targets around, say, teenage pregnancies or smoking cessation was seen as unlikely to threaten the careers of the HA staff responsible for those areas.

'Success' is where you find it

Within HAs there were few incentives to look critically at performance. As goals may be expressed in broad terms ('coping with
winter pressures') or in terms of process (contracts signed) as
opposed to tangible outcomes, HAs were in a position to claim
credit where it may not have been due. This makes economic evaluation problematic. In the absence of, for example, objective
measures of 'coping', it is difficult to assess the extent to which
investments in coping strategies were justified and, given the uncertainties of cause and effect in the system, to assess the likely outcome in the absence of HA intervention. The lack of explicit
success criteria, however, meant that success could be defined post
hoc and in an arbitrary manner.

In addition, the problems associated with getting things done
through other organizations meant that where the HA staff were
able to forge agreements on the ground this was treated as an end in
itself. Similarly, activity in terms of increased patient numbers or
enhanced staffing levels was equated with success regardless of the
outcomes of this activity. For example, investments in additional
nurses to work with CHD patients in primary care were welcomed
by the practices served. The GPs were unlikely to question the
wisdom of such investment for fear that it may jeopardize future
development opportunities. Patients who were seen by the nurses
were grateful for the attention, regardless of whether or not health
outcomes were improved. HA managers who championed such
developments were keen for them to be declared a success and the
nurses themselves were keen to feel that they were impacting on the
health of the community. Additional hospital doctors were declared
a success on the grounds that they were 'boosting morale' and when
reporting on the success of the Baxby locality smoking-cessation
scheme, the manager cites the enthusiasm of the health-care assist-
ants who 'love it' and 'say it's going very well' as evidence of its value.

It is important not to see such actions in terms of self-serving
bureaucrats seeking budgetary enhancement and overprovision of
services (Niskanen 1971). First, those who seek additional
resources are motivated by the desire to provide better (or at least
more) services for patients. These resources are not necessarily
under the control of those who request them and are not a form of
bolstering power bases. Second, in relation to overprovision of
service, there is no general agreement about what constitutes a
'correct' or 'adequate' level of provision, due to the inherently

uncertain nature of the health-care investment process. Indeed, one could argue that given the very high CHD mortality in Poppleton HA, there is some justification for increasing investment in CHD services. However, the latter argument would rely on effective as opposed to merely 'visible' care being provided.

HA objectives and performance monitoring – balancing, not maximizing

Individual members of staff had written objectives which were, in theory at least, subject to regular review, by their line managers. These individual objectives were intended to stem from and reflect organizational objectives. The role of the HA in terms of needs assessment and securing health care to meet local needs was enshrined in legislation, but the policies pursued to achieve these aims differed between purchasers. HAs have different needs, services and populations, so priorities may differ, but HAs facing similar problems do not always produce similar policies for dealing with them.

Although health economists have taken the maximization of health or of health gain as the objective of the NHS (Culyer 1997), it is not clear from the targets that health maximization is the objective of the NHS. The revised performance measurement criteria define six aims of the service (NHSE 1998a). These six areas are intended to give a clear signal of what matters in the NHS and to provide a way of making a rounded assessment of whether the new NHS is performing in line with the expectations set out in the White Paper. In addition to health improvement and health outcomes, performance is now monitored in relation to fair access, effectiveness, efficiency and patient/carer experiences. This suggests that the view from the Department of Health is that the NHS should attempt to achieve a balance between competing demands of maximizing health, providing value for money, meeting the needs of customers and ensuring 'fair access' to services. Another Department of Health publication *Our Healthier Nation* (Department of Health 1998b) focuses on improving the health of the most disadvantaged members of society.

Uncertainty exists about the measurement of health outcomes where only outputs (such as hospital admissions) are identified and this leads to problems in evaluating service changes. Taken together with an inability to answer questions such as what constitutes an 'adequate' level of service provision, the result is an environment in which 'policy *results* – it does not get *made*' (Heclo, 1975: 153, original emphasis).

Puzzlement at Poppleton HA arises, not just because of a lack of data, but because the issues involved are so complicated. The objectives contained in the cardiovascular strategy are 'prevention', 'optimum management of acute and chronic pathways of care' and 'minimize disability'. Public sector organizations need to reconcile multiple interests, build stakeholder support, and take credit for 'success' which may explain why goals are often specified in deliberately vague terms (Ranade 1997). These objectives are not useful when attempting to answer questions such as 'What do we mean by optimum and how would we recognize optimum care?' When questioned on what the CHD strategy was trying to achieve, the MD replied 'We're not looking for immortality here. We are about preventing premature death from CHD.' However, he went on to add 'People have to decide whether they are trying to save lives or buying life years.' This implies that the issue was still open to debate amongst the stakeholders concerned. On ten occasions within 2 weeks the MD repeated his advice that cholesterol-lowering drugs should not 'be given to 80-year-olds' on the grounds that 'we are not buying immortality here'. However, when asked 'If we're into preventing premature deaths, does that mean we should spend less resources on elderly patients who turn up in A and E with a suspected heart attack?' The MD said emphatically that this was not the intention. 'You see, people have got to make up their mind about what it is we're trying to achieve here. Are we saving lives or life years or what? We can't do everything.'

At a neighbouring HA I watched as a consultant gastroenterologist met with HA purchasers to discuss the construction and implementation of a guideline for patients with dyspepsia. During the 2-hour meeting, the consultant asked repeatedly 'What is the aim of the guideline?' At first, the DPH replied that the aim was to 'do the best for patients'. 'But what does that mean? Is it the best we can afford? Or is it to cut drug costs? Isn't the whole thing to get the PPI[3] bill down?' He asked a further five times during the meeting, but nobody answered his question. As the meeting was drawing to a close, the DPH said 'The main aim now is to get the guideline drawn up and we can start rolling it out.' Apparently, it did not perturb HA decision-makers that no clear aim was specified for the guideline. This theme of 'puzzlement' or confusion around objectives is developed in Chapters 4, 5 and 6.

COMMISSIONING HEALTH CARE

Each HA bought health services for its resident population from local service providers, predominantly NHS trusts. Contracts for care were settled annually and the process for agreeing the content was one of rolling forward the services currently provided, with small changes at the margin. For existing services, no attempt was made to evaluate the cost effectiveness of the health care provided, but new services, for which additional resources were sought, were subject to greater scrutiny.

Providers were requested to make a business case for service developments, but often the benefits were not quantified and purchasers had no clinical evidence on which to make judgements of effectiveness or cost effectiveness. For example, the request from the local NHS trust within Poppleton HA for an additional consultant cardiologist was prompted by a growing waiting list for outpatient cardiology appointments. The outputs from this investment were identified in terms of additional outpatient capacity, but the likely impact on health outcomes was not quantified.

The problem for HA decision-makers was that of uncertainty in relation to the likely health outcomes and knock-on effects on other aspects of the service of such an investment. Health economic evaluation entails assessing evidence of effectiveness and calculating the cost-effectiveness of candidates for investment. This approach, which involves methodical calculation of costs and benefits in accordance with rational decision-making models, does not fit easily with the needs of HA decision-makers facing high levels of uncertainty and short timescales. In many cases evidence of effectiveness does not exist (Stocking 1995). This is not simply due to the informational barriers referred to in the health economics literature and cannot always be rectified by the collection of further data.

Making judgements about what would constitute an adequate level of service was difficult, particularly since ideally notions of adequate or acceptable service levels need to be considered within the context of affordability and the overall balance of investments between services. Targets for cardiological procedures and resources have been produced by the British Cardiac Society (BCS), but these do not address affordability and the BCS, hardly a disinterested party in this process, is not concerned with the demands on resources made in other disease areas.

DECISION-MAKING UNDER UNCERTAINTY – THE POTENTIAL FOR DISCRETION AND DECEIT

There were clear and formal structures for making decisions in Poppleton HA which related to meetings of the HA and its sub-committees. Outside of these formal mechanisms, decisions would be taken by individual directors or their staff. Defining the characteristics of those choices which can be resolved at an informal or individual level is difficult as there are often inconsistencies in the process. For example, at Poppleton HA the size of the financial commitment involved in a decision did not appear to bear any relationship to the level at which the decision is taken. Contracts in excess of £50 million were agreed by the CD and FD, whereas extra contractual referrals (ECRs are patient referrals which are not covered by existing contracts) for relatively small sums would be referred to a sub-committee of the HA.

Although the HA was the formal decision-making body, most decisions were made outside of the HA meetings by individuals acting on their discretion. With large workloads and tight deadlines to manage, HA staff were sufficiently occupied with their own area of responsibility to limit the extent of their involvement in issues which fell outside their remit. The lack of information and uncertainty within the system led some HA managers to follow a process of change avoidance. In an environment where action may have unintended consequences, the policy decision may be to do nothing. Alternatively, for HA managers who were keen to promote change, such as the MD at Poppleton HA, a policy vacuum existed to be filled by those with enough nerve to do so. Where outcomes are not clearly specified, evaluation is almost non-existent and success defined post hoc, the risk of making 'bad' decisions is small. The atmosphere of secrecy combined with a lack of time on the part of HA employees served to reduce the extent of critical scrutiny and create opportunities for managers to misrepresent and manipulate in order to achieve their desired outcome. This misrepresentation could be used as a tactic between purchaser and provider or purchaser and NHSE. However, the focus on secrecy and divisions created by the internal market ignores the potential for division and deception at HA level, which was a very real feature of life at Poppleton HA.

The emphasis on uncertainty and lack of control illustrates the difficult task faced by the HA MD, but the portrayal of a powerless MD struggling against the odds does not present the whole picture.

Whilst the MD's power in relation to GP prescribing and referral activity was limited, in areas where control was more direct (the management of his team, the provision of 'specialist' advice to HA colleagues, the establishment of a new service for cardiac patients in primary care) the MD turned uncertainty and a paucity of data to his advantage.

Flyvbjerg's observation that 'power is knowledge' turns the Baconian dictum 'knowledge is power' on its head. Those who possess power can define what counts as knowledge and rationality, and ultimately what counts as reality (Flyvbjerg 1998). In an environment where data is unavailable, one response may be to commission a data-gathering process. However, the lack of data creates the sorts of opportunities for knowledge definition to which Flyvbjerg refers. For the MD at Poppleton HA, the mantra that younger patients should receive priority over older patients (see Chapter 4), that heart failure treatment produces only small health gains (see Chapter 6) and that cardiac nurses in primary care are a huge success (Chapter 5) was repeated often enough to ensure that its contents were accepted in certain quarters as inviolable truths. This acceptance was not just a function of the number of times these 'truths' were stated, but stemmed from the MD's specialist knowledge as a clinician, and importantly, *the* clinician responsible for the HA's CHD strategy.

Although the potential existed to analyse data collected by the cardiac nurses, the MD refused to provide the data on the grounds that he wanted to wait until the nurses had reviewed several thousand patients in order to assemble a large data set. Meanwhile, the MD presented data which, he claimed, indicated the success of the nurses. My suggestion that if the nurses were not successful it would be better to find out sooner rather than later left him unmoved. This has echoes in Flyvbjerg's study, where a manipulated evaluation is undertaken in relation to a proposed bus terminal development in order to produce the result which the powerful bus company wants. Flyvbjerg points out that 'knowledge kills action; action requires the veil of illusion . . . Better knowledge . . . when combined with a more balanced evaluation might destroy the illusion and "kill" the action the company wants'. The fear that knowledge will 'kill' action means that for the MD, knowledge is not always desirable, as Flyvbjerg writes 'power, quite simply, often finds ignorance, deceptions, self-deceptions, rationalizations and lies more useful for its purposes than truth and rationality, despite all costs' (1998: 34). The MD had decided that as the standards of care for CHD patients in primary care are so variable, leading to unacceptable inequalities in service provision, nurses should systematically apply protocols in reviewing CHD patients. He was not prepared to consider the possibility that the nurse scheme would not improve standards. This illustrates both the MD's confidence in his own judgement and his capacity for self-delusion in an environment where motivation is obtained from action which is regarded as an end in itself and is assumed to equal 'success'.

THE NHS AND NEW LABOUR

In 1997 the government issued a White Paper entitled *The New NHS: Modern, Dependable* (Department of Health 1997) which announced a set of reforms in the NHS. The White Paper talked of paving a way for the 'new NHS', which involved neither a 'return to the old centralized command and control systems of the 1970s' nor 'a continuation of the divisive internal market system of the 1990s'. This 'third way' encompassed six key principles:

1 to renew the NHS as a genuinely *national* service; patients will get fair access to consistently high-quality, prompt and accessible services right across the country;
2 to make the delivery of health-care against these new national standards a matter of *local* responsibility; local doctors and nurses who are in the best position to know what patients need will be in the driving seat in shaping services;
3 to get the NHS to work in *partnership*; by breaking down organizational barriers and forging stronger links with local authorities, the needs of the patient will be put in the centre of the process;
4 to drive *efficiency* through a more rigorous approach to performance by cutting bureaucracy;
5 to shift the focus onto quality of care so that *excellence* is guaranteed to all patients, and quality becomes the driving force for decision-making at every level of the service; and
6 to rebuild *public confidence* in the NHS as a public service, accountable to patients, open to the public and shaped by their views (Department of Health 1997: para 2.4).

Although the 'divisive internal market' whose defining features were described as 'unfairness and bureaucracy' was to disappear, the separation between the planning of health care and its provision was to be retained. A 'stronger, clearer strategic role' was envisaged for HAs which would 'overcome the fragmentation which characterized the internal market' (para 4.2).

PCGs were to be created which involved all GPs in an area together with community nurses taking responsibility for commissioning services in the local community. HAs were still to be responsible for assessing health needs and drawing up strategies for meeting these needs in the form of a health improvement programme developed in partnership with all the local interests and ensuring delivery of the NHS contribution to it. Emphasizing the partnership and public involvement theme and reflecting the government's declared aim of tackling inequalities in health, Health Action Zones (HAZs) were created to target extra funding to areas of greatest health need and offer opportunities to explore new ways of involving local people. In addition to improving NHS services, the aim of the HAZ initiative was to deal with broader issues which affect the health of local people such as housing, income, transport and the environment. In order to develop and implement a locally agreed strategy for improving the health of local people, HAs would be required to work with local councils, voluntary organizations and local communities in addition to local NHS providers.

HAs were to allocate resources to PCGs and hold them to account. PCGs came into being in shadow form on 1 October 1998, going 'live' in April 1999. The creation of PCGs was expressed in terms of retaining 'what has worked' about fundholding and discarding what has not. The White Paper spoke of PCG 'incentives', since PCGs could reinvest savings to improve services. *The New NHS: Modern, Dependable* portrayed the creation of PCGs as giving maximum freedom to use the resources available for the benefit of patients. However, the creation of PCGs can also be seen as an attempt by the government to force GPs, whose referral and prescribing decisions resulted in resource commitments, to take responsibility for balancing local health-care budgets. An important feature of PCG budgetary responsibility was that under the new regime prescribing budgets would be cash limited.

Funding for hospital and community health services, prescribing and general practice infrastructure was to be brought together into one unified budget at HA and PCG level. The imposition of a hard budget constraint on prescribing (replacing the previously non-cash-limited indicative budget system) and the introduction of the unified budget meant that overspending in one area of the budget would have to be covered from savings elsewhere within the budget. GPs were not given any choice in relation to PCG membership and many GPs expressed opposition to the idea. Importantly, GPs were to retain their cherished independent contractor status in terms of the provision of health care. The government later reversed its decision to include GP infrastructure funding within the unified budget. Instead this resource, which relates to things close to GPs' hearts (that is practice staff and premises costs) was ring fenced, which meant that it could not be used to make up shortfalls in other areas of the budget. This illustrates the government's awareness of the need to ensure GP cooperation and make some concessions in order to obtain this cooperation. Although GPs welcomed this decision, the news was less warmly received at Poppleton HA. (See Chapter 5.)

A new system of 'clinical governance' was to be introduced, aimed at ensuring that clinical practice was in accordance with minimum standards. This process would increase accountability on the part of clinicians and received a lukewarm response amongst local Poppleton HA GPs, who feared that this would erode clinical freedom. The clinical governance agenda would be backed up by a new Commission for Health Improvement (CHI) to 'oversee the quality of clinical services at local level, and *to tackle shortcomings*' (Department of Health 1997: para 3.7, emphasis added). The latter role caused the HA MD to refer to CHI as the 'stormtroopers' who would tackle poorly performing doctors. The representative of the NHSE at local level was keen to present clinical governance in a positive light, stressing the benefits to patients and the opportunities from 'lifelong learning'.

A new National Institute for Clinical Excellence (NICE) was created to 'give a strong lead on clinical and cost-effectiveness, drawing up new guidelines and ensuring they reach all parts of the health service' (1997: para 3.5). NICE was established in April 1999, putting health economic evaluation at the centre of the process designed to assess the relative clinical cost-effectiveness of new health technologies (NHSE 1999b).

NEW LABOUR AND FORMAL RATIONALITY

The theme of guidelines and standards runs through much of the White Paper. This reflects the government's declared aim of reducing variations (inequalities) in access to health care and health outcomes. These guidelines advise clinicians on how to treat patients and represent a stark contrast to the exercise of clinical judgement by reflective practitioners within the confines of the consulting room. The assumption underpinning the promulgation of guide-lines is that by following these rules efficiency will be improved and that the best possible outcome under the circumstances will be achieved. Guidelines, in theory at least, are based on some exter-nally generated evidence of efficacy and, ideally, this evidence rep-resents the accumulation of high-quality research. These can be seen as a form of 'calculable rules' as the existence of evidence on which to base guidelines provides an external referent of the likely outcomes of alternative courses of actions. As such, guidelines embody the sort of rule-driven behaviour which is the essence of Weber's formal rationality. Similarly, NICE is expected to be able to quantify costs and benefits of new drugs and technologies and provide local decision-makers with top-down standard rules for allocating resources in the most efficient manner. This implies a faith in formally rational processes and brings to mind Weber's words on the ' "Objective" discharge of business [which] primarily means a discharge of business according to *calculable rules* and without regard for persons' (1978: 975, original emphasis).

As part of the drive to improve quality, evidence-based national service frameworks (NSFs) were to be produced for major areas and disease groups to bring together 'the best evidence of clinical and cost-effectiveness, with the views of service users, to determine the best ways of providing particular services' (Department of Health 1997: para 4.9). Subsequently, it emerged that the first two NSFs would focus on CHD and mental health. The NSF for CHD was planned for launch in April 1999, but only appeared in March 2000. Anecdotal evidence suggests that the delay was due to the funding requirements of implementing the proposed minimum standards. The NSF for CHD contains clear rules for treating patients, together with a strict timetable for implementing these rules and for achieving national standards of care.

Whether the government's focus on the production of bureau-cratic rules is due to its faith in the ability of formally rational processes to resolve the dilemmas of health-services resource allocation is not always clear. For some observers, the capacity to present decisions as the product of 'science' rather than politics and the handing over of problems to technical experts provides the government with a mechanism for distancing itself from unpopular decisions. The need to adhere to centrally promulgated, uniform standards (for example an 'end to postcode prescribing') runs counter to the aim of local priority-setting and accountability.

Guarantees contained in *The New NHS: Modern, Dependable* that 'patients will be treated according to need and need alone' (Department of Health 1997: para 2.13) may be intended to create the perception in the minds of the electorate of an NHS which is dependable. However, meeting the competing aims of treatment based on need, ensuring fair access, local flexibility in priority-setting within fixed resources and so on places enormous demands on HAs and risks raising unrealistic expectations amongst the public.

White sees the creation of NICE, an 'independent body', as enabling the government to absolve itself of responsibility for potentially unpopular rationing decisions (White 1999: 17).

> NICE is not an instrument of the democratic will, but of expertise – an instrument, moreover, created at arm's length from ministers. If Professor Rawlins'[4] team recommends . . . say, the costly use of beta interferon to treat multiple sclerosis, Frank Dobson . . . will be able to say 'Sorry guv, nothing to do with me.' Parallels are drawn with 'New Labour's' handing over responsibility (for which read blame) to the Bank of England for monetary policy.

Since the list of technologies for appraisal by NICE are agreed by ministers, with the final decision made by the Minister of State for Health, it is difficult to see how ministers can distance themselves from the process in the way that White describes. Elsewhere, New Labour's health policies have been seen as part of a return to a 'command and control' NHS model. Klein (1999: 9) perceives the process as shifting responsibility (and blame) back to ministers who 'appear to be operating under the delusion that they can actually control what happens in the NHS'. The focus on bureaucratic rule-following and top-down directives embodied in recent NHS policy documents provides support for Klein's argument. It also raises a number of questions, however, in relation to the extent to which formally rational approaches can deliver solutions to complex policy problems. Some of these questions relate to the cognitive limitations on formal rationality discussed earlier in Chapter 2. In addition, there is also the issue of how, if at all, substantive rationality or the role of social values is to be incorporated within such a framework. Whilst the NHS under New Labour is to be shaped by the public's views, it is not clear how this will work in practice. In addition, if medical professionals are led by social values, such as altruism or the good of the individual patient in front of them, the professional values may clash with the rule-based conduct of formal rationality (Ritzer and Walczak 1988). This raises the question of how such conflicts can be resolved and who is to be the final arbiter in such a clash.

HEALTH ECONOMICS AND CHD IN POPPLETON

Nationally, CHD accounts for one in four deaths. In recognition of this, HAs were required to meet targets in relation to CHD morbidity and mortality (Department of Health 1992, 1998b). In Poppleton, mortality from CHD was substantially above the national average and CHD was a key priority area for the HA. Although the HA commissioned health care from hospital and community service providers, little was known, prior to the start of the project, about the extent of expenditure on different healthcare programmes. The annual contracting round at which service requirements for the forthcoming year were agreed tended to roll forward existing services with minor changes at the margin. Providers requested additional resources for CHD services, but there was little data from which to assess competing demands for funds in terms of benefits to patients. The MD described the problem thus:

> If we had £100,000 tomorrow to put into [CHD] services, I wouldn't know what to spend it on to get the best use of the resource. Even when I had spent it, I wouldn't know how to measure whether it had been a successful intervention.

In order to improve the way resources were allocated for CHD services, the HA commissioned a piece of work to use health economics in informing the decision-making process. The aims of the work were:

1 to define CHD services and quantify investment, processes and outcomes within these services for Poppleton HA;
2 to identify areas for realignment of resources based on evidence of effectiveness and resource requirements;
3 to recommend areas for change based on economic criteria (that is to identify the solutions which generate maximum health gain from a fixed budget); and
4 to develop success criteria to enable the monitoring of service changes in practice.

The impetus for commissioning the work came from the MD, who was keen to employ health economic techniques in formulating

CHD policy. It was agreed that responsibility for day-to-day direction of the project should rest with the HA MD. I was treated as a member of staff from the outset and introduced as 'our new health economist' throughout the organization. The fact that my previous career had been as a health-service manager probably helped in terms of their perception of me as 'one of us'.

USING HEALTH ECONOMICS AT POPPLETON HA – GETTING STARTED

The MD enjoyed considerable control within his day-to-day work environment by presenting his view of the world to the members of his team. Pharmacists working for the MD and other team members, myself included, looked to the MD to provide clinical advice. My role as an academic researcher meant that I was able to test out the information given to me by the MD, unlike the other team members who had little time or opportunity to do so. In a system where information is sparse, the MD explained that sometimes it is necessary to use guesswork or 'what little information there is'. Under these circumstances, the MD used a combination of both to confirm his views of the service and often rounded up numbers for impact. In 6 months of confident assertions on the basis of guesswork and some crude information, I never once saw anybody challenge his figures or what he was saying.

When I had asked what happens to patients with chest pain who stay in the local trust for 2 days, the MD had replied 'Nothing! They just sit around, some of them on orthopaedic wards for a couple of days and then they kick them out again.' He had also presented the same information at talks to others outside the HA. In addition, he would point to the fact 'only 10 per cent of chest pain patients have had an MI . . . what are the other 90 per cent doing? They should never have been let in in the first place!' The impression given was that a large number of patients were inappropriately admitted to hospital and that many of these patients received little or no treatment once inside the hospital. MI patients were seen as having legitimate claims on a bed, whereas other 'chest pain' admissions were due to inexperienced junior doctors. Although figures on prevalence and mortality were reeled off easily and the importance of using local data stressed, this contrasted with the willingness of the MD to accept anecdotal evidence 'people tell us' in support of what he believed to be true. The MD also quoted the modal length

Table 3.2 Cardiovascular-related non-elective activity Poppleton Hospital Trust (1996/97)

Discharge diagnosis	Deaths and discharges (%)
Angina	21
Acute myocardial infarction	17
Heart failure	13
Other chest pain	21
Other confirmed heart disease	14
Other unconfirmed cardiovascular	14
Total	100

of stay for angina patients at a trust in a neighbouring authority of 1 and held this up as a shining example for local trusts to achieve. When I pointed out to him that the average length of stay was 12 days and that the readmittance rate within 6 months was 30 per cent, compared with 5 days and 25 per cent respectively at the first trust, he continued to quote the 1 day stay and to ignore the information which conflicted with the messages he had already given out within the HA.

When I spoke to staff at three different sites about the '90 per cent of patients' who were 'inappropriately' admitted, they gave me a different story. All sites had set procedures and care protocols for dealing with chest pain patients. Those with suspected MI were given a standard battery of tests, regardless of whether they were in a medical ward or, due to pressures on beds, on other wards. Others, with unstable angina for example, would need to be admitted in order to be stabilized. An examination of the data for 1996/7 revealed that included in the MD's 'chest pain' category were patients who needed to be admitted. Only 35 per cent were discharged with a diagnosis of 'other chest pain' or unconfirmed disease.

The 10 per cent figure for acute myocardial infarction (AMI), quoted by the MD, was for one hospital which admitted 19 Poppleton HA residents with a diagnosis of AMI. At the local trust, where around 600 AMI patients were admitted, the percentage of total 'chest pain' related emergency admissions was 17 per cent.

The MD had confidently explained when discussing CHD that 8000 people with chest pain attend annually at the local trust. On examination of the data, I found that for 3000 of these patients, the chest pain was, on presentation, of a non-cardiac nature (such as musculo skeletal or pulmonary oedema). When I asked the MD which figures should be used for illustration, he told me 'Always use the bigger ones, it'll have more impact that way.'

The first task was to obtain a clear understanding of CHD services in terms of activity and costs. However, this reliance on existing data, manipulated for dramatic effect and anecdote made the process difficult as I was unable to rely on what the MD told me, but was conscious that trust clinicians may be equally inclined to put their own particular 'spin' on these issues.

THE CHANGING FOCUS OF THE RESEARCH

Almost from the start of the project, the work began to depart from the original design. These changes were influenced by the following factors:

1 the reluctance of the MD to involve other stakeholders;
2 the problems of dealing with uncertain, dynamic systems in health services; and
3 information deficits.

Stakeholder involvement

The original intention had been to construct a programme budget for CHD services and establish a working group, comprising local stakeholders to examine service changes at the margin (MA). I had met twice with the CD to discuss details of the project before starting at Poppleton HA and, like me, she was aware of the need to establish a stakeholder group at the earliest opportunity. However, when we raised this with the MD, he gently refused to do this, explaining:

> We have to get the data to get them interested . . . We can't go to them until we have something interesting to show them . . . some of these guys are consultants and the way to get them interested is to produce some local data that gets them to look at their own services. It's no good getting them involved too early. We need to have something concrete to show them.

In most areas of his work the MD was clear in his own mind on the course of action to be pursued, however, as he had explained, he was unsure what to do in relation to CHD services. Since the MD's style was to promote a clear 'line' to local stakeholders, his reluctance to involve other clinicians from primary, secondary and tertiary care may reflect his desire to firm up solutions in his own mind before attempting to persuade other stakeholders to adopt his way of thinking. Although this issue was raised repeatedly in the first month, the MD steadfastly refused to change his mind.

Dynamic and uncertain systems

The second issue which influenced the work was the changing nature of service provision. In order to monitor or model changes to baselines it was necessary first to establish a baseline position. However, measuring the baseline was difficult as the HA was already starting to invest in schemes which would impact upon baseline figures. Therefore, the baseline was a moving target which would change according to the point at which it was measured. The HA was investing in cardiac nurses to work in primary care with CHD patients, and, in addition, it was about to recruit senior medical staff to assist with emergency pressures. The Medical Audit Advisory Group was running an aspirin audit in primary care designed to increase aspirin prescribing, and in one locality a primary care initiative aimed at tackling readmissions for cardiac and respiratory problems had been underway for some months. As the CD explained, 'We can't just hold everything still while you go around measuring it!'

This problem was not insurmountable, but what made me apprehensive was the fact that the CD and MD wanted me to evaluate the impact of their investments, despite the paucity of baseline data and despite the impossibility of disentangling cause and effect relationships in the complex and uncertain system. For example, when I asked the MD how I should evaluate the contribution of medics in A and E, he cheerfully responded that we could look at admissions and if these are 'down on last year' then the scheme would be a success. When I pointed out that sending all chest pain patients home could reduce admissions, but that this would increase mortality, he said 'Obviously we've got to look at other indicators too'. He was not clear, however, on how this would be done, since equating changes in mortality rates with the introduction of the new doctors seemed to be stretching a fairly tenuous link a little too far. Reductions in admissions were unlikely to be achieved in any case as capacity problems at a neighbouring trust resulting in overflow activity being redirected meant that other patients would probably fill the empty beds. Similarly, if admissions reduced, calculating how much of this reduction was attributable to each of the initiatives (that is nurses, doctors, aspirin and primary care) would be an impossible task.

The CD and MD thought that I was worrying unnecessarily and were at pains to stress that in the 'real world' that data were crude and things were messy. They recognized that the quality of the study would not be on a par with something published in the *British Medical Journal*, for example, and at one stage mistook my concerns as being for satisfying external examiners in relation to my PhD research. The MD was satisfied that if the overall trend was 'roughly going in the right direction' then he would be happy, regardless of whether or not individual cause and effect relationships were delineated. The MD also introduced the idea of asking hospital clinicians how things had fared as a 'softer' measure of success. In other words, the MD wanted me to declare the investments a success if admissions reduced; and if they were unchanged or had increased, the fact that trust clinicians felt that 'morale' or some other 'soft' variable had improved could be used to justify the investment.

During these discussions I felt as though I was talking in another language, as I could not make the CD and MD aware of my concerns. Their attitude was not one of cynical data manipulation, but they genuinely appeared to believe that such an evaluation was acceptable for their purposes. It should be remembered that in other areas, evaluation was non-existent, so in a sense they were attempting to introduce some measure of performance rather than merely throwing money at problems and crossing their fingers. If they had wanted merely to present their schemes as a success, the skills of the MD could have been easily applied to achieve such an end without recourse to a health economist. However, it may be that what they really wanted was an evaluation to confirm the success of their decisions.

Barnes and colleagues in their study of user groups' attempts to influence health services describe how the 'professed role as umpire in a pluralistic game is a source of legitimacy for the [HA's] official managerial role . . . [which] frequently spilled over into micropolitical manipulation' (Barnes *et al.* 1999: 119). They note the way in which HA policymakers invoke the views of service users, playing the 'user card' (Mort *et al.* 1996) when it suits their purpose. It may be that the 'health economics' card would be played when it supports the choice made by policymakers or disregarded, as in the case of cholesterol-lowering drugs in Chapter 4, when it is expedient to do so.

Information deficits

One of the barriers to the use of health economics highlighted in the economics literature was a lack of relevant information. At Poppleton HA the 'understanding' of the services commissioned was based largely on anecdotal evidence and a superficial reading of the situation. The MD did not have any data regarding the cardiac rehabilitation service, nor was A and E information routinely available. Although the HA had information on cardiac deaths and discharges, lengths of stay, admission and readmission data, there was little understanding of what happened to patients once they entered the hospital. For example, there was no indication of the number of MI patients admitted to the Coronary Care Unit as opposed to other beds which were seen as being less suitable.

However, where information was available, it was not being used. The focus on MI patients who were seen by the MD as legitimate users of beds meant that the problem around angina patients was largely ignored. A glance at the deaths and discharges at the local trust indicated that angina patients represented 21 per cent of cardiac-related emergency admissions compared with 17 per cent for MIs. Angina readmissions were 27 per cent at 6 months compared with 19 per cent of people readmitted post-MI within the same period. Since the MD had defined priorities in terms of MIs, his response to the angina figures (and at one trust angina readmissions were 21 per cent within 1 month and 41 per cent at 6 months) was to apply pressure to the providers to restrict admissions and reduce length of stay.

MI patients were a high-risk and highly visible group. The label 'angina' was applied to a spectrum of symptoms from mild chest pain on exertion to patients experiencing chest pain at rest and requiring intravenous heparin treatment in hospital. Although numbers were available for angina deaths and discharges, getting behind the data to reach an understanding of the sub-groups of angina patients and the reasons for admission was difficult. The hospital was developing a pathway of care for MI patients designed to ensure that all patients received a minimum standard of treatment, but there was no such pathway for angina patients and it was not possible to track these patients through the system using available data. This was not due to the hospital withholding information, but to the data-collection systems which were geared largely towards producing minimum data sets for contract monitoring purposes.

The ability and, indeed, the requirement of the hospital services to produce contract data contrasted with the situation in primary care. There was no information on the number of patients with CHD within the HA, and if the trust represented a 'black box' into which patients entered and most emerged alive, primary care was a 'black hole' into which patients disappeared on leaving hospital to an altogether uncertain fate. Although by now most practices were computerized, a number of data systems proliferated and the quality of the data held on the systems was variable. Hospital activity was highly visible, being concentrated mostly within large buildings in which care was of a more standardized nature. Hospital activity was measurable and, in true NHS fashion, the measurable had become the important. Primary-care activity was not measurable and, despite the knock on effects of primary care activity in other parts of the system, was not the subject of scrutiny.

This information deficit was further complicated by the fact that relationships with providers ranged on a continuum from no trust to high trust, which meant that where information was provided by some hospitals it was not seen as credible. This was particularly relevant in the case of the tertiary cardiology centre which, according to the MD, asked for more resources every year despite failing to deliver contracted activity, blaming increased costs on case mix changes. The clinical audit/R and D manager for the trust was equally suspicious of the HA. This trust was able to produce very detailed data on the activities undertaken, partly because of the narrow range of work conducted and the high level of R and D activity within the unit. The manager felt penalized compared with other providers who produced only superficial data, which did not allow HAs to challenge their activities.

Despite these information gaps, a programme budget was calculated based on estimated costs for primary, secondary and tertiary care for CHD patients. The MD was pleased with this as it gave him another number to quote in public presentations and in reports on cardiovascular disease services. When I questioned his enthusiasm, he told me that this was a useful piece of information as it aided understanding of the service. I asked how this would be used and the CD explained that this methodology could be applied to calculating programme budgets for other disease areas, although the ultimate aim of such an exercise was not forthcoming. I pointed out that a common appreciation of services which would allow stake-holders to understand the services provided outside of their own sector would be more conducive to making progress. It was at this point that I started to get involved in all sorts of activities beyond the scope of the original proposal.

Getting in deeper and wider

The issue of whether health economists should be based in HAs is one of the unresolved dilemmas of health economics. Those who argue in favour of an NHS base do so on the grounds that a closer proximity to decision-makers will increase the relevance of the advice provided by exposing the economist to the practical diffi-culties faced in the real world away from the ivory tower. Oppon-ents argue that health economists risk 'going native' and getting embroiled in issues which are not concerned with health economics (Mulkay *et al.* 1991).

In Poppleton the MD's reluctance to proceed with a stakeholder group exercise meant that I was left pondering the prospect of 2 years with little to occupy myself. Resource allocation issues do not present themselves in neat bundles for the health economist to unwrap and the attention of the MD and CD varied in relation to the other commitments they faced. The project board for the research stopped meeting after the first month and the original design was not discussed thereafter. For the next few months I found myself in contract meetings, team meetings, CHD stake-holder and locality meetings whilst the MD and CD appeared unsure as to what to do with me. A health economist who had recently left a HA-funded post explained why: 'Health economists are like bidets – everyone wants one, but they don't know what to do with one once they've got it.'

My insistence on the need to understand what happens to CHD patients, as opposed to merely collecting some crude data on deaths and discharges and my fears that the impact of the additional medical staff in A and E would be difficult to evaluate, particularly as it was unclear what these doctors would do, led to more meet-ings. At the insistence of the CD, I was to convene and chair a group comprising the local consultant cardiologist and others which would develop protocols for the new doctors and define a pathway of care for chest pain patients. The group included a local GP and this led to my being involved in sorting out reimbursement issues and even designing a claims form for the purpose. In April, May and June I did very little work which could be described as 'health economics', although I did begin to understand the health-care system in relation to CHD patients. However, in June, the issue of statins (cholesterol-lowering drugs for CHD patients) began to drift towards the top of the MD's agenda. The problem of affordability in relation to these effective drugs was causing increasing anxiety within the medical directorate and this led to my finally getting my opportunity to apply health economics to a live issue within the HA.

NOTES

1 By common aims, I mean in a broad sense of commitment to the symbols of the NHS and providing the best care for the patient, as opposed to some 'rational' decision-making criteria.
2 Myocardial infarction or heart attack.
3 Dyspepsia drugs which are very effective at providing symptom relief.
4 Chairman of NICE, 1998–.

CASE STUDY I:
A COST-EFFECTIVENESS
ANALYSIS OF CHOLESTEROL-
LOWERING DRUGS

INTRODUCTION

Statins are drugs which have been shown to reduce cholesterol and coronary events in the general population (Shepherd *et al.* 1995) and in patients with established CHD (Scandinavian Simvastatin Survival Study Group 1994, Sacks *et al.* 1996). The evidence comes from large, long-term trials and the impact on clinical end-points is significant.

In November 1996 a working group, comprising members of Poppleton HA and hospital and primary care representatives, drew up a guideline for the use of statins in relation to Poppleton HA residents. The guideline was evidence based, and having taken on board research findings about guideline ownership, implementation and sensitivity to local circumstances, the HA pharmaceutical adviser (PA) prepared to commence the process of disseminating the guideline. Previously, with the other HA prescribing protocols, no attempt had been made to assess the financial impact of the guideline at the construction stage. However, the HA PA had recently learned from the health economics component of a prescribing guidelines course of the importance of costing guidelines. A quick calculation was performed based on 15,000 estimated residents with CHD and a large number of these patients fulfilling the eligibility criteria for statins which created alarm and resulted in the shelving of the guideline. The figure of 15,000 patients was a 'guesstimate' by the MD.

Some PBMA studies highlight the attractiveness of the 'do noth-ing' option for policy-makers unwilling to 'rock the boat' by chang-ing the nature of services purchased with associated resource consequences (Miller and Vale 1997). Preserving the status quo by doing nothing was not an option for health authorities in relation to statins. The uptake of this emerging technology was increas-ing alongside a large-scale campaign by the various statin manu-facturers to promote their product to GPs. Coronary care nurses were being recruited to undertake a systematic review of CHD patients in primary care and would require advice on how to manage patients with raised cholesterol. In addition GPs (and 50 per cent were GP fundholders in Poppleton) were approaching the HA PA to request advice and information about statins in order to identify which patients would receive maximum benefit from the drugs. The HA's medical advisers and PA had already devised and delivered a programme of prescribing education to GPs. This illus-trated the issue of cost-effectiveness and the concept of 'numbers needed to treat' in the area of CHD drugs generally. It is possible that this increased awareness raised expectations among GPs regarding the HA's ability to provide a simple answer to the ques-tions raised by the availability of statins.

BRINGING THE STAKEHOLDERS ON BOARD

In June 1997 the members of the HA convened a small working group to examine the issue of statins. Prior to the meeting, two 'tac-tics' discussions with the PA and myself were held, the first at the request of the MD. At the first discussion, the aims of the wider meeting were defined by the MD as, first, 'to agree that primary prevention in its entirety is not affordable' and, second, 'to agree to focus on secondary prevention'. Secondary prevention refers to the treatment of patients with disease, namely with angina or post-MI. Primary prevention, by contrast, is the treatment of patients who do not have CHD.

As a strategy of secondary prevention was not affordable, it was necessary to select some patients from the total CHD population with raised cholesterol as being more 'deserving' than others. Judgements in relation to the deserving or otherwise status of patients were to be made on the basis of cost-effectiveness, or at least that was the MD's declared aim. Whilst the increased risk for those with CHD would be likely to ensure a consensus that these patients should receive priority, denying treatment to some CHD sufferers at high baseline risk, would be less likely to gain agreement amongst clinicians.

Following the first discussion, the PA and I discussed the agenda and plan of campaign for the meeting and met again with the MD. This time the aim of the larger meeting was described as 'to achieve ownership of the overall problem' and 'to make statins affordable'. When I asked 'How much is affordable?', the MD replied:

> Well we've got no extra money from anywhere, so really we've got nothing, but I suppose if you pushed me, maybe one or two million . . . If we don't have a guideline, we'll probably spend three-and-a-half million anyway, so by having some sort of guideline based on rationing and stratifying risk, at least we can be more certain that the right people will get the statins. Our aim has got to be to get them to the people who'll benefit most . . . Some GPs are putting 80-year-olds on them and that's a complete waste.

I asked if this was because of the lack of evidence of statins in relation to 80-year-olds, but the MD replied that he thought it likely that there would be benefits in this group, but these were not a priority.

Prior to the tactics discussions, the PA, MD and I had spent at least 2 hours a week in informal discussions or ad hoc meetings, often with the CD, discussing ways to make statins affordable. 'Statins' was a regular item for discussion at the weekly team meetings in the MD's department. All of these meetings forced us to discuss the published evidence and likely epidemiological pattern. (How many people have CHD and, of these, how many have raised cholesterol?) Attempts were made to squeeze from the evidence and published data on epidemiology some magical 'solution'. The 'if we work systematically and follow the evidence, we'll get the right answer' approach of the PA and MD contrasted with scepticism of the evidence and judgements about deservingness or otherwise of patients on the part of the CD and project manager (PM). Arguments were presented based on anecdotes about patients or relatives. 'My mother's 80 and her doctor tested her cholesterol and now she's worried about having butter on her scones! I mean, if she's going to die I'd rather she had a heart attack in her sleep than had a stroke and stayed alive for 5 years in a really bad way.' Both were keen to use dietary modification as a device to delay the prescribing of statins and the MD was inconsistent on this point. In early meetings he had said 'Let's put barriers in the way, we'll call them "filters" and we'll say anybody who fails to comply with dietary modification is excluded from having a statin.' However, having read the evidence on the extent of reductions in cholesterol likely to be achieved as a result of diet, he was less keen to support stretching out diet beyond 3 months.

The CD stated on several occasions that she would rather spend the money on something else and that as raised cholesterol was 'only a risk factor' the HA had no obligation to treat it. 'I've got an ECR for a young spinal patient,' she told me, 'I'd rather spend the money on nursing care for him than on statins.' When I asked her why this was the case, she replied 'At least I can see something for the money. The improvement in quality of life will be enormous . . . That's really what it's all about. I mean these people [potential statins recipients] aren't in pain. The statins won't make them feel better or anything . . .'

The fact that raised cholesterol was 'only a risk factor' and that many people who have heart attacks do not have raised cholesterol added to the uncertainty surrounding statins. The CD was not alone in her view that treating risk factors was less important than other more visible priorities. This suggests that there is a difference in perception between an intervention which influences risk factors in asymptomatic patients and those which represent reactive, immediate treatment. In the case of the latter, the relationship between cause and effect is often much clearer cut and the outcomes are highly visible. Cost is also an important factor, as in the case of aspirin, which is very cheap in comparison to statins, the issue of treating a risk factor was not questioned.

During these meetings we clutched at straws, trying to find an 'answer' to a problem the goal of which we could only specify as 'making statins affordable'. Everybody agreed that part of this aim was to target the drugs to those who would benefit most, but beyond this reaching a clear objective or notional budget proved impossible. The MD and PA were keen to use evidence, particularly if it would support a restricted use of statins, but both remained ambivalent on the question of whether statins were seen as something to be promoted or discouraged. I offered to conduct a cost-effectiveness analysis of statin treatment aimed at stratifying patients and using local data where possible and this was greeted was some enthusiasm. The method would be to replicate a recently published study and I produced a summary report of this study for distribution at the meeting (Pharaoh and Hollingworth 1996). The

MD was keen to propose this to the stakeholder group, but only after a discussion of the issues which was intended to lead them to support rationing of statins.

THE JUNE STAKEHOLDER MEETING

In addition to the MD, PA and myself, the stakeholder working group included primary and secondary care clinicians and the FD from both the HA and the local secondary care trust. The MD informed the group that growth funds were already committed and that although there was 'overwhelming evidence that statins will work . . . we are talking telephone numbers . . . and we just don't have that sort of money'. He explained the need for the group 'to be able to sign up to an ethical and affordable guideline'. The diabetologist and cardiologist were familiar with the published cost-effectiveness analysis on the use of statins which sought to stratify patients according to age, sex and cardiac health (angina or MI status) to illustrate the relative cost-effectiveness of treating different cohorts of people. The FD, however, expressed complete ignorance of the statins issue and alarm at the likely financial consequences. The tendency at Poppleton HA had been to retain prescribing issues within the medical directorate and this included the financial aspects such as budget-setting. At the trust the FD had no involvement in and, therefore, little knowledge of prescribing issues in primary care. This compartmentalization of workloads made it easier for the FD to focus on balancing the cash limited books, which at the time in practice meant ensuring expenditure on HCHS services remained within budget, so this ignorance is understandable.

Control over prescribing policy by the MD and his staff whilst bolstering the position of the department within the HA now carried with it the disadvantage that other members of the HA saw prescribing as a peripheral issue. Previously the MD had a set policy and had a fairly free reign in this regard. Such a position would be attractive when clear objectives could be specified, but in the case of statins, the MD was keener to involve others in the process. However, he was less convinced of the need to raise the issue at the weekly management team meeting attended by the CE and other HA directors. The MD explained that treating all patients with established disease and raised cholesterol in Poppleton HA would prove unaffordable as there were no additional resources available for statins.

The PA proposed that, using local data where possible, efforts should be made to further stratify patients in order to identify those at greatest risk. The declared aim was to make statins 'affordable', but since there were no additional resources and no plans for disinvestment, the HA representatives were unable to say what sum might be deemed 'affordable'. The MD, when pushed on the likely sum required, replied 'We don't know how much, it could be £5 million', which caused the HA FD to jerk forward and complain excitedly 'We can't afford that!' The MD explained that any overspending on prescribing would have to come from HCHS budgets in order to encourage the hospital staff to consider the wider implications of prescribing statins. It is not clear how this threat was perceived, as the link between the HCHS and prescribing expenditure was fairly indirect. In any case, it was unlikely that priority services such as diabetology or cardiology at the trust would be subject to funding cuts.

The diabetologist opposed the restricted use of statins on the grounds that 'If I were a drug company I'd take up the case of somebody and sue the Health Authority . . . it's not you who's going to be dragged through the courts.' When the MD replied that 'We have no choice . . . we need to be able to sign up to a guideline that is ethical and affordable', the diabetologist replied 'We do have a choice, we could cut back on other areas like cervical cytology and breast screening' and began to read out costs per life year gained for these treatments which compared unfavourably with statins. The MD dismissed this option, explaining that cutting back on these services was politically unacceptable.

The diabetologist had spoken at length about how important his patients were and how he must put patients first and it seemed unlikely that he would agree to restricting statins use to exclude some patients with CHD. The PA, knowing of the diabetologist's interest in research, suggested that there 'might be a paper in it if we can model it' and this persuaded him to sanction the modelling exercise. He was sufficiently enthused to offer to contact a professor of pharmacology in Yorkshire who had expertise in the area of risk and CHD. It was agreed that the economic analysis would be conducted.

Outside the meeting, the MD expressed his satisfaction with the outcome. The MD had no direct control over any of the people present other than the PA, who was perceived as an ally. This explained the need for careful planning and tactics intended to promote a sharing of the problem and acceptance of the need for targeting. He had obtained agreement to the modelling exercise from the diabetologist, a forceful advocate for statins use. The young and recently appointed cardiologist had said little during the meeting and had not opposed the modelling proposal. By not informing the FD of the problem prior to the meeting, the MD's message achieved maximum shock value in terms of its effects on the normally subdued HA FD. However, acceptance of the modelling exercise did not imply that clinicians would act on its findings and none of the clinicians had agreed to ration statins in practice. Although the issue of affordability of the guideline was unresolved, the MD proclaimed the meeting a success. No problems were resolved by the meeting, yet compared with alternative outcomes which may have included outright rejection of risk stratification and considering the limited range of levers at the disposal of the MD, the outcome was perhaps the best that the MD could hope for.

THE RIVERVIEW GUIDELINES

In July 1997 a neighbouring HA (Riverview) launched its guidelines on cholesterol-lowering drugs. This HA, faced with similar problems, costs and evidence chose to issue a guideline with no upper age limit and offered HA support in systematically calling in all CHD patients in order to secure maximum uptake in the population. The launch meeting panel comprised purchaser representatives as well as primary and secondary care clinicians and delivered a common message of secondary prevention (that is patients with established disease) regardless of age. This decision was based on the evidence of effectiveness and the HA acknowledged that the resource implications of guideline implementation were not easily affordable. However, the meeting was informed that 'the HA is committed to this policy' and GPs were urged to identify CHD patients systematically and proactively and apply the guidelines. In response to GP questions about the implications of overspending, the audience was given a vague reassurance: 'We will take statins into account, but you will need to demonstrate that there are no areas of waste within the rest of your prescribing expenditure . . . We are committed to the guideline, but . . . no, we don't have any spare funds to resource it.'

When I asked the HA representative outside the meeting how the policy would be funded, she explained that previous experience indicated that guideline uptake would be low and this would reduce the potential cost of the guideline. She was genuinely keen to promote statins prescribing and feared that having no guideline would lead to inappropriate prescribing. However, although she accepted that costs would rise even at low levels of implementation, she admitted that at present there were no available funds identified for statins prescribing. The approach was to do the 'right thing' now and deal with the consequences as they arose.

THE STANDING MEDICAL ADVISORY COMMITTEE GUIDELINES

In August 1997 the Department of Health issued the Standing Medical Advisory Committee (SMAC) guidelines to HAs and GPs on the use of cholesterol-lowering drugs (Standing Medical Advisory Committee 1997). These recommended secondary prevention as a priority, specified the level of cholesterol at which individuals should be considered at risk, but gave no clear guidance on age. In the accompanying letter, the Department of Health made it clear that no new money would be forthcoming to fund the implementation of such a policy. The phrase 'the purpose of this statement is to help doctors to set priorities for treatment with statins' appeared in bold type, but the words that the guidance was 'not intended to replace or override clinical judgement in individual cases' appeared also. The summary guidance, again in bold type, was to 'prescribe statins to those who have had a heart attack and have total cholesterol of 4.8 mmol/l or more, or have angina and total cholesterol of 5.5 mmol/l or more'. The latter group has a risk of coronary events of approximately 3 per cent per year and the guidance indicated that that represented a 'high risk of major coronary events'. In other words, the guidance was suggesting a policy of secondary prevention. Any guideline which restricted statins to a sub-group within the secondary prevention group would, therefore, contravene the guidance.

There will be individuals with a risk of 3 per cent or over who do not have CHD. This group was the third priority for statins, after post-MI and angina patients. Since some CHD-free individuals will be at the same level of risk, or higher than some angina sufferers, the guidance to treat the latter first would suggest that level of risk is not the only factor being considered when constructing the guidance, although the impression given in the paper is that risk is the determining factor. Affordability and the need to contain costs may explain the prioritization order. The guidance estimates that post-MI and angina patients represent 4.8 per cent of the population aged 35–69. The high-risk primary prevention group comprises a further 3.4 per cent of the 35- to 69-year-old population and treating this group would increase the statins bill by around 70 per cent. Those with CHD are more immediately visible and denying treatment to CHD-free individuals is less likely to create public concern than restricting statin use in CHD patients.

The guidance also points out that 'there is little trial evidence of benefit or harm from starting statin treatment in people over the age of 70 for the primary prevention of CHD', but ducks the age issue entirely in its consideration of secondary prevention. However, by giving estimates of the eligible population in terms of the 35–69 age group, there is an implicit assumption relating to the age at which patients should be treated. The Sheffield risk tables, which relate to primary prevention only and provide prescribing advice for patients up to the age of 70, were attached to the guidance.

The MD complained that this was yet another case of the centre interfering in local affairs whilst leaving the HA responsible for the fallout from its irresponsible actions. He stated that the health economic analysis would be used to identify priority groups in the population. On the same day, all GPs in the UK received a copy of the guidance.

THE ECONOMIC MODELLING EXERCISE

During July and August 1997, I undertook an economic analysis to ascertain the costs and benefits of treating sub-groups of patients with CHD. Local coronary mortality and population mortality rates data were used to construct life tables to model life expectancy and identify patients at the greatest risk of death. In the absence of detailed data and extrapolating from efficacy data in published trials, benefits were calculated using baseline risk as a proxy for capacity to benefit. The age cut-off from the trial data was 70 years, but patient benefits and costs for over 70s were modelled assuming benefits commensurate with the younger age group.

The results showed that as risk increases with age and assuming benefits commensurate with the trial evidence, the greatest benefits accrue to those at highest risk. This means that costs per life year saved are lower for older patients and this result is in accordance with other studies on this subject (Johannesson and Jonsson 1997).

(This does not mean that this result is inherently 'valid', but merely reflects the similarity in methodologies used in published studies on this subject.)

The aim was to provide a simple model which would build on readily available data and the message produced was a relatively simple one, namely that older patients with established disease should receive priority for statin treatment.

DECISION-MAKING WITHIN POPPLETON HA – A CHRONOLOGY

When presented with the results of the economic analysis on Wednesday 13 August 1997, the MD and PA agreed that the concept of treating older patients with a preventive measure contradicted their intuition and decided to shelve the results of the evaluation. The MD's response was 'Right, we'll ignore that . . . we'll have a cut-off at age 70 and we'll say there's no evidence . . . then we need to look at barriers, let's call them filters . . . we'll say diet first. .we'll get them [the GPs] to look at inappropriate prescribing and we'll get into therapeutic tendering.'

Neither person sought to challenge the technical accuracy of the analysis, but the MD defended his opinion on the grounds that the aim of the NHS is to prevent premature death. Once individuals have reached 'three score years and ten plus a bit', priority should be given to 'younger patients'. The PA felt that 'It makes sense to go for younger people [rather than] . . . going into detail fiddling around with some arty farty model to try to work it out and then coming up with a ridiculous answer.' When asked to explain his views, after a moment's thought, he cited the economic contribution to society of younger individuals who are in employment, compared with their retired counterparts. This may be due in part to a desire to provide a clear justification, based on explicit criteria for what is a gut reaction. His response may also have been influenced by the fact that the questioner was an economist. When pressed further 'Does this mean that the long-term unemployed receive a lower priority?', the pharmacist (again after thinking) further answered that younger people are more likely to have young children and that this gave them priority status. 'The family is really important to me, so I think people with children should be treated first.' Far from identifying all the possible prioritization criteria, narrowing them down to a sub-group of relevant criteria and then applying these to the CHD population, the PA appears to start from the visceral and work back to try to explain (to himself as much as to me) on some cerebral level why he feels as he does. The process of seeking reasons to justify action or beliefs already held and disregarding alternative information is, if we are to believe the psychological research on the subject, part of the human condition (Sutherland 1992). However, such an approach is hardly justifiable as grounds for wider policy formulation.

At a meeting the following week, the CD expressed her belief that:

> a life year saved at 40 is worth more than a life year saved at 80 [since] society would value this [the 40 year old] more ... we are not capturing quality of life in any of this ... I know that there are always exceptions and the young person may have no job or no money ... but generally speaking, most people would say that young people should receive priority.[1]

At around this time, the CD was involved in making choices about growth-hormone treatment for adults. The evidence of benefit for this treatment was an improvement in quality of life as measured by the Nottingham Health Profile, but the CD stated elsewhere that she was disinclined to invest in this: 'They want us to put money into it because the patients *feel* better ... I can think of better things to spend the money on.' When I asked how she justified the £100,000 she was considering spending on residential and nursing care for one spinal patient (she had earlier said that this would be money well spent), she replied that 'It's all about quality of life ... with the growth-hormone saying the patient feels better isn't a good enough reason to spend the money.' This illustrates the factors which influence the CD in her decision-making. It also demonstrates the extent to which she uses her own judgements in allocating resources on behalf of the community.

Throughout August and September 1997 the team wrestled with the issue of how to manage statins and the message to be sent out to local prescribers. The MD was critical of Riverview HA's actions. In his opinion, the HA was relying on poor implementation to contain costs whilst appearing to be following evidence-based medicine in a proactive fashion. This contrasted with the actions of the team at Poppleton HA, which would now suffer financially for its success in implementing service changes in CHD. Poor implementation in the NHS in general was a constant complaint of the MD's. On my first day he explained to me that unlike managers in other HAs, who spent a lot of time talking and got nowhere in terms of making changes (in his view, most NHS managers 'couldn't implement their way out of a paper bag'), he was actually getting involved in making changes at the sharp end.

Following the receipt of the SMAC guidelines, there were five meetings, most of them informal, in August 1997 and eight meetings in September 1997 prior to a wider evening meeting on 17 September 1997. This was in addition to statins being raised as an item at Monday morning directorate team meetings. The PM was keen to discriminate against patients who smoked or whose lifestyle was unhealthy. When I pointed out that these were the high-risk patients who should be targeted, she defended this position on the grounds that the public would support this view.

This judgement, presented as fact rather than opinion and repeated on many occasions, is indicative of the gap between the theory of evidence-based care and reality, the level of debate in these discussions and the extent to which unaccountable individuals feel comfortable with making decisions on the deserving or otherwise status of patients. There was a tendency to preface remarks with 'the public thinks' or 'if you asked the patient, they'd say' in order to justify opinions presented, but the basis for such claims was unclear. One member of staff, whose role at the HA included undertaking consultation with groups of service users, complained to me that she felt uncomfortable with undertaking user consultation because it raised expectations that views would be fed into the policy process, but in practice these views were usually ignored. She had recently undertaken such an exercise to determine user and carer views for the review of mental health services and this had not been considered by those (HA and others in a multi-agency forum) defining policy.

There were genuine concerns about the lack of knowledge surrounding the precise relationship between risk factors and events for individual patients. There were no sub-group analyses available to examine, say, smokers versus non-smokers to ascertain whether the extent of benefit in these two groups was similar. The relationship between compliance and effectiveness was unknown and the effectiveness of statins outside of the sanitized confines of a randomized controlled trial (RCT) were uncertain. It was not clear that if revascularization requirements were reduced in statins patients, these patients would not simply be replaced by others, merely reducing the threshold for tertiary cardiology interventions. However, the fact that such uncertainties caused fewer difficulties in the case of much cheaper drugs suggests that the cost of the drugs was a major factor influencing thinking. The recourse to inconsistent and, at times, incoherent argument suggests a panicked response to a looming financial crisis, rather than anything resembling the rational decision-making process.

Investment in spinal patients where benefits are more immediate may have more appeal than treatments which are characterized by uncertainty and where benefits are less immediate. The view of economists that immediate benefits are valued more highly than those arising in the future would appear to be borne out in relation to HA investment. However, an alternative explanation may be that HAs have little control over emergency care for which an immediate response is required and the spinal patient's needs are urgent in relation to asymptomatic CHD patients.

The September Statins Meeting

A meeting to which all GPs in Poppleton HA were invited was held on 17 September 1997. The speakers included only medical staff and these were drawn from the HA, primary care and secondary care. The meeting was chaired by a local GP, who described the purpose of the evening as being not to produce guidelines but to 'flesh out issues'.

The consultant diabetologist spoke first. The opening words of his speech (entitled 'Evidence-based Medicine – A Medical and Ethical Dilemma') were:

> Ten years ago life was simple. When you treated patients you relied on gut feeling and you were usually right. Sometimes you were disastrously wrong, but nobody could prove it . . . Now things are different, there have been several major shifts in the direction of evidence-based medicine.

He then went on to present four emotive case studies of patients and asked the audience (rhetorically) whether or not each patient would receive a statin from them. His approach was to raise the spectre of litigation as a means of frightening GPs into prescribing statins.

He went on to suggest cutting back on breast screening, cervical screening, inappropriate prescribing and management costs to fund statins. He was critical of the SMAC guidelines as being full of 'shoulder shrugging sentences . . . When you ask "Who should I treat?" it says the answer is up to you . . . it's clear there's no more money for this.' He then referred to a letter from the Department

of Health which contained the phrase 'the amount of money available for NHS prescribing budgets is informed by an assessment of
trends and pressures, including new drugs'. His interpretation of
this phrase was that 'if anybody goes and spends lots of money on
statins then this will feed through into the spending round'. He did
not mention that the guidance also states that 'for many patients, a
change in diet will be sufficient to bring their cholesterol down to a
safer level' and that 'there is no intention that the threshold recommended by SMAC will be imposed in any way'. Having stressed
litigation earlier, he now returned to the subject, asking 'What
defence can we use for not prescribing statins?' to which he
answered that lack of evidence, peer standard, guidelines, moral
obligation, the General Medical Council (GMC) or 'only obeying
orders' were all unacceptable. As a parting shot, he read from guidance on disciplinary measures in relation to medical staff reminding
the audience that doctors 'should always seek to give priority solely
on the basis of clinical need'.

The MD spoke next, pointing out that aspirin saves ten lives for
every £6000 spent, compared with over £1,000,000 with statins and
that since the number needed to treat (NNT) for statins is 30, 29
patients who don't need the drugs would receive them. Local
'cottage' hospitals had been the subject of discussion at HA level,
but GPs had fiercely attacked the HA for discussing the potential
closure of these community facilities. Knowing the deep attach-
ment of the GPs to these hospitals, the MD continued 'If we shut
Newbold cottage hospital and Pelham Hospital, we'd still not save
the £8 million to treat all CHD patients with raised cholesterol . . .
The important question is how do we make it affordable?' (The £5
million from the June meeting is now £8 million, for maximum
effect.)

The MD then went on to ask 'Are we trying to prevent death or
get everybody to 100 when the natural lifespan is 75?' This cleverly
avoids using terms such as 'fair innings', which suggest that a value
judgement is being made and presents the ageist argument in terms
of a 'natural' course of events. However, this is a little disingenuous
since many aspects of medicine are precisely about interfering with
'nature', but when this interference takes the form of low-cost drugs
such as aspirin, it may be more acceptable.

The MD did his best to present the arguments for restricting
statin prescribing, pointing out that statins are a preventive
measure aimed at modifying a risk factor, not treating a disease. He
did not mention that statins will delay disease progression in people

with established disease, which is in effect treating disease, although he did go on to say that preventive measures are 'different from giving people aspirin post-MI'. He suggested that the phrase 'multifactorial' in relation to the causes of CHD means 'We don't have a bloody clue what causes it!' and stressed that the long-term, potentially adverse effects of statins were unknown, as the trials were around 5 years in duration. Responding to the diabetologist's calls for disinvestment in breast screening and cervical cytology he told the meeting that these would save only £310,000 and that all the medical beds in Poppleton hospital would have to close to fund statins for all CHD patients.

The summing-up for the entire meeting was provided by a local GP, who stressed that doctors as personal physicians were not look-ing at the needs of the whole community, but had to do the best for the individual patient. He was keen, however, to limit statins to secondary prevention.

This meeting contrasted markedly with that held in Riverside to launch statin guidelines. Mixed and conflicting messages were pre-sented and no action was agreed or suggested other than in general terms, with the MD appealing for restraint, the diabetologist advo-cating much broader statin use and the local GP somewhere in the middle. Although questions were raised in relation to age, dietary and lifestyle status, there was never any attempt to define the pur-pose of a statin prescribing strategy. The vague 'making statins affordable' aim alluded to in earlier meetings by the MD was never placed within the context of agreed values or priorities. In the absence of agreed criteria on which to base policy, individuals were free to suggest how affordability might be pursued.

Widening the decision process

Following the failure of the evening meeting to reach any consen-sus, the MD decided to inform the management team of the statins issue. The 'Statins position statement' presented to them on 25 Sep-tember 1997 identified the 'target group emerging' as:

- patients with ischaemic heart disease;
- younger age group; and
- those who have not responded to a properly applied diet.

A paper outlining the likely cost of implementing the SMAC guidelines was presented to the HA in October 1997. This included a range of scenarios based on varying assumptions around compliance, implementation, prevalence, cholesterol, age and the impact of dietary advice on risk factors. The likely annual expenditure on statins ranged from £2.5 to £5.5 million and the same meeting was informed of the projected overspend on prescribing of £0.5 million for the current financial year based on pre-SMAC prescribing trends. The paper advised that patients believed to benefit most were 'in the younger age group', although no indication was provided as to the nature of this benefit or the evidence base to support this remark. 'Younger' was not defined. The HA members were asked to 'note this significant financial pressure and the need to identify how this will be managed'.

The discussion on the issue lasted 15 minutes, which included the MD explaining the contents of the paper. The chairman commented 'There's no doubt that these drugs are very effective' and expressed relief that this was a pressure on the prescribing budget. This reflects the preoccupation of HA directors with the cash limited budgets and the fact that prescribing was seen as the MD's responsibility. The director of primary care asked 'Shouldn't we be asking if we had £3 million to spend tomorrow whether we'd choose to spend it on statins?' I asked whether we shouldn't look at disinvesting in services in order to pay for the statins, but the questions were treated as comments and no answers were forthcoming. The situation was noted and no further action was taken.

Ironically, at the same meeting, immediately prior to the statins paper, a report was presented to the HA by the MD on the proposed arrangements for managing new technologies at HA level. If this process were applied to statins, following agreement that they were 'a clinical effective/cost-effective technology with a financial impact that will distort existing HA priorities', a recommendation would be made. The matter would then be debated in full by the HA and a decision made on the subject. This report was 'noted' by the HA and yet the statins item had received little or no debate before moving swiftly on to the next item. The paper itself illustrates the efforts of the MD to use a systematic protocol and to do 'the right thing', but in a system characterized by informal decision-making, lack of clarity about objectives and non-decision-making, such an approach may not be possible.

Clutching at straws and losing interest

In November 1997, we met with representatives from the pharmaceutical industry in an attempt to find an innovative solution to the statins problem, but to no avail. Professor John Sims from Sydney University came to the UK and spoke on the LIPID trial, another statins RCT, which confirmed, if confirmation were needed, the beneficial effects of statins. The PA was focusing his attention on getting a job outside the HA and left in December 1997. By now, the weather was getting colder and HA managers' thoughts were turning once again to winter pressures. The combination of emergency admissions dominating the agenda and the absence of any obvious way forward led the statins meetings to fizzle out altogether. Poppleton HA never did develop a statins guideline, but by 1999 one PCG had developed its own guideline and another was looking at this issue. The MD claimed later that it was always his intention to encourage the localities (now shadow PCGs) to develop their own local statins guidelines. So not only is ambiguity a feature of organizational objectives ('What is it we are trying to achieve?'), understanding ('What are the precise relationships between risk factors, statins and CHD?') and attention ('Statins are yesterday's problem given the central directives to manage emergency pressures'), but ambiguity now applies to recent history. The past is not so much another country in the Poppleton HA, as another planet.

NOTE

1 Several studies have shown the public to be in favour of discriminating against 'older' patients, so the CD may be right in her claim. However, this is not a universal finding, see for example Dolan *et al.* 1999.

5

CASE STUDY II: SYSTEM-WIDE MODELLING OF CHD SERVICES IN POPPLETON HA

INTRODUCTION

This chapter describes attempts to use health economics to examine the whole of CHD services in Poppleton HA. This economic analysis was different from the statins issue in terms of size and scope, but there are other important differences between the two exercises which are worthy of mention.

First, statins were seen as an immediate 'problem' for the HA. Cardiac nurses in primary care, increased awareness of the drugs, pharmaceutical industry marketing and central guidance from the NHSE had all served to move the drugs higher and higher up the MD's agenda. The need to tackle health services for people with CHD was much less urgent in terms of requiring a reactive response.

Second, the MD was responsible for the HA prescribing budget. In a system where performance is often difficult to measure, the ability to balance budgets is one of the few 'hard' markers by which managers are judged. Compared with the broad aim of tackling CHD, the statins represented immediacy and urgency and the increased expenditure on these drugs was very visible.

Third, cause and effect relationships with regard to statins prescribing (as opposed to the impact of statins on CHD in Poppleton HA) were relatively simple to grasp. If the aim is to control the growth of statins prescribing, then something must be done to influence the prescribers. Decision-makers were uncertain of what happens to patients when they reach hospital and the relationships between primary, secondary and tertiary care with regard to CHD were altogether less amenable to conceptualization.

Fourth, because statins was a prescribing issue, the PA was actively involved in trying to drive the process forward. After he left in December 1997, there was no input from any of the pharmacists into the health economics system-wide project.

Finally, the modelling work required literature reviews, off-site meetings with stakeholders, data collection at the tertiary trust and meetings with health economist colleagues at the university. This meant that I spent more time than previously outside the HA and I looked forward to these visits as much of my time was spent at the HA reading circulars or journal articles, in the absence of other things to do. In terms of drawing wider conclusions, this experience is important because it supports the idea of economist as 'bidet' raised earlier (see Chapter 3). It also highlights how problems do not present in neat packages for economists to tackle and illustrates the fact that the mainstream HA business was carried on elsewhere, outside the orbit of the health economist.

BACKGROUND TO THE SYSTEM-WIDE MODELLING PROJECT

Alongside the statins work, there was a whole host of initiatives being pursued by Poppleton HA as part of its wider CHD strategy. These are described in Tables 5.1 and 5.2, together with a short description of the nature of each in terms of reactive or proactive initiatives. What this illustrates is that although life at the HA is depicted as one of reacting to pressures and problems, there are proactive schemes which HAs either initiate or support. All measures are in some sense a response to a perceived problem, but reactive measures respond to immediate or urgent problems. The term 'proactive' is used to denote schemes which are less 'knee jerk' in nature, although the final outcome may be the same as would have been the case if timescales were truncated or immediate pressures increased. The idea that the reactive nature of decision-making in HAs is not conducive to the use of more proactive health economic approaches may be an oversimplification.

Although the HA was pursuing a range of initiatives in primary, secondary and tertiary care, the volume and case mix at the tertiary centre was a constant source of argument between the MD and HA contract staff on the one hand and the tertiary trust on the other. In

Table 5.1   CHD initiatives in and around Poppleton HA – proactive

	Description of initiative	Rationale
(i)	Nurses undertaking a systematic review of CHD patients in primary care, delivering evidence-based interventions (lifestyle, medication review and so on)	Proactive measure, MD's idea, designed to address perceived 'unsystematic' treatment by GPs; funded by HA and drug-industry money
(ii)	An audit of all patients receiving angiography to determine severity of disease and post angiography treatment according to a severity scoring system developed and used in New Zealand	Proactive measure designed to address constant complaint by MD (and other HAs) that tertiary clinicians are not systematic in prioritization of patients; made possible by development of New Zealand score; funded by HA audit monies
(iii)	An aspirin audit in primary care intended to increase aspirin prescribing in eligible CHD patients	Proactive measure involving most practices
(iv)	A primary care initiative in one locality following up patients frequently readmitted to hospital with chest pain	Proactive measure designed to investigate why patients attend and what happens when they are discharged, together with reasons for frequent reattendance; focus also on alternative ways of practice organization in primary care; HA funded
(v)	A rapid chest pain assessment project, funded by R and D resources, intended to speed up the process of MI diagnosis in low-risk patients in the A and E department of the local trust	Proactive measure, joint R and D project between local district general hospital and large teaching trust in 'Cityville' HA; funded by regional R and D money

1997/98 the trust had performed only 85 per cent of coronary artery bypass grafts (CABGs) contracted for with the HA, despite having received additional resources for extra activity. This fuelled the MD's view that the trust was 'ripping off' the HA. The situation led to heated conversations between the trust and the MD and a

Table 5.2 CHD initiatives in and around Poppleton HA – reactive

	Description of initiative	Rationale
(i)	Direct access exercise tolerance testing (a diagnostic technique) at the local trust, aimed at reducing bottlenecks in secondary care	Reactive measure proposed by trust clinicians, funded by the HA
(ii)	Appointment of additional physicians (staff grade) at the local trust intended to reduce emergency activity pressures	Reactive measure; HA's response to suggestion by the trust

worsening of relations between the two parties. (A brief note on terminology in relation to procedures undertaken at the tertiary centre is provided in Table 5.3.)

On closer examination, it became clear that part of the reason for the reduction in tertiary sector activity was due to the appointment of a consultant cardiologist in the secondary care sector. The HA had funded this post at the local trust in 1996/97 because, prior to this, in the absence of consultant cardiology staff, patients were seen by one of a number of general physicians. The HA had anticipated that the appointment of the cardiologist would generate increased referrals to the tertiary sector and had contracted for additional tertiary activity on the basis of this assumption. However, referral patterns changed after the appointment so that GPs now referred patients to the lone cardiologist (where previously these referrals had been spread across a number of general physicians), whose waiting time for outpatients was 6 months and growing. In addition, the secondary care cardiologist preferred to perform angiographies on his patients personally on a sessional basis using tertiary trust facilities, but could only perform four per week at the tertiary centre, which added to the backlog. The reduction in the number of patients undergoing angiography meant that there were fewer patients available to undergo tertiary procedures. For example, fewer than 500 angiographies were performed compared with a planned activity of over 600 cases in 1997/98.

The HA-funded primary-care project, which followed up patients who were frequently readmitted with cardiac or respiratory problems, found that patients discharged from hospital often had no follow up in primary care. When their symptoms worsened, they presented to A and E as they had done previously, establishing a

Table 5.3   A brief guide to the main procedures provided for patients with CHD at the tertiary centre trust

Artery	A blood vessel that carries oxygen-rich blood.
Atheroma	Deposits of fatty material and cholesterol inside the arteries.
Coronary Angiography/ Angiogram	Also referred to as arteriograms or catheterization. An image of the coronary arteries is obtained in this procedure by passing a delicate tube (catheter) through the blood vessels under local anaesthetic. X-ray opaque fluid is injected to outline the blood vessels, showing up any areas of narrowing (stenoses) due to atheroma. This test is a pre-requisite for CABG or PTCA.
Coronary Artery Bypass Graft (CABG)	This is an open-heart operation in which a fresh blood supply is brought to the heart muscle using arteries within the chest or segments of vein from within the leg.
Coronary Stents	Coronary artery stents are small mesh cylinders placed in ballooned arteries at the time of angioplasty. They act as permanent prosthetic linings to maintain the patency of the artery. Stents, therefore, may have significant advantage in overcoming the problems that limit the full potential of PTCA.
Percutaneous Transluminal Coronary Angioplasty (PTCA)	This procedure involves the introduction of a catheter through the skin (percutaneous), into a blood vessel (transluminal) and to the arteries of the heart. A very fine deflated balloon wrapped around the tip of the catheter can be inflated to enlarge the artery at an area of stenosis.

Notes:

CHD is caused by the build up of cholesterol, containing plaque, in the walls of the coronary arteries. This reduces the width of the artery and, therefore, reduces the flow of blood and the supply of oxygen to the heart muscle. This may cause pain in the heart, which is known as 'angina'.

Heart attacks (MIs) occur when the diseased artery becomes blocked, cutting off the flow of blood and oxygen to the heart muscle. Partial blockages, caused by clots which form and dissolve again, result in transient periods of unpredictable pain. This is known as unstable angina.

Elective patients may be referred to the tertiary centre from the secondary care for further investigation. Many patients arriving at the tertiary centre will undergo angiography and this may be followed either by coronary artery bypass (CABG) or percutaneous transluminal coronary angioplasty (PTCA), depending on the extent of atheroma observed at angiography.

pattern of discharge and readmission to secondary care with little or no contact with the primary-care team. During the initial stages of the project, the GPs involved had expressed the view that the hospital was at fault as it had not 'sorted out' the patients and that discharge documentation was poor. The project showed that despite improvements in discharge documentation, the fact that there was no pathway of care for patients following discharge meant that in most cases the documentation was filed on the patient's record and no further action was taken.

What these examples illustrate is, first, the difference between the anecdotal or superficial analysis of the patterns of care in Poppleton HA, based on little or no information, and the picture obtained from a deeper reading of the situation, based on more robust data. Second, the striking feature illustrated is the interconnectedness of the elements of the health-care system in relation to CHD patients. A blockage which manifests itself as reduced activity in the tertiary sector is actually the product of shifts in referral patterns in primary care following changes in the secondary-care sector. Cardiac readmissions, characterized as a 'hospital problem' by observers outside the hospital, reflect in part the lack of care in the primary sector. Perceived inequalities in access to care at the tertiary centre may be more a product of processes in primary and secondary care, and so on.

The realization that small changes in one part of the system can have unintended consequences elsewhere illustrates the importance of looking across the system, as opposed to tackling problems in isolation. However, this made the prospect of tackling CHD issues so much more daunting. For chronic conditions such as CHD, patients within the system flow between primary, secondary and tertiary care without being 'cured'. Interventions may provide relief from symptoms and improved quality of life for a time, but the process cannot be expressed as a linear progression starting in primary care and ending in secondary or tertiary care. There are complex loops as patients attend and reattend, with new patients adding to the pool of morbid individuals and deaths reducing the numbers. When I asked people at the HA and in primary and secondary care about the impact of effects in one sector on the rest of the system, they agreed that system effects were important, but felt unable to predict what these might be in most cases.

I began to contemplate the idea of constructing a system-wide model to simulate the effect of different service changes for CHD patients in Poppleton HA. The MD thought this an excellent idea, but the harder I thought about it the more daunting the task appeared. On 13 November 1997 I met with the researchers from the National Prescribing Centre who were working on computer simulation models in relation to prescribing. They advised me against pursuing a modelling route unless I had a few years to spend on the process. The researchers were later to abandon their attempts in this area.

The MD was undaunted. He asked me to sketch out a 'rough outline' of patient flows in the system to serve as the basis for a model, which I attempted to do. At first I used a computer to try to create a pictorial representation and then resorted to pencil and paper as the drawings expanded. I tried to capture the various patient permutations possible in the system. For example, patients attending A and E either self-refer or do so at the request of their GP, then they are either admitted or sent home. In the latter case they may be called back for outpatient follow-up or not. In the former, they may be in a general medical bed or a coronary care bed and in either case they may die, be discharged with outpatient follow up, discharged completely or transferred to the tertiary centre. On arrival at the tertiary centre, emergency patients will undergo an angiography followed by either a regime of medical management under the supervision of the consultant or with GP follow up only or they may undergo CABG or PTCA. At any stage in their stay at the tertiary centre, they may die or be discharged. Following an MI, patients may have cardiac rehabilitation or no rehabilitation or some follow up by their GP. Things are not this simple, however, as the tertiary centre's small secondary-care facility accepts patients who will be assessed and admitted straight to the tertiary centre.

There are also elective flows to be incorporated into the picture. An increase in emergencies will reduce capacity for elective care and vice versa, so the relationships between these two types of care (the tertiary centre classifies patients as 'emergency' 'urgent' or 'elective' adding to the complication) must be mapped. The major problem, however, is that patients who are discharged may come back within a matter of weeks or months. These patients may be the same patients who underwent tertiary procedures, or those discharged on medical management from secondary or tertiary care or patients discharged with a diagnosis of 'chest pain non-specific' and so on. The only simple concept to map is that those patients who die will not come back into the system!

Although health economists use decision tree software to model complex linear relationships which typically have 'cure' or 'death' at the end of tree, the chronic nature of CHD and the number of possible treatment permutations means that decision trees are not useful in modelling this disease. Instead, I spent several hours on different occasions drawing lines on paper that was spread across the office floor.

The MD and I met five times in December 1997 and at each of these meetings, we tried various strategies for capturing the CHD patient flows. Invariably, at these meetings the lines on the (by now A2 size) paper began to resemble spaghetti as I attempted to capture the admission and readmission of patients within the system and the flows between the various sectors. The meetings were usually abandoned at this point, only to be resumed the next time at the start of the process. I wanted desperately to provide something useful to the MD, but was acutely aware of the difficulties I faced in attempting to model the whole system. I was advised by colleagues at the university that constructing such a model would take several years of work and was encouraged to pursue alternative strategies for my research. I began to contemplate abandoning the study altogether.

Shortly after this low point in the project, Adrian Bagust, from the York Health Economics Consortium, joined my host department at the university on a part-time basis and he suggested another, altogether more appealing strategy.

THE YORK CHD MODEL

In March 1997, just a month before starting at Poppleton HA, I had visited Adrian Bagust in York to discuss a CHD model which he and his colleagues had developed to simulate system-wide effects for CHD strategies. The purpose of my visit was to discuss the model and more generally to learn from Adrian's experiences. When Adrian joined my department at Liverpool in October 1998, he offered me the use of his model for my work with Poppleton HA.

He met with the MD and the MD's team and myself at Poppleton HA on 22 December 1997, explaining to them the workings of the model in general terms. Adrian talked for about an hour about the background to the model and the assumptions underpinning it, together with its limitations, before giving a very brief demonstration of the input screens. He refused the MD's request for a copy of the model to 'play with' over the Christmas break, because the modelling exercise was part of a wider process of thinking and communicating. He explained to me outside the meeting that the idea that this 'black box' would produce a solution, as if by magic, was something he would rather not encourage. Within the main meeting, Adrian explained that the modelling process with other HAs had been an iterative one based on the following steps.

Step 1 – informing/consulting with stakeholders about the proposed modelling process.
Step 2 – discussion of options for service changes with local stakeholders (an expert group of a few carefully selected committed individuals).
Step 3 – data collection and input to establish a baseline position for CHD services locally.
Step 4 – modelling of service changes.
Step 5 – feedback of preliminary results.
Step 6 – amendment of results, based on feedback.
Step 7 – presentation of model results.

Steps 6 and 7 were to be repeated once or twice to arrive at a consensus.

The MD agreed that these steps should be followed, but was keen to have a larger working group for the process than suggested by Adrian. The strengths of a small group, as outlined by Adrian related to the commitment of those involved to attend meetings and collect data. The greater the number of people involved, the more likely it would be that individuals would become 'passengers', attending some meetings, but not contributing greatly to the overall process. The MD recognized these potential problems, but expressed the view that clinicians would not implement changes unless they were involved in the process from the outset. Citing once again the failure of the NHS around implementation and the ability of trust clinicians to disregard the views of the HA, the MD insisted that certain individuals, as a minimum, should be invited onto the working group (step 3). This would mean a membership of ten or more, in addition to myself.

Step 1 – informing the stakeholders

In April 1998 an evening meeting was held to inform local primary-, secondary- and tertiary-care representatives of the proposed modelling process and to raise the subject of the working group. Twenty people attended the meeting and these were representatives of primary, secondary and tertiary care who had been selected by the MD and CD. The CE gave a brief introduction, outlining the problems of stretching scarce resources, and stressing the need for collaboration and, importantly, the 'messy' nature of HA decision-making in an environment where data were limited, evidence was lacking and political and resource constraints placed great restrictions on the options available.

I then spoke, covering issues such as the need to address system-wide effects, the multiple competing and unclear goals ('Are we trying to prevent deaths or is tackling premature mortality a higher priority?' 'Where does quality of life feature in all of this?') facing the HA and the need for a shared understanding based on more than anecdotes of the services provided. I also drew attention to the fact that the model was not being touted as 'the answer' to the CHD problems and that no magic solution existed. Instead, I was proposing that we use the model to get a clearer picture of where we were at that point and to shed some light on where we might be heading if we pursued certain paths in the future. Despite all the mess in the system, decisions about resource allocation were still being made and, I suggested, the model might help us think through some of these issues in a more systematic and explicit manner.

Preparing the talk had been difficult because I wanted to stress some of the problems with the current system using the unintended effects of the cardiology appointment as an example, but the CD did not want this discussed for fear that it would reflect badly on the HA. Similarly, the MD and CD were not keen for me to highlight the fact that they had invested heavily but had failed to secure additional activity at the tertiary centre, partly due to external pressures from the NHSE. My brief was to describe the difficulties of the current 'muddling through' approach in order to make a case for a more systematic way of working, but without giving specific examples of these difficulties as this might portray HA staff in a poor light.

Adrian spoke on the assumptions underlying the model and explained the PBMA approach of which the model was a variant. He described the steps to be followed, ideally culminating in a consensus view. A representative from the tertiary trust, the clinical audit manager, who was largely in favour of anything which could make decision-making more systematic, asked about the implementation of findings in previous exercises. Adrian replied that, as an academic, his brief had been to facilitate the modelling process, but his involvement had not extended to issues of implementation.

The MD was the last to speak, presenting figures showing variations in clinical practice across the three secondary-care trusts and highlighting the need to look across the system in a proactive way as opposed to 'throwing money at problems' and 'hoping they would go away'. The CE addressed the meeting from the floor, deliberately, so that the process was not seen as the HA telling the stakeholders what to do.

The questions from the audience largely concerned process issues such as the amount of time commitment, the level and knowledge required for participation in the working group and the steps and timescale to be followed. Two clinicians from the tertiary trust independently suggested that the project should be supported and the questions on the process were framed in positive terms. I had met most of the members of the audience during my time at Poppleton HA and had established fairly cordial relationships with them. However, the MD of the local trust expressed the view that 'We all know who the problem patients are in the system.' The issue could be resolved, he suggested, by applying 'common sense' and without recourse to a complicated modelling process. Such a view is perhaps understandable given that the pursuit of this approach had enabled the local trust to extract large sums of development funds from the HA in the recent past. Similarly, the tertiary-centre clinicians had expressed confidence at contract meetings in relation to the evidence base for the procedures conducted at their hospital in contrast to much of the activity taking place in secondary care. It may be that their enthusiasm stemmed from a desire to see other centres subjected to the sort of scrutiny which they had experienced. Certainly, they would be unlikely to anticipate a reduction in resources from such a process.

In the hotel bar afterwards, my HA colleagues agreed that the meeting had gone well. I was pleased that there had been no violent objection and some support for the process. Basking in the sense of camaraderie and listening to the anecdotes about various personalities, I felt cheered at the prospect of making progress. Much later, when I reflected on my notes of the meeting I was struck by the way I had obtained so much satisfaction from this meeting. Making progress at the HA had felt like wading through treacle, so that the sense of achievement from this event was totally disproportionate to the actual progress (if any) made. I was reminded of how, when I first attended the key clinicians meeting with the CD, MD and FD, I could not understand their expressions of satisfaction at the 'success' of the meeting, when no progress in terms of concrete actions had been made. The fact that confrontation had largely been avoided was clearly seen as progress by the HA representatives.

Step 2 – discussion of options for service changes with local stakeholders

The first meeting of the CHD working group was held over lunch in a local hotel. Sixteen people including myself and Adrian, two secondary-care consultant cardiologists, two FDs, two GPs, a cardiac surgeon, a tertiary-care cardiologist, a consultant in A and E medicine and the CD, MD and information manager from the HA attended the first meeting on 1 June.

At the evening meeting only one GP had attended and he told the PM outside the meeting that he felt intimidated by the presence of the hospital consultants because he was the only representative from primary care present. In May, I invited three GPs to join the working group. Two of the GPs later confirmed their attendance, but the third telephoned and asked if he would be paid to attend. When I explained that there was no budget for this and that the cardiac surgeons and cardiologists were giving up their lunch hour to attend for free, he was unmoved. When I pointed out that his GP colleagues were attending, he explained that their role as a member of the local medical committee meant they could claim financial recompense. Getting GPs to participate in HA projects often met with this response. The economic literature on incentives would suggest that GPs are likely to respond to financial incentives. However, the disadvantage of this is that if GPs are paid to participate in some instances, they may be unlikely to participate on occasions where payment is not offered.

I introduced Adrian who spoke briefly about the model largely for the benefit of those who had been unable to attend the evening meeting. He went on to explain that we were keen to model service changes, but that proposals for modelling would need to be accompanied by information or judgements about the likely immediate impact of such changes. For example, instead of saying 'more medical staff in A and E', we would need to know what exactly these staff will do differently. For example, will it be to admit more patients or to improve care so that mortality reduces? The intention was to model the immediate impact based on the views of the working group and to examine the system-wide implications using the dynamic York model.

I then asked for suggestions of service changes and was greeted with silence. I did not feel that this was a stony silence and it may have been that the condition that suggestions should be accompanied by an assessment of impact in terms more precise than 'improve care' had temporarily stumped the group.

To get the ball rolling, I suggested that we should look at the impact of the primary-care nurse project initiated by the HA, which was being hailed as a success despite the fact that it had not been evaluated. The MD suggested that we should look at an initiative at the secondary-care trust intended to diagnose or quickly rule out a heart attack in low-risk chest pain patients. One of the GPs suggested that 'I'd like to see something to deal with these patients who keep coming back ... things like open access to echo and ECGs would help.'

(An echo or echocardiography refers to a test that uses sound waves to create a picture of the heart. The picture is more detailed than on X-ray image, and there is no radiation exposure. An ECG is a test that records the electrical activity of the heart. It is used to measure the rate and regularity of beats as well as the size and position of the chambers, any damage to the heart, and the effects of drugs or devices to regulate the heart. An exercise ECG provides a recording of the electrical activity of the heart during physical stress to test the heart's reaction to increased demand for oxygen. A recording of the activity of the heart (ECG) and blood pressure readings are taken while the patient walks on an exercise treadmill or pedals a stationary bicycle.)

There was some debate about the benefits of open access to diagnostic tests as this extract shows:

Cardiologist A secondary care: But it's a question of targeting the right patients because open access will just open the flood gates ...

GP: Yes, but I'd quite like to have access to these tests to rule out cardiac problems... If I can say to somebody 'You've got a normal ECG' then this will help me deal with them ... There's nothing worse than these patients who keep coming back and they say they've got to wait months for an ECG at the hospital ...

Cardiologist A secondary care: I don't agree with open access stress testing [exercise ECG test] . You need to understand the type of patient you're dealing with and the nature of the test ...

Cardiologist B secondary care: But maybe we could have direct access. It would be worth doing in low-risk patients to exclude a diagnosis ... Maybe we could decide how many people we want treated at the [tertiary centre] and work backwards to say how many tests we need and other things so people don't wait too long.

Cardiac surgeon tertiary care: It might not be a bad thing to have a long waiting list at your end. It might be better at the exercise test stage because once they get to me I've got to do something about them. There are some patients I'd rather not see, but once they're referred I have to see them ...

Cardiologist B secondary care: Well I think we should start by saying what's the impact of treating people with prognostic disease [that is those with an immediately life-threatening disease] first of all? If we start by saying 'We want to operate on these people' then we can work back.

What this exchange highlights is the difference of opinion amongst the clinicians, all of whom have a tendency to see things in terms of their own workload. The GP is anxious to reduce the number of patients returning to him. The phrase 'this will help me deal with them' suggests that the test may be beneficial in reducing GP stress, rather than providing reassurance to the patient. Cardiologist A's resistance to open access means that he wants to see patients before any test is ordered, since the GP is not in a position to decide on who are the appropriate candidates. The test carries a risk, so it may be that Cardiologist A is seeking to reduce the risk to patients or that he is protecting his 'specialist' role. His hobby-horse is the development of a rapid access chest pain clinic for patients with recent onset chest pain. This 'one-stop' clinic would provide diagnostic tests under the cardiologist's direction and patients would be seen within 4 weeks. The development of an open access diagnostic service would undermine the case for the new clinic slot.

The surgeon's preference for patients to wait at the early stage of the process is not expressed in terms of patient anxiety. It could be argued that if patients wait later in the process, when they have a confirmed diagnosis ('You need an operation, but you'll have to wait 6 months so don't do anything strenuous!'), this would place enormous strain on them. This surgeon was acknowledged by the centre managers to be one of the most proficient, but this meant that his case mix was skewed towards the more complex and high-risk patients. In the past he had explained that the 12-month waiting list target was putting pressure on him to undertake difficult cases when he would prefer to defer some patients because of the complexity of their cases.

The recently appointed secondary-care cardiologist suggested that we model the impact of treating patients with prognostic disease (that is life-threatening triple vessel or equivalent disease) in tertiary care first of all and then work back to assess the level of resources required for this in secondary care. The cardiologist's waiting list was long and getting longer. He had explained to me earlier in the year that as he was a recently appointed member of staff, he was fairly low down in the pecking order compared to the other consultants. He felt that the more established consultants had more resources in terms of junior staff and that, for the population served, the hospital should have another cardiologist. The hospital was keen to obtain funding for a second cardiologist and so his interest in focusing on secondary-care capacity is understandable.

I interpreted the cardiologist's proposal to model the treatment of those with prognostic disease first as a way of moving forward. It seems extremely unlikely that he was advocating that only these patients should receive tertiary interventions, particularly since he had at first suggested that all patients be included. However, the MD responded to the suggestion saying that 'That's what we want to do, but the waiting list targets mean we have to treat people who don't need it. We could work out the effects of blunderbuss waiting list directives and send a message to the centre.' The use of rhetoric and drama in an attempt to unite the group around the common enemy – 'the centre' – merely produced audible sighs. The trust MD disagreed: 'We already know that waiting list targets are skewing things, but we'd be better concentrating on things we can do something about.'

The tertiary-centre cardiologist, whose main interest is research suggested that his own scheme which was experimental, cheap and successful at reducing or eliminating pain in patients with severe disease should be expanded along with the other interventions which comprised his unit's 'comprehensive programme for the treatment of intractable angina'. The cardiologist went on to elaborate about the nature of the pain mechanism and the lack of any clear association between pain and level of disease. 'Doesn't it strike you as odd,' he asked rhetorically, 'that we don't have the faintest idea how the angina pain mechanism works?' The trust MD replied that he did not find this odd:

> What you're talking about is uncertainty and it doesn't just apply to cardiology . . . that's what medicine is all about. Most of what we do is pretty uncertain . . . Maybe we should forget looking at disease processes and concentrate on patient groups . . . we all know the patients who keep coming back to A and E we should target these . . . We know where the problems are.

At the earlier meeting, this clinician had suggested that problems could be tackled by applying 'common sense' and without recourse to a complicated modelling process. So it appears that an elaborate process is too complex due to the enormous uncertainties surrounding medical decision-making and, at the same time, the issue is really quite a simple one as 'we all know' the important aspects as individual clinicians.

The focus in the model is with patient flows, rather than carefully mapping out rates of progression of disease. This has been explained to the trust MD at two meetings by now, so it seems unlikely that this is a misunderstanding on his part. It may be, however, that from his point of view, since frequently admitted patients are a 'problem' now, there is a need to tackle this problem at the point of presentation because that is what the clinicians in the trust do. The emergency care work is about the tackling rather than the resolution of problems. The trust MD is unenthusiastic about the modelling process, but he does not suggest what should be done for these 'problem patients' nor does he perceive a link between what happens in emergency medicine and elsewhere in the system.

I explained that the locality project, which looked at frequently admitted patients had identified these people, but the question remained of what to do for them once they were identified. The more experienced of the secondary-care cardiologists picked up on the theme of uncertainty explaining 'The test we're using is not very good. You can't just say because somebody has a negative test that they're fine . . . the whole process is pretty uncertain . . . the ECG result is poor in many circumstances.' I asked 'If this is the case then why do you use the test?' The cardiologist replied, 'Well you can pick up patients who need urgent treatment and fast track them.' At this point the cardiac surgeon repeated his view that 'You might be better to have delays at that end because once I see them I'm forced to do something about them.'

After some discussion about diagnostic tests and the issue of whether it is desirable for patients to be delayed at the start of the process to reduce the pressure on tertiary services, I began to panic. We were approaching the time at which clinicians would have to leave and we had few suggestions for the modelling process. I repeated my suggestion that we model the cardiac nurses in primary care and Cardiologist A agreed. He suggested that we should model a directed access echocardiography service. This would be 'pro forma' based access allowing the consultant to make the final decision on eligibility for directed access as opposed to GP referred. I then suggested to Cardiologist A that we model a chest pain clinic since he had repeatedly requested that the HA fund such a clinic and he agreed, explaining that he would like us to model a clinic for high-risk patients.

The CD suggested that the earlier proposal to 'work backwards from the number of people we want to revascularize' be modelled, building in maximum waiting times. One of the GPs (who had been asking for a statins guideline from the HA since August 1997) suggested 'I'd like a guideline on statins because this would give me something to hide behind ... at the moment I've got the SMAC guidelines or nothing.' The CD suggested that statins should be left out of the exercise for the time being as there were other issues which would be better addressed using the system-wide approach.

This prompted the MD to remark 'It's like the 85-year-olds who are getting revascularization, it's ridiculous.' To which the cardiac surgeon responded 'Well, if they're not referred it makes it a lot easier.' The MD returned to a recurring theme of his, saying 'We need to make choices about what we're here to deliver. Are we trying to get everybody to their natural lifespan or prevent deaths?'

The CD wanted to see the additional activity, for which the tertiary centre had requested funds, modelled in terms of the system-wide effects. As people were gathering their papers to leave, I summarized the options to be modelled as:

- chest pain clinic;
- primary-care nurses;
- directed access echocardiography;
- capacity and waiting time issues across the system;
- additional activity at the tertiary centre;
- rapid chest pain / MI diagnosis scheme; and
- pain relief for intractable angina.

Step 3 – data collection and input

Local mortality data for CHD were held within the HA, but no data were available for CHD prevalence locally at this time. The model contained prevalence data from Newcastle, where it had been used previously and it was decided on the advice of Adrian Bagust, to adjust the prevalence values to the point at which the mortality rates predicted by the model corresponded to the local mortality data levels. Outpatient data were not available and, in the absence of any other option, were estimated by inputting all the other information, leaving the outpatient activity as a balancing figure

Local data were available for admissions, readmissions, length of stay and waiting times. Prescribing data based on a limited sample of patients reviewed in primary care by the cardiac nurses were used to estimate the proportion of patients receiving various drugs.

Step 4 – modelling of service changes

Chest pain clinic

Following the meeting, I went to discuss the chest pain clinic proposal with the secondary-care cardiologist. He outlined his idea for a chest pain clinic for 'high-risk' patients, saying that this would provide a one-stop service to 'sort out' patients and would be run one afternoon per week on an outpatient basis. The key to success would be rapid access to diagnostic tests and consultant expertise designed to ensure that these patients were assessed promptly and referred on as appropriate.

The consultant explained that although he ran a chest pain clinic for patients from Shoreville and Riverview, Poppleton HA did not buy into this service. This clinic was for all patients, but the proposal for modelling would be for high-risk patients only. However, when asked about the likely outcomes from the clinic in terms of the impact on key model parameters ('What happens to the patients following the clinic?' 'Where do these patients come from?' 'Are these patients currently frequent A and E attenders?' 'What would the impact be on mortality, on MIs and on admissions?') the cardiologist was unable to provide even a guesstimate response to the question. There were no data available from the current clinic as the two funding HAs had never requested this. The cardiologist suggested that the way forward would be for Poppleton HA to fund the service for 1 year to allow data to be collected, but in terms of the immediate modelling exercise, it appeared that little progress could be made on the issue.

Pain relief for intractable angina

I visited the tertiary cardiologist to discuss his pain-relief development for intractable angina. He told me that he was developing an experimental technique which involved injecting patients who were severely limited in their activities by angina, with some form of anaesthetic which successfully contained their symptoms for between 3 and 6 months. The cardiologist was amazed at the success of this process since the fact that the anaesthetic did not wear off after a matter of hours defied scientific logic. However, the technique had allowed patients requiring bed rest to go on holiday and had freed up beds in neighbouring trusts. The cost of the injection was £14 and the cardiologist performed this in-between angioplasties, which meant that workload was contained within existing capacity. The scheme, although interesting, was not modelled because the number of patients involved was small and there were no plans for changes to the service. The scheme was not a priority for the HA, which was unaware of its existence prior to the meeting and, surprisingly, was unconcerned by the development of this ad hoc experimental process conducted on their patients. The cardiologist was concerned mainly with bringing the scheme to the attention of others ('This is what's going to get me my Nobel Prize,' he told me!), rather than seeing it incorporated into the modelling process.

Rapid MI diagnosis in secondary care

This scheme was a regionally funded R and D initiative which was being evaluated on two sites within the region over a 2-year period. As this was the subject of an in-depth evaluation intended to follow up patients for a prolonged period, the MD agreed to exclude this option from the modelling process.

Cardiac nurses in primary care

The aim of this scheme was to review every patient with a diagnosis of CHD in primary care. Six nurses were recruited to work in each of the six localities in the HA, reviewing patients at baseline, then at 3 and 6 months after the initial review. The role of the nurse was to deliver six interventions, namely:

- advice on
  - (a) Smoking cessation
  - (b) Exercise
  - (c) Diet
- review of medication to promote GP prescribing and patient concordance in relation to
  - (d) Aspirin
  - (e) Beta blockers
  - (f) Lipid-lowering drugs (statins).

Data were provided by the HA, but they showed results at baseline for approaching 1700 patients and at 6 months for less than 500 patients. Statistically significant increases in aspirin and beta-blocker prescribing were observed (around 8 per cent and 6 per cent respectively), together with a significant drop in plasma cholesterol of around 0.5 mmol/l.

The first important thing to note is that, because the baseline and 6-month sample are not the same people (the smaller group are a sub-set of the initial cohort, and may not be representative of the cohort) no conclusions can be drawn from the data. Secondly, there was an increase in aspirin prescribing across the HA because of a local aspirin audit initiative. Similarly, in practices where the nurse had not yet visited, statins prescribing increased regardless, due to increased awareness of the drugs.

In other words, the data were useless in this format and I asked the MD for another data set which showed a comparison of like with like. The MD suggested that I use the existing data 'for now' and update the model when a matched pairs data set could be produced. The information department which was currently otherwise occupied would produce this in the near future.

Directed access echocardiography

This scheme was intended to provide a diagnostic facility to allow GPs to obtain a diagnosis for patients with suspected heart failure. The MD was of the firm opinion that heart failure should be excluded from the modelling exercise which should concentrate on angina and MI. This was the subject of an ongoing debate between the MD and myself and is discussed in more detail in Chapter 6.

Additional tertiary-centre activity

Relations between the tertiary centre and Poppleton HA were acrimonious. Although the HA had been unhappy at the failure to meet contracted activity on the part of the trust, the relations between the parties worsened following the intervention of the NHSE regional office. In early 1998, the MD was keen to recoup his investment in respect of the underperformance on contract, however, his bargaining position was weakened when the NHSE put pressure on him to ensure that no patients were waiting more than 12 months for their treatment. Coming up to the year-end the trust was under pressure from all purchasers to meet waiting list targets and was struggling to cope with patient volumes. The position had been exacerbated by a recent outbreak of the methicillin-resistant staphylococcus aureus infection, which had reduced the number of procedures performed. The agreement reached between the MD and the trust was that no money would be withdrawn if waiting list targets were met. The MD was unhappy at this position, expressing the view that the NHSE had forced his hand in the matter, stressing the need to meet targets at any price. From the MD's perspective, the trust, aware of the NHSE's involvement, had used the MD's weakened position to maximum effect, enabling them to underperform without being penalized for doing so.

The volume and case mix at the tertiary centre had been the matter of ongoing discussions since (and before) I started at Poppleton HA. The introduction of new technologies (in particular expensive coronary stents for use in angioplasty) had been causing concern amongst local purchasers who had expressed the view that stents should only be used when absolutely necessary. An Effective Health Care bulletin *The Management of Stable Angina*, published in October 1997, contained the statement 'Despite little evidence that coronary stents are more cost-effective than standard angioplasty they are increasingly being used. The adoption of this or other new technologies should be managed in line with the results of reliable trials.'

The trust agreed to a request from a united group of purchasers to conduct an audit of all patients undergoing angioplasty over a 3-month period with and without stents in order to provide local data on the effectiveness of this procedure. The purchasers were unhappy to pay for coronary stenting during the audit period, which was planned for completion in July, and the consensus view amongst them was that only emergency use of stenting should be paid for. The cardiologists were less than happy with this state of affairs as can be seen from their letter of 27 April 1998 which contains the sentence 'Medico-legally, we believe it to be indefensible not to stent a coronary artery after PTCA when a sub-optimal result is present or threatened closure is apparent since this is what our peer interventionists would do.' The authors also 'robustly reject' the Effective Health Care bulletin statement and suggest that:

Purchasing decisions based on this single flawed review will thus result in direct detriment to patients.

If despite our opinions, purchasers of coronary interventional procedures choose not to pay for this work, then the reasons why individual patients cannot have the treatment that we recommend or have to be placed on ever-increasing waiting lists must be made clear to them, their general practitioners and their referring consultants.

Although the letter mentions benefits to patients, much of the argument concerns 'medico-legal' issues or the centre's 'international reputation' and its role in establishing new technologies. It is doubtful that giving information to patients which suggests that they have received sub-optimal care will be in the patient's best interest, although it may protect the cardiologist in the event of litigation. These inflammatory remarks had little effect on purchasers, who awaited the outcome of the stent audit.

The HA CD was suspicious of stenting and the centre generally. Whilst the surgical capacity of the centre was limited, making increased numbers of CABGs impossible within current working hours, there was potential capacity for increased angioplasty. The CD viewed stents as yet another example of the cardiologists 'doing more of what they want to do' and she was much keener on getting the centre to deliver the planned activity figures on CABGs. The CD appeared to have little grasp of the clinicians' argument, which was that CABGs should be delayed as long as possible as the risks of the procedure were high and the opportunities for repeat CABG were much lower than for PTCA. She also viewed CABG and PTCA as interchangeable, when, as the Effective Health Care bulletin explains, CABG is 'more appropriate for patients with more severe or extensive disease'. As CABG is more efficient at relieving pain than PTCA and has a much lower repeat intervention rate, the CD viewed CABGs as better value, on the mistaken assumption that she was comparing like with like.

On 3 July 1998 the MD and I met with the centre's R and D and clinical audit manager. The results of the stent audit showed that repeat intervention was required in 13 per cent of PTCAs, compared with 8.5 per cent for PTCA plus stents, a statistically significant difference. We left the meeting to go straight to a meeting of contract directors from local HAs to discuss the allocation of a tranche of zonal 'whole systems' money which the government had allocated to allow HAs to tackle 'waiting-list pressures'. The MD presented the audit findings, reading out numbers from the sheets provided by the centre, without expressing a view one way or another. Generally, the reception was sceptical. My impression was that regardless of the findings the results would have been challenged, as the response was knee jerk. After making uncomplimentary remarks about the unit, one of the contract leads said exasperatedly 'All we want to know is how many CABGs and PTCAs to buy, but how can we tell?'

Various decisions were made at the meeting, rather hurriedly, about carving up the new monies, largely on the basis of who had already received money and often without any clear criteria. The timescale was short and the amount available was unclear, but the group assumed that it would get roughly one-third of the regional total based on population. There were conditions attached to the money, which meant that minimum volumes of activity had to be achieved ('We can't afford clinical sense . . . let's just go for volume').

Eventually, it was agreed that the tertiary centre should receive £100,000 for 'infrastructure' relating to new beds. (The centre's ability to respond to short-term waiting-list initiatives had always been constrained by the number of high-dependency beds to accommodate patients immediately after surgery or angioplasty.)

The MD suggested that 'It'll take the noise out of the system for a bit', which caused one of the other CDs to comment that 'Ian Greatorex had plenty of noise in the system and look where it got him'. This was a reference to the plight of the CE at Salford and Trafford HA. The HA had planned to close beds at the local hospital (which 50 years earlier had been the setting of a famous picture of Aneurin Bevan, with a child heralded as the first NHS patient), during the fiftieth anniversary year of the NHS. *The Independent* newspaper reported on 2 July:

> Plans to close a hospital children's unit were shelved just before Frank Dobson, Secretary of State for Health, was due to make an NHS 50th anniversary visit, it emerged yesterday . . . Yesterday Mr Dobson said he had told the NHS North West regional executive which, he said, was made up of Conservative appointees, to withdraw the plans [saying] there had been no proper consultation . . . A statement issued by North West NHS Executive yesterday said: 'Regional health managers have now required Salford and Trafford Health

Authority to withdraw proposals to change children's services at Trafford General Hospital. This will not affect the planned development of services at Salford Hope Hospital, which were approved following the earlier consultation in 1996.

The meeting concluded with agreement to give the Poppleton HA CE a copy of the suggested funding items, so that she could 'go to the region [NHSE] with a signed-up scam'. At this point, the MD reminded the group that I was writing this up for my research on decision-making and health economics. None of them raised any objection to my using the material. There was some laughter and comments relating to what on earth a reader would make of this process and one comment that health economics had nothing to do with the NHS, since it was all about 'politics'. The important thing for the purpose of the modelling exercise was that the 'evidence' from the audit had been largely ignored.

A week later, a meeting was held at the tertiary centre at which presentations were made by the cardiologists and the clinical audit manager emphasizing the benefits of stents, but no agreement could be reached on the subject between the trust and its purchasers.

The upshot of all this is that for the purposes of the modelling exercise, the CD advised me that I should leave the stents out, as the improved effectiveness was still subject to debate, and merely model the overall increase in activity requested by the centre. As the model included actual as opposed to planned activity and the trust had underperformed generally, the request that the HA fund planned activity plus the revised stent figures meant an increase requested of 49 CABGs, 109 cardiac catheters and 17 PTCAs.

Capacity and waiting-time issues across the system

Under this heading, various options were modelled addressing the following questions.

- What will happen if we reduce the waiting time for the first consultant cardiology appointment to 2 months?
- What will happen if we ensure that no patient waits longer than 12 months from GP referral to leaving the tertiary centre? (Because of the disagreement on where patients should wait, we assumed three equal waits of 4 months each, in other words primary to secondary care, secondary care to angiography and angiography to PTCA or CABG.)

Do nothing

Here we examined what would happen over the next 10 years if no changes were made, but building in the trend towards increasing numbers of elderly patients from the population estimates locally.

During the summer and into September 1998 the PCG developments ('Like the Northern Ireland peace process, but harder' was how the primary-care director had described getting agreement to PCG configuration) and Frank Dobson's pronouncements on Viagra were focusing minds in the Medical Directorate upon the seemingly impossible task of getting GPs to change their prescribing behaviour. ('I've got one GP who says it takes too long to write amoxicillin [a cheaper antibiotic], so he prescribes augmentin. How can you get through to people like that?' asked the most vocal of the PAs, two of whom after 6 months were looking for other jobs.)

The MD had been hoping that the GMS budget (which relates to the things 'closest to home' for the GPs, such as practice staff and premises costs) would be part of the overall cash limited budget. The implication would be that if GPs could not remain within budget on prescribing, then some downward adjustment would have to be made on their GMS budget. This would mean losing practice staff or topping up the deficit from their own pockets. As at a 'time out' to discuss prescribing in June, the team had all agreed that the only way to balance the prescribing budget was to 'appeal to their [GPs'] greed', a refusal to protect the GMS budget was more than an attractive policy – for the MD and his team it was the only hope!

At the end of June 1998, Alan Milburn, then a Minister at the Department of Health, wrote to the HA advising that the GMS budget would be protected. This was perfectly understandable given the Minister's attempts to corral reluctant GPs into PCGs. A refusal to ring fence the GMS budget would have antagonized the already unhappy GPs even further. However, the policy had pulled the rug from under the MD and his team, removing the only lever available to them and forcing them to rely on the appeal to the 'greater good' in their conversations with GPs.

The 'winter' pressures were still in evidence at the end of June when the team meeting learned that the local trust had 'no beds again today' and that they had to open up the day case wards for emergencies.

In August 1998 I attended the first meeting of the regional working group for the development of invasive and tertiary cardiac services chaired by a professor of cardiology from outside the region. The learned professor had been recommended by the BCS and the appointment of a cardiologist as chairman of the group signalled to myself and the MD at least, that the review was likely to be somewhat influenced by the interests of both parties which lay in increasing the number of tertiary procedures and cardiologists. The intention of bringing in an 'objective' outsider, rang a little hollow.

Step 5 – feedback of preliminary results

On 5 October 1998 the modelling group was reconvened at a local hotel. The exercise showed that there would be an increase in demand of approximately 12 per cent based on population projections. In other words, even in the steady state scenario, things would become a little 'unsteady' if no action were taken.

The additional activity requested by the tertiary centre could not physically be accommodated within the model. Of the 49 CABGs, 109 catheters and 17 PTCAs extra requested, the centre would 'run out' of patients by the time it had performed 40 more CABGs and 40 extra catheters. (PTCAs were not a problem.) This was because without any action in secondary or primary care to fill the extra slots, the waiting times would be reduced to 0 months before the tertiary centre reached its requested additional workload.

Reducing the outpatient wait for cardiology in secondary care to 2 months would require an increase in capacity of 13 per cent (in consultant cardiologist time), and would leave all other waiting times largely unchanged. If an extra cardiologist was taken on in secondary care to reduce waiting times, the 'blockage' in secondary care would now be moved through the system, with patients waiting 4 months less between secondary and primary care, but 4.5 months longer between secondary and tertiary care.

Imposing a waiting time of 12 months from GP referral right through to completion of tertiary-care procedure would reduce CABG waits, but increase PTCA and catheter waits. This would require increased investment in secondary and tertiary care. None of these options would make a significant impact on emergency attendances or mortality. This is partly due to the fact that they largely transfer waiting periods between sectors or between groups of patients (for example CABG to PTCA). In addition, because for many patients tertiary procedures are life enhancing rather than immediately 'life saving', the mortality benefits from the additional procedures are assumed to be small in the context of the Poppleton

HA CHD mortality as a whole. For the individuals receiving CABG or PTCA, benefits may be substantial. As only a small percentage of all CHD patients receive tertiary procedures in any 1 year, however, the impact of these interventions on the whole Poppleton HA CHD 'problem' is limited.

The cardiac nurses in primary care showed by far the greatest benefits to patients in terms of fewer emergency admissions, reduced waiting times across the board and reduced mortality. The assumption made in the modelling exercise was that beta-blocker and aspirin prescribing had increased, which the flawed data provided had suggested. Additionally, the nurse intervention was modelled *as if* all patients were covered by the nurse intervention. The reasoning behind this was that as there were six nurses, in a steady state situation all newly diagnosed CHD patients would receive the nurse intervention. One of the problems with this approach is that it did not reflect the drop-out rate from the intervention. The MD suggested that we assume no drop out initially and revise this on receipt of the second data set, as the PM had asked the nurses to record this prospectively following the initial modelling meeting.

Apart from the suggestion by the tertiary-centre FD that the unit would be able to meet all of the extra workload, the discussion was one of clarification and elaboration rather than a rejection of the findings. I explained to the FD that the problem was not with his unit, but elsewhere in the system. Buying additional activity without generating more referrals would, once the waiting lists had been cleared, eventually result in no more patients flowing to the tertiary centre.

I explained that the nurse data were flawed and that the conclusions were extremely tenuous. However, the audience did not appear to be particularly concerned by this. The intention at this meeting was to give people something to pull apart and get them to provide better data or scenarios for the next round of modelling. The MD agreed to provide a matched pairs data set and the secondary-care cardiologist, who now wanted a more explicit modelling of one extra cardiologist, offered to submit data to enable me to incorporate this scenario into the next round of modelling. The meeting concluded with general agreement that the results were interesting and with clinicians offering to give them some thought and contact me with either data or requests for modelling scenarios.

Later that week, I received a letter from the secondary-care cardiologist with assumptions stated and data provided (the waiting time was now 8 months and not 6 as had been the case earlier in the year). The letter asked for the system-wide implications of recruiting an extra consultant cardiologist to be considered.

RUNNING OUT OF STEAM

As will be recalled, the next phase of the process was a revised modelling, based on amendments suggested by the group. As the only substantive amendments were the revised cardiac nurse data and the cardiology post, I planned to input the two at the same time, together with any other suggestions I received in the interim. However, in practice, no data were received and the process ground to a halt.

The modelling had lost momentum in a similar way to Colin Green's PBMA work at Rotherham HA (see Chapter 2). In the Rotherham case, working papers were produced for the HA, suggesting how things might proceed in the future, as a means of completing the project. In my case, I raised the nurse data periodically at meetings with the MD. His responses were to evade the question, to suggest that data would be more useful when several thousand patients had been reviewed or to promise the data at some time in the future when the information department had the time to attend to this. He blamed his inability to produce the data on the fact that the information staff were not under his control and had other priorities. In May 1999, when these members of staff were under his direct control and there was a large volume of data collected, he gave me vague reassurances, but nothing materialized. Eventually, I stopped asking.

6

CASE STUDY III: STATINS, HEART FAILURE AND CHEST PAIN IN BAXBY

BAXBY – THE RESEARCH SETTING

Baxby PCG, the smallest of Poppleton's PCGs, secured PCG status despite its size, because the HA recognized the distinct identity of the locality and the track record of independent working within the area. Additionally, the main provider of secondary care for the area is a trust outside the HA boundary ('Ashurst NHS Trust') which handles only 20 per cent of secondary-care activity for Poppleton HA, almost all of which is for Baxby residents.

Baxby's locality manager, who subsequently became Baxby PCG's CE, was well regarded by the HA and local GPs. In May 1996, the PA from the HA had moved to Baxby to become the full-time PA for the locality, making Baxby the only locality within Poppleton HA to have its own full-time PA. The Baxby PA had gained experience which he was able to build on within the locality, working with local GPs and developing relationships whilst based at the HA.

Baxby's organization and infrastructure, coupled with its relationships with Ashurst NHS Trust and its strong sense of local identity made it different from other localities. Initially when I expressed an interest in working with a locality the HA Director of Primary Care suggested that it should not be Baxby on the grounds that 'Baxby gets everything'. For example, Baxby was one of the first two localities to take on one of the MD's cardiac nurses. When the HA funded a pilot project to examine innovative ways of using additional GP time in primary care, the practice chosen was one from Baxby.

The Baxby PA and the locality manager, had worked hard at bringing GPs together to share data and change practice since the arrival of the PA. Both worked at maintaining good links with the HA, recognizing the importance of these links in securing the maximum resources available for Baxby.

The locality manager lived near to the MD and they would meet outside work over a drink occasionally. Although these were social occasions, the MD and the locality manager would sometimes discuss work-related issues. This and the latter's attitude of positive working with the HA meant that he was 'closer' to the HA in terms of communication and constructive relationships than any of the other locality leads.

In October 1997, the PA convened the 'Baxby Cardiac Focus Group' which later became the Baxby PCG cardiac sub-group. The letter of invitation to join the group outlined that this was intended to be 'a dynamic multidisciplinary group, with expertise from both secondary and primary care' to 'meet on a regular basis' with the aim of considering 'making recommendations for the care and management of patients with cardiovascular disease in Baxby'. The first meeting on 15 October 1997 was attended by five GPs, the consultant cardiologist from the trust, the Baxby PA, the HA PA, a health visitor, the locality cardiac nurse, a business manager from the trust and myself. The Baxby PA had invited interested parties to attend the meeting in an effort to attract local GP input, and membership of the group changed little over the next 18 months, with most of those present at the first meeting continuing their involvement.

DEVELOPING A STATINS GUIDELINE

The Baxby PA chaired the meetings and organized the note-taking and other administrative tasks. Having spent his time in Baxby building links with local clinicians, he was aware of the need to involve local stakeholders in the process. He welcomed open discussion and was not inclined to offer his own opinion. His style contrasted markedly with that of the MD.

The first issue for consideration by the group was the management of hyperlipidaemia (excess of fat in the blood) in Baxby and the thorny issue of statins prescribing. The Baxby PA opened the meeting, explaining the need to 'agree a consistent and integrated care approach to the management of hyperlipidaemia' in Baxby.

He identified what he saw as the issues for consideration by the group:

- whether they were meeting the needs of their patients;
- what the gaps were;
- who the target groups should be;
- the issues for GPs: age and which statin; and
- SMAC guidelines

The Baxby PA suggested that, as time was limited, the group should start to work through this list and continue at the next meeting. He then asked for comments on the subject of patient needs and target groups.

The cardiologist expressed the view that guidelines were needed and raised the issue of the SMAC guidelines, suggesting that these might provide a basis for discussion. The mention of the SMAC guidelines provoked energetic responses from the GPs present. One GP suggested that we needed help in interpreting the guidelines and another said that an understanding of the evidence would be helpful. There was general agreement on these issues and conversations around the table on the difficulties of making informed choices on the issue, particularly when faced with conflicting 'evidence' from pharmaceutical company representatives. The cardiologist spoke eloquently on the evidence base for statins, outlining the various RCT findings. He also urged the meeting to ensure that statins were available for these 'high-risk' patients as the health gain was so large and the evidence base so robust. He drew attention to the fact that Riverview and Shoreville HAs had produced statins guidelines, which were implemented by secondary-care cardiologists at the trust and argued that, in the interests of equality, these drugs should be available to all patients who needed them. On a practical basis, he suggested, it would 'make sense' to have a common approach to enable trust clinicians to follow one common guideline, rather than different protocols for different HAs. The GPs listened carefully to the cardiologist.

There was some discussion on the Sheffield risk tables which were appended to the SMAC guidelines which the GPs found confusing. 'I mean this doesn't even have family history as a risk factor,' said one GP, which prompted a discussion of what constituted 'family history' of CHD, with GPs offering vignettes from their practice population (for example 'I've got one patient in his forties and his brother and his father are already dead . . . surely he needs to be on a statin?').

The HA PA, keen to limit the use of statins, pointed out that the Sheffield tables were for patients without CHD. He suggested that it might be better to concentrate on patients with CHD first ('the high-risk group') and then go on, at some point in the future, to consider primary prevention. This suggestion prompted discussion on what constituted 'high risk', with GPs offering yet more examples of 'high-risk' patients with no CHD but other risk factors. (For example 'I had a patient in the other day who smokes, he's very overweight and his cholesterol was 9 . . . if he's not a candidate for a statin, I don't know who is.') The meeting started to break up into discussions of 'risk' and which patients to treat, so at this point the Baxby PA called the meeting back to order and made some attempt at moving forward. 'So what are we saying on this? What do you think?' he asked the cardiologist.

The latter accepted the PA's suggestion that a target group be identified, but he added that guidelines were only intended to give 'guidance', that 'there will always be patients who fall outside of the guidelines' who will need statins and that GPs should exercise judgement in interpreting the guidelines.

There was general agreement with this suggestion. The HA PA suggested that alongside any guidelines there would need to be an implementation strategy which would address issues such as what to do with patients who do not 'fit the guidelines'. The cardiologist spoke of his own involvement in the construction of the Riverview guidelines (see Chapter 4) which targeted patients with CHD. These guidelines were clear in their message (secondary prevention only) and simple to understand and implement, he felt. However, this provoked further discussion about the need to treat patients without CHD but who were perceived by the GPs to be 'high risk'. The discussions of risk perception revealed that each GP had their own ideas about what constituted risk. In addition, the mention of risk factors prompted a discussion on smoking and lifestyle which divided the GPs. Although one of the GPs felt that patients who were unwilling to stop smoking should not be eligible for statins, another GP disagreed and the cardiologist drew attention to the high-risk nature of such patients. The discussion of risk once more led GPs to the conclusion that any guideline should address the issue of high-risk patients with no known CHD. For this reason, four of the GPs were unhappy to adopt the Riverview guidelines whose focus on secondary prevention was seen as too narrow. The minutes of the meeting record agreement that 'health professionals in Baxby and Ashurst should be adhering to one set of guidelines', but that compared to the Riverview guideline 'the group would probably wish to give more information and advice about primary prevention'.

The Baxby PA then asked for views on an age cut-off for statins. The HA PA suggested that as they could not afford to 'give them to everyone', younger patients should be targeted. This provoked responses from the cardiologist and one of the GPs. The former pointed out that older patients were at greatest risk and expressed the view that it was not sensible to invoke a blanket age cut-off. The latter spoke of an elderly patient ('in his eighties') who, the meeting was told, was fit and active and cared for his infirm wife. For this GP, treating such patients was good medicine and potentially saved resources because if 'anything happens to this patient' his wife would require costly care. The discussion on age continued, with the clinicians attempting to resist an age cut-off and the PA pressing for some reference to age in the guidelines.

The cardiologist pointed out that in the Cholesterol and Recurrent Events (CARE) trial, older patients had benefited from statins. The CARE trial included 4159 patients aged 21 to 75 years, the majority of whom were under 69 years of age (mean age, SD 59 ± 9) and the follow up was for 5 years. The investigators found that the effect of pravastatin on the rate of major coronary events was not substantially altered by the patients' age at baseline (Sacks *et al.* 1996). After a discussion in which another GP presented a thumbnail sketch of a patient in his eighties with a high quality of life and much nodding in agreement from the GPs and cardiologist present, it was agreed that there should be no age limit.

One of the GPs expressed ignorance in relation to the choice of statin, the evidence base for statins and the choice of cholesterol measurement (total cholesterol, full lipid profile with low-density lipoprotein ratio, triglycerides). Other GPs echoed these sentiments, directing questions on the subject to the cardiologist (for example 'Does it have to be fasting lipids?' 'Should we use all this other information or just total cholesterol level?'). The Baxby PA suggested that this be covered in discussion of patient management.

The HA PA was unwilling to recommend one particular statin, but suggested that the evidence-based approach was to use simvastatin or pravastatin, as only these two statins were backed by evidence from large multicentre randomized controlled trials. However, for patients with raised cholesterol requiring a reduction of over 40 per cent only atorvastatin would produce the desired effect. The PA was suggesting an evidence-based approach, then ignoring the issue of evidence for patients with very high cholesterol levels, but nobody commented on the inconsistency of the approach.

This inconsistency is understandable when one considers the difficulty of adopting 'hard and fast' criteria in relation to what is to constitute 'acceptable evidence'. Is the 'rational' approach to pursue systematic and clear criteria on evidence (that is large RCTs only) and deny patients access to atorvastatin, the only drug shown to reduce cholesterol to target levels for some patients? GPs can prescribe atorvastatin and observe at first hand from their own patients the extent to which the drug is effective in reducing cholesterol. However, this assumes that it is the reduction in cholesterol which is directly responsible for a reduction in coronary events. If the relationship between cholesterol and coronary events is more complex (in other words it turns out not to be a 'class effect') then prescribing atorvastatin may not be justified. If local experience suggests that atorvastatin can achieve a 40 per cent reduction in cholesterol levels, should this be ignored because the results do not come from a large multicentre RCT?

The Baxby PA then asked the meeting to consider the subject of target groups. The SMAC guidelines (see Chapter 4) had set a clear priority ordering, with post-MI patients receiving higher priority than angina patients. The cardiologist suggested that both groups were at high risk and it made little sense to deny statins to angina patients and make them wait until they had an MI. The HA PA, agreeing with these views, went on to state that the first priority should be to treat patients with CHD regardless of whether or not they had previously had an MI. By ostensibly supporting a broad approach to statins prescribing he had succeeded in obtaining agreement to a strategy of secondary prevention, thus narrowing down the potential patient population. Earlier, on the subject of local guidelines, the minutes report that 'The Riverview guidelines ... did not fully address primary prevention issues. The Group would probably wish to give more information and advice about primary prevention.' Later, on the subject of target groups, the minutes record that 'It was agreed that the Group's advice and recommendations should concentrate on the group of individuals who have clear evidence of [CHD].'

Up to this point I had said nothing, but I was struck by how the discussion had proceeded thus far with little mention of affordability. This does not mean that the clinicians present were unconcerned by the cost of statins. Indeed, their concerns to understand the evidence and participate in guideline development were fuelled by an awareness of the potential consequences of this new drug within the context of limited resources. Prior to the start of the meeting, whilst chatting over sandwiches and coffee, the GPs had spoken of the need for a guideline because of fears around the financial consequences of statins.

When I raised the issue of affordability, the HA PA pointed out that statins costs would be much higher if the guideline encompassed patients over 65 years of age. 'What can we afford?' asked one GP, to which the HA PA replied, 'Well, there's no new money.' The cardiologist optimistically pointed to the potential for cost savings 'in the future' in the health sector and the wider society. I reminded him of the need to balance the annual budget and explained that although costs and benefits for the health-care sector could be modelled, estimating wider impacts would be a more complicated process.

As an economist based in Poppleton HA, I was always conscious of 'real world' constraints such as the need to balance annual budgets and the difficulty of freeing up resources from hospital services characterized by high levels of fixed costs. My background as an accountant and my awareness of the HA environment no doubt influenced my approach to these discussions. I wondered how I would have behaved if I had been an academic health economist based at the university. Would a HA health economist in those circumstances take the long view and see all costs as variable in the long term? Should I take a wider societal perspective and consider costs and benefits outside of the HA, in more detail?

I wondered how other health economists based in HAs dealt with such dilemmas and couldn't help thinking that life would be easier if I adopted a purist approach. Taking a societal perspective has a much more humanitarian and holistic 'ring' to it. Not having to worry about 'details', for example the HA financial framework, would allow me to argue unreservedly for the proactive dissemination of cost-effective interventions such as statins. Any criticism from HA managers about my failure to acknowledge constraints could be answered with the suggestion that a programme budgeting exercise to include all CHD services and stakeholders be undertaken in order to identify areas for disinvestment. As the system-wide modelling exercise in Chapter 5 illustrated, however, in the real world life is much more complicated.

The discussion of patient management revealed a lack of knowledge on the part of the GPs present and a heavy reliance on the advice of the cardiologist. His advice in relation to cholesterol measurement was to request a full lipid profile on the grounds that this would give the maximum information on which to base a decision. However, given the statements made by the GPs earlier with regard to the confusion created by receiving several different measurements (total cholesterol, low-density lipoprotein ratio, triglycerides), it was by no means clear that additional information would improve clinical decision-making in primary care.

The GPs asked the cardiologist the following questions on patient management. 'Should I wait until the patient has had a diagnosis confirmed before starting him on a statin?' 'What if the total cholesterol is low, but triglycerides are high?' 'Does it have to be a fasting cholesterol?' 'What if it's just over the 5.0 mark?' 'Should I start the patient on a low dose first?'

Keen to move the discussion forward, the Baxby PA asked the cardiologist for his views on the plasma cholesterol level at which statin prescribing should be initiated. The SMAC levels were seen as impractical and confusing because the suggestion was to prescribe statins to post-MI patients with a cholesterol level greater than or equal to 4.8 mmol/L but use 5.5 mmol/L for angina patients. These levels were based on those used in clinical trials and were a fairly arbitrary measurement rather than representing an absolute point at which it would be correct to intervene in each of these two groups of patients. There was general agreement that one cholesterol level should be used. The cardiologist suggested that the aim should be to reduce cholesterol to below 5.0 mmol/L, which would be consistent with providing one clear measure and with the Riverview guidelines. However, he went on to suggest maximum acceptable levels for low-density lipoprotein and triglycerides. We deferred to his clinical expertise.

After some discussion on the merits of dietary intervention, the meeting closed with the Baxby PA agreeing to draw up a draft cholesterol management algorithm for the next meeting. A summary of the meetings process which culminated in the launch of statins guidelines in April 1998 is presented below.

15 October 1997: agreement of the need for a guideline;

4 November 1997: draft guideline produced suggesting prioritization of patients with CHD; draft states that it is 'not usually appropriate to lower cholesterol in patients 75 years and over. In patients 70 to 74 years decisions to initiate cholesterol-lowering drug therapy should be made by doctors on an individual patient basis, taking into account health gain and social care implications';

19 November 1997: draft guideline produced, suggesting particular consideration should be given to patients under 60 years of age;

10 December 1997: the HA PA had left the group, the wording suggesting an age cut-off was removed; primary prevention management plan to be produced;

21 January 1998: group agrees to defer primary prevention management plan;

11 March 1998: final guideline agreed stating that in 'older patients' decisions 'should be made on an individual patient basis . . . It may not always be appropriate to lower cholesterol in patients over 75 years of age'

22 April 1998: PCG-wide guideline launched, with the HA MD providing support for the guideline.

The final guideline resembled closely the Riverview guideline, suggesting intervention for patients with CHD at cholesterol levels of 5.0 mmol/l. No age cut-off was included and primary prevention was to be deferred to some unstated time in the future. On the issue of primary prevention, the cardiologist had spoken eloquently of the need to target patients with CHD first. His intervention on the subject had been sufficient to persuade the GPs on the matter. Indeed, the GPs listened carefully to his advice at each meeting and were willing to be guided by it. At no time did any of the GPs present seek to challenge what he said and, for the most part, GP contributions were questions directed to the cardiologist, or anecdotes to reinforce what the cardiologist was saying. Although the whole guidelines process was prompted by the financial implications of statins, very little consideration was given to the issue of affordability.

The health economics input to the process was minimal, consisting of costing the secondary-prevention guideline and estimating the likely costs of expanding the guideline to those at high risk of developing CHD at the request of the Baxby PA. The costings were tentative, as the likely extent of guideline implementation was uncertain.

Following the first meeting, the group members began to feel more comfortable with each other as we settled down to meeting and working on the statins issue with some unity of purpose. The purpose was the production of a statins guideline, which was itself only a means to some unspecified end. For the cardiologist, the guideline would serve to simplify matters at the trust as well as targeting statins to high-risk patients. GPs welcomed advice which would enable them to overcome their lack of expertise in this area. There was also agreement that a guideline would provide reassurance for GPs who wished to deny patients statin treatment. From my perspective, the guideline would, if implemented, provide some means of reducing wasteful prescribing of statins to low-risk patients.

Observing the GPs at the group, at the evening HA wide statins meeting and at the launch of the Riverview guidelines, it had become clear to me that many GPs knew little about the evidence base for statins and even less about calculating 'risk' in patients presenting. At the December meeting of the group, one GP had justified treating patients at low risk of developing CHD on the grounds that the practice nurse referred patients with raised cholesterol, but no other risk factors to him. 'Once they have their [cholesterol] result they come to me . . . and I have to do something about it,' he complained. When I asked why the practice nurse was measuring cholesterol in healthy patients, he further complained that the practice nurse training encouraged nurses to measure cholesterol. The other GPs present agreed that this was also a problem for their practices, and although they expressed disagreement with this approach, none was keen to tackle the issue.

I had raised the subject of affordability at the first and second meetings of the group, but this had not been addressed in constructing the guidelines other than indirectly in the discussions on deferral of primary prevention. At the March meeting, at which the launch of the guideline was discussed, I again raised the issue of affordability, pointing out that at the launch of the Riverview guideline much of the discussion from the floor centred on this question. It would be reasonable to assume, therefore, that GPs locally might want to know whether there was support for overspending on their drugs budget if the cause of this was increased statins prescribing.

The cardiologist's view was that statins were a priority and that rather than denying these 'cost-effective' drugs to high-risk patients, it would be preferable to cut back on other areas. He was not willing or able, however, nor did he see it as his role to suggest what these 'other areas' might be. He pointed to the slow uptake of guidelines in primary care, suggesting that even with the guideline poor or delayed implementation would mean that expenditure would rise only gradually as a result. He even suggested that the financial impact would be limited as 'It's just formalizing what's already happening in practice anyway'; although one could be forgiven for asking why the group has spent months on this issue if this was the case.

The Baxby PA agreed that affordability was an important issue, but that without the guideline the statins expenditure may be higher and the health gain lower due to inappropriate prescribing. The minutes record that:

> there was a brief discussion about priority-setting and impact on prescribing expenditure. It was felt that sound clinical practice would still need to be balanced with what was affordable. It was felt that it may take some years before the maximum impact on expenditure was realized.

The guidelines were launched at an evening meeting in April 1998, which was attended by the MD who gave his full support to initiative.

HEART FAILURE MANAGEMENT PLAN FOR BAXBY

At the March meeting of the group, consideration was given to the production of heart failure guidelines.

Heart failure is a life-threatening disorder which may occur following an MI. Indeed, an estimated 50 per cent of MI patients will go on to develop heart failure as a result of their MI. Mortality (50 per cent within 5 years of diagnosis) is high, as is morbidity (locally, mean length of stay was 12 days, with readmissions within 6 months at 17 per cent). Annual admissions of Baxby patients to the trust for heart failure were similar to those for MI (85 per annum), but in-hospital mortality was greater for heart failure patients (21 per cent versus 17 per cent). (All figures are based on 1996–7 activity.)

Angiotensin-converting enzyme (ACE) inhibitors are drugs which have been shown to reduce mortality and morbidity in heart failure (SOLVD Investigators 1991, 1992). However, several studies have shown that many heart failure patients are not being prescribed these drugs, whilst others have highlighted the difficulty of correctly diagnosing heart failure in primary care based on presenting symptoms alone. The result of this is that a false positive diagnosis may be made in as many as three-quarters of patients (Wheeldon *et al.* 1993). The use of echocardiography greatly increases the accuracy of diagnosis in relation to heart failure (Dargie and McMurray 1994).

Both Shoreville and Riverview HAs had produced heart failure guidelines which involved the provision of open-access echocardiography services to promote accurate diagnosis and increase ACE inhibitor prescribing for heart-failure patients. The Baxby PA introduced the subject by explaining that there was a strong body of evidence to support the use of ace inhibitors and that the group might like to consider developing a heart-failure guideline.

The PM explained that 'as far as the HA is concerned, there is a big issue to tackle with CHD patients . . . [the MD] suggests that before we start with heart failure we should finish the CHD patients'. To which the cardiologist replied:

> It's all very well to say we'll plan for the nuclear holocaust next year, but the nuclear holocaust is here now! . . . Heart failure is fundamentally different to statins because it's much more complex and involved . . . we need to put what's being done in the practices on an evidence base.

He went on to explain that as Shoreville and Riverview had already constructed guidelines, the task would be easier for Baxby as we would not have 'to reinvent the wheel'.

During the previous group meetings, I had developed an impression of the cardiologist as a knowledgeable clinician who would use every opportunity open to him to promote service developments within cardiology. Although he acknowledged the need to prioritize, he was unwilling to offer up service reductions to pay for expansion in other areas of cardiology. Over time, the opinions and contributions of group members could be predicted with some accuracy. For example, the health visitor in the group wasted no time in highlighting the benefits of lifestyle advice for CHD patients and the potential role of health visitors in delivering this. The Baxby PA's role was to umpire the proceedings and move the meeting on whilst being as inclusive as possible and all without ever offering an opinion of his own. The PM's contributions were as an enthusiastic advocate of the HA strategy and as a conduit for the MD's message that heart failure should not be tackled yet. The GPs could be relied upon to welcome enthusiastically the cardiologist's suggestions for service expansion and reject as meaningless any proposed measures of performance in primary care. For my part, I always found myself asking where the additional resources would be taken from to fund new services. This was a role with which I was all too familiar and reminded me of my previous existence as an NHS accountant. The difference was that now I was also keen to question the evidence base for service developments and able to research this for myself without having to rely entirely on clinicians.

An awareness of the effect of the cardiologist's persuasive rhetoric on the GPs led me to raise my guard and question the validity of any suggestions he made. He in turn treated me as a representative of the HA, intent on pouring cold water on whatever scheme he suggested in the interest of cost-cutting. This relationship of mutual suspicion and caution was to be temporarily replaced by a more collaborative and supportive approach as the heart-failure issue developed.

The cardiologist explained that Riverview HA had invested additional resources in open-access echocardiography at three sites, and that this had resulted in a two-tier service as Baxby patients were being denied access. However, as I knew something of the background to events at Riverview, I pointed out that the £100,000 required to fund the echo service had been removed from tertiary cardiology services such as CABG and PTCA. These services were regarded as a high priority within our group. I suggested that before rushing headlong into adopting Riverview's guidelines, the costs and benefits of such a strategy should be assessed as we did not have £100,000 to invest. I offered to investigate the matter further and to estimate local echo requirements using the literature and any information I could glean from Riverview HA.

Heart failure in Baxby: conflicting views

On 16 June 1998 I met with the cardiologist to discuss his ideas for a chest pain clinic as part of the system-wide modelling process (see Chapter 5). In addition, I discussed the potential expansion of echo services at the trust which the cardiologist had suggested could be obtained at a modest cost. He explained that the high level of investment required by Riverview HA was necessary due to high-capital equipment costs at one site. The cardiologist had purchased equipment from charitable funds for his service and only the marginal cost would be payable as there was capacity available to deal with Baxby patients.

He expressed concern that the HA was funding nurses to call in patients who had previously had an MI and dealing with only part of the disease. The MD's policy of only treating part of the problem, of 'this bit of the heart will have to wait until we get round to that priority' was, he felt, ludicrous.

I met with a representative of Riverview HA, who explained the approach taken there and confirmed what the cardiologist had told me. The literature on the diagnosis and management of heart failure made a strong case for ACE inhibitors in heart failure on the grounds of effectiveness and cost-effectiveness (Hart *et al.* 1993, Van Hout *et al.* 1993). I used some prevalence and incidence data collected by an ex-colleague of mine from a local HA to estimate likely incidence and prevalence, by 10-year age bands, for males and females in the Baxby population. This produced estimates of around 45 to 50 new cases each year, which would suggest that in the worst-case scenario of a 75 per cent false positive rate, the maximum number of echoes required to diagnose all new cases would be 200 per annum. In reality, the figure would be unlikely to reach this level due to poor implementation. I also contacted a local GP and academic who confirmed what the cardiologist had told me and that my understanding of the literature was correct.

I then spoke to the MD to ask why he was so resistant to tackling heart failure. I had asked him this question previously as the issue of what was to constitute CHD for the purposes of the modelling exercise in relation to statins and the system-wide model had raised differences of opinion amongst the participants. Local cardiologists had been keen to include heart failure, whereas the MD had resisted its inclusion. The reasons given for this varied.

First, there was the issue of implementation. The MD feared that by changing the focus of the strategy to include heart failure, the impact of the cardiac-nurse intervention would be reduced. When I discussed this with him in July, he explained that we would tackle heart failure when CHD had been 'finished'. My own feelings were that since tackling CHD was like painting the Forth Bridge, we would never get around to heart failure. The MD replied that my approach would be like starting to paint the bridge, painting the first pillar blue and then stopping to argue about the colour scheme when we got to the next bit.

In addition, the MD was keen to prioritize 'younger' patients and saw heart disease as primarily a disease of old age. (In Riverview the estimated prevalence for age bands 55 to 64, 65 to 74 and 75 plus years was 10.1, 25.3 and 60.8 per thousand respectively.) For this reason, heart failure was low on his list of priorities.

Another factor was the MD's aversion to the prescribing of ACE inhibitors which stemmed from an incident involving a local GP some years previously. The GP had been prescribing expensive ACE inhibitors as first line treatment for uncomplicated hypertension, when cheaper equally effective alternatives were available. This had resulted in Poppleton HA having a very high rate of expenditure on these drugs. Since then, however, some brands of ACE inhibitors had become available in cheaper generic forms. Yet having made up his mind on the subject, the MD was reluctant to change it despite the changed circumstances.

Finally, the MD was not acquainted with the evidence on ACE inhibitors in heart failure and was unaware of the extent of benefits in terms of reduced mortality and morbidity. Despite this, the MD was the only source of medical advice to the HA on the issue.

The July group meeting

At the July meeting of the group, I relayed the results of my literature search on evidence, cost-effectiveness and estimated prevalence before giving my support to the need to tackle heart failure. I pointed out that any guideline would need to be adequately resourced and additional funds would not be available from the HA given the MD's resistance. I also informed the group of work undertaken by a PA in Derbyshire which cautioned against encouraging increased prescribing of ACE inhibitors in the absence of an echo service. Given the extent of false positive diagnosis, such a strategy could be more expensive and less effective than an echo-based approach. I suggested that as awareness of ACE inhibitor treatment increased, expenditure on the drugs would rise regardless of whether or not echo was provided.

There are parallels with the statins guidelines here, as there was no new money for increased prescribing of cost-effective drugs. However, expenditure on these drugs would be likely to increase in the absence of a guideline as GP awareness increases.

The answer to the question 'How much can we afford to spend on increased ACE inhibitor prescribing?' is 'Nothing at all', in the absence of additional resources. However, by providing no guidance the overall increase in expenditure could be greater still. This raises the question of whether it is 'rational' to promote a strategy for which no resource exists. Or is a better alternative to pursue a line of action which says that, in the absence of additional funds, guidelines should not be issued, even if the health gains are lower and the costs higher under this scenario?

The GPs were easily persuaded to support a policy of open-access echocardiography. They listened with interest when I explained that not prescribing ACE inhibitors to the three in four patients who would otherwise be incorrectly diagnosed as having heart failure would save enough money to pay for the cost of the additional echoes. The damage done to patients in terms of labelling and inappropriate medication would be reduced and benefits to patients with heart failure but not yet receiving ACE inhibitors would be increased from a more systematic approach underpinned by echo facilities.

The minutes record with reference to heart-failure management that 'it was recognized that investment in diagnosis and treatment now was important' and it could be claimed that this crude health economics was the reason for the group's support for developing a heart-failure guideline. However, looked at from the perspective of the GPs, the echo strategy offered an additional service development which removed from them some of the pressures of diagnosis and treatment. The guideline would be evidence based and the health economic analyses indicated that this was a cost-effective use of resources. However, it is not clear that if an alternative analysis supported additional workload for GPs and reduced access to secondary care on the grounds of health gain and cost effectiveness, that this would receive the same level of support from the GPs present.

In other words, over the life of the group, the GPs had shown their enthusiasm for service expansions, regardless of whether or not evidence of effectiveness or cost-effectiveness existed. Additionally, support for initiatives which supplied GPs with more information was usually forthcoming, even if this information would not change patient management. For example, shortly after my arrival at Poppleton HA, I became involved in a project centred on emergency cardiac and respiratory admissions for patients from one practice in Baxby. The project focused on the reasons for frequent readmissions and the interface between primary and secondary care.

The two GPs from this practice who were actively involved in the project were also members of the cardiac group. Initially, data were collected on the number and characteristics of patients. The GPs welcomed the information. When one of the GPs praised the initiative on the grounds that the information was 'useful', I asked how he would use it. His reply was that it 'tells us a lot'. The GPs complained that because of poor communication procedures on the part of the trust (specifically, failure to issue timely and relevant discharge letters), they were often unaware of a patient's admission and subsequent discharge. A great deal of effort was spent on improving discharge communications and this improvement was verified by an audit of the process. At a subsequent project meeting, the trust business manager and a nurse manager grinned as praise was heaped on them in recognition of the success achieved around the letters.

'So what happens now when the letters arrive?' I asked. The GP explained that the faxed discharge letters were now filed by the practice clerical staff with the relevant patient record on receipt. 'So what do you use this information for?' I asked. The GP explained patiently to the new and obviously clueless health economist that many of these patients never visited the surgery. The practice could not follow up these letters and, if it tried to, by the time the letters were read there was a good chance that the patient would be back in hospital again.

So, I asked, why is it important to have the letters in the first place? The GP explained patiently that if the patient did attend the surgery (and the audit data showed that for these patients they rarely, if ever, visited the GP, choosing to self-refer instead to A and E at the onset of symptom exacerbation), then it was 'useful' to have the background information. 'Useful or interesting?', I asked, fearful of pushing my luck with my questions. To which he replied that it was certainly very interesting to have all of this information together when the patient attended. Resisting the urge to say 'You mean all this effort's gone into the discharge letters so that you can file them? Don't you think that there might be some connection between the fact that the primary-care team has no contact with these patients and their frequent reattendance at A and E?', I thanked the GP for his patience.

The episode was revealing because it highlighted the way in which these GPs valued information for its own sake, just as Detsky's clinicians valued 'pure information' which did not change the management of the patient (see Chapter 2). In the context of subsequent comments made by GPs in the cardiac group about the difficulty of measuring performance and their powerlessness to make an impact on the burden of disease locally, the GP's attitude made some sense. If the GPs see no connection between what happens in primary care and the impact in other areas, there is no reason to 'interfere' with the revolving-door patients. The value placed on 'pure information' is discussed further in the context of the proposed chest pain clinic below.

a research collaboration between the Prescribing Research Group (my academic 'home') and a third party. I had volunteered to search the literature to derive model parameters (such as prevalence, false positive diagnosis and percentage of patients on ACE inhibitors having had an echo) as this would allow me access to the model to adapt to the Baxby setting. As my original calculations based on up to a 75 per cent false positive rate had been rather 'back-of-the-envelope', I suggested that this more sophisticated approach might provide more meaningful results. Keen to reflect the fact that life in Baxby would be different from the rarefied clinical trial environment, I suggested that local GPs might want to substitute their own values where appropriate.

The model also contained the facility to examine the impact of the heart-failure nurse based at the trust on costs and outcomes using data obtained from a Scottish pilot, or local data if available. The other feature of the model was its ability to illustrate the impact of beta-blocker prescribing on costs and consequences. Beta-blockers are drugs which previously were thought to be harmful to patients with heart failure. At the time of the meeting, however, there was good evidence of the beneficial effects of these drugs (Cleland and Swedberg 1996) and the computer model showed a strategy which incorporated beta-blockers to be cost saving under a range of feasible assumptions.

However, although the group members passed around a hard copy running to about ten pages illustrating model parameters and data-input fields, there was agreement that this approach was perhaps a little too sophisticated for the group at present (or, as the minutes described it, 'it could be useful in the future to the PCG'). One of the GPs approached me at the end of the meeting to explain apologetically that she and her colleagues were not ungrateful for the work I did for the group, but as they (GPs) were only 'simple souls', the model was too complicated for their purpose.

November saw the publication of the *National Service Framework on Coronary Heart Disease Emerging Findings Report* by the NHSE (1998b). *The New NHS: Modern, Dependable* (Department of Health 1997) had announced the development of NSFs to improve quality and consistency of services in a number of areas, including CHD (see Chapter 3). The *Emerging Findings Report* included heart failure in its definition of CHD. It also gave examples of clinically effective interventions for which there is good evidence of clinical and cost-effectiveness, but which are incompletely applied in practice. These include 'appropriate investigation and treatment, e.g. with angiotensin-converting enzyme inhibitors of people with suspected heart failure'.

In December, the HA public-health specialist, the Baxby PA and CE and I met to discuss further the issue of a heart-failure guideline. We intended to use the Riverview guideline, but as we examined the laminated double-sided A4 flow diagram, we noticed that at one point the instructions read 'refer to atrial fibrillation guideline'. Baxby had no atrial fibrillation (AF) guideline, but at this point we decided that delaying the heart-failure guideline while we embarked on a whole new project to develop AF guidelines would result in unacceptable delay.

In AF the two small upper chambers of the heart, the atria, quiver instead of beating effectively. Blood is not pumped completely out of them when the heart beats, so it may pool and clot. If a piece of the blood clot in the atria becomes lodged in an artery in the brain, a stroke results. About 15 per cent of strokes occur in people with atrial fibrillation. The potential for 'knowledge' to 'kill' action while a whole new data collection exercise was undertaken for AF was resisted. Apart from our desire to make progress, there was also the issue that AF would not strictly be the remit of the cardiac group. (At this time, there were only two sub-groups reflecting Baxby's two health improvement programme priority areas of CHD and chronic obstructive pulmonary disease. This meant that there was no forum for developing policy in relation to other disease areas such as strokes, other than the PCG board meeting itself.)

This episode illustrates the difficulty of compartmentalizing health problems. It is important also with respect to rationality, as the rational comprehensive approach would be to collect all the information necessary for the construction of an AF guideline, and presumably any other guidelines which stem from the AF guideline itself. Such an approach may result in there being no conclusion within the lifetime of the group to the heart-failure guideline process. Although health economic approaches assume rationality is desirable, here it may be better to pursue the short-term guideline completion, ignoring AF, or glossing over the issue, in order to secure health gain in the short to medium term.

The next meeting in January agreed that as access to echocardiography was a high priority, proposals for funding approximately 40 to 50 open-access echocardiograms (around £3,000 to £3,750 on a cost per case basis) for Baxby be submitted to the HA CD and MD and the PCG board.

THE RAPID ACCESS CHEST PAIN CLINIC

The January meeting also discussed the rapid access chest pain clinic provided by the trust for Shoreville HA patients. This item had been deferred at each meeting since September due to lack of time, although the cardiologist had managed to raise the issue under other items at each meeting he had attended. The issue was raised now, despite his absence because his lobbying of the HA had succeeded in £10,000 being earmarked in the HA's draft financial plan for 1999–2000. The item was ranked 2 on a scale of 1 to 3, where 1 was an unavoidable commitment. The HA was now consulting with the PCG and other stakeholders on the proposed list of developments.

Although the cardiologist and I were in agreement on the need for a heart-failure guideline, I was less persuaded by the rapid access chest pain proposal. When the issue was raised in the cardiac group, the cardiologist suggested that the service be funded for Baxby patients and that once up and running, the information would be collected. I spoke to the consultant in public health with lead responsibility for CHD services in Shoreville, but she was unable to provide information of the service purchased. The decision to fund this development had been taken before her arrival at Shoreville and nobody at the HA was clear about what the service provided.

There were several unanswered questions in relation to the proposed clinic which was to provide rapid access to a full set of diagnostic tests for chest pain patients. First, no indication was available of the likely volume of referrals which made it difficult to estimate the number of slots required in order to maintain a short waiting time for the clinic. The outpatient waiting times for cardiology were running at 6 months, despite the fact that the trust now employed four cardiologists compared with one at the Poppleton DGH which served a similar sized population. In other words, increasing capacity had not reduced waiting times, but had merely increased volumes.

Additionally, there was no information available on what might be the benefit of such a clinic in terms of future emergency attendances and admissions. As the cardiologist had not audited the current service, his argument that the clinic would 'sort out' patients who frequently reattended A and E by ruling out CHD or providing a clear diagnosis and appropriate follow-up remained untested. Although it had been pointed out in meetings that providing reassurance by ruling out CHD in some patients was worthwhile,

GPs acknowledged that some CHD-free individuals continue to present despite reassurances of their disease-free status.

I took advantage of the cardiologist's absence to stress the need to obtain data on the current service before committing to this for Baxby. The GPs present agreed with this, but the offer of £10,000 from the HA deserved consideration. Although the group would have preferred to use the money to fund echocardiography, there was no possibility of this. The Baxby PCG CE expressed the view that any offer of additional resources for Baxby patients should be greeted with enthusiasm.

This tension between not wanting to lose the chance of obtaining resources and not wanting to spend these resources on chest pain is illustrated in this extract from the minutes:

> It was noted that there was little evidence of the effects and benefits of a rapid access chest pain clinic ... Access to rapid chest pain services has been a priority for Baxby GPs for some time. After discussion it was felt that the Baxby CE should write to the HA indicating the support of the group for the use of growth moneys suggesting it should be of the highest priority.

As regards funding for the development of the echocardiography service, the MD was no longer openly opposed to the development of the heart-failure guidelines. The NSF had made it clear that heart failure was included in the definition of CHD and this made it difficult for the MD to maintain his line without losing face. However, in response to requests for funding for the echocardiography service, the MD insisted that the current services should be revised in order to release resources for the echocardiography development.

At the meeting, we discussed provisional dates for the launch of the guideline. Until now, I had been swept along with the enthusiasm of the group and motivated by what I saw as the need to counter the MD's indefensible decision to deny cost-effective drugs to patients who would benefit greatly from them. How would a HA health economist whose accountability was to the MD rather than the group have felt, I wondered. Although I was aware of the need to identify resources to fund the service, I had hoped that the HA would make funds available for 1 year initially. As was so often the case at the HA, once a service had been funded for 1 year, it became difficult to deny funding in subsequent years. Small additional items such as this were then usually incorporated into the main block contract with the trust.

It was clear by now that the NSF document was not having the effect upon the MD which I had hoped for. In response to my concerns about funding, particularly so close to the guideline launch, the PCG CE reassured me that fundholder savings would be used to pay for the development for the first year.

There was never any attempt to assess competing candidates for this resource. Instead, as with other investments by the PCG, items were dealt with as they arose. Each item was considered on its own merits and criteria. The HA resource document had contained a long list of developments, no doubt intended to focus minds on the trade-offs to be made within the budget. However, it is not certain that this proactive, wider approach results in a 'better' decision in terms of health gain (or whatever criteria HA managers might be aiming to fulfil) than the incremental approach. In the case of the HA's list, it was not clear why certain items were included. The ranking for schemes assessed as priority 2 and 3 was based largely on the disease area addressed and in response to the lobbying of the local consultant, rather than the proven benefits of the scheme (as is illustrated by the inclusion of the chest pain clinic for which benefits are uncertain).

As it turned out, only schemes graded as '1' were funded. At the February meeting, the group learned that the £10,000 for a chest pain clinic at the trust was not available, as all the resources for schemes graded 2 and 3 had been used to support 'pressures' within the system, including meeting waiting list targets.

The issue of funding for the echocardiography service was discussed again within the group. The PCG CE had written to the HA CD on 29 January 1999 requesting that the service be funded, but had as yet received no reply. Additionally, the funding issue had been further complicated by information provided by the trust finance department, which suggested that the cost of the echocardiography service would be higher than estimated by the cardiologist. This was because the revised cost was based on reapportioning the total cost of the service over all users rather than providing access to the spare capacity at marginal cost. The cardiologist blamed the trust finance department for the 'misunderstanding' and agreed to offer the service at the price originally quoted.

LAUNCHING THE HEART-FAILURE GUIDELINES

On the evening of 3 March 1999, the guidelines were launched at a meeting at a local hotel. The cardiologist spoke on the issue of guidelines and answered questions from the floor. The PM outlined the 'achievements' of the cardiac nurses based on the flawed data set (see Chapter 5). Perhaps anticipating criticism from myself, she did include the phrase 'these are not matched pairs' in her talk, but it is unlikely that anybody in the room apart from the PM, the MD and I understood the significance of this phrase. In any case, she then proceeded to draw conclusions from the data and inform the audience of the 'success' of the nurses.

The MD was to speak on the performance indicators. So many of us had heard the talk so many times before that I could not help saying to him 'You're not going to do that talk again are you?' He said that he would give the matter some thought and gave a lively presentation bringing in the issue of performance monitoring and linking it to clinical governance, the NSF and the local strategy. He then went on to present the local data on CHD deaths which showed a decline in numbers and claimed that this 'success' was 'down to the strategy and to the efforts of all of you in this room'. The style was evangelical and the message was well received. I understood the need to raise the spirits of the people present who would be instrumental in delivering the NSF and felt it would be churlish of me to point out the secular decline in CHD, which was a national and international rather than purely local phenomenon.

The PCG chairman stood up to respond. He gave a broad grin, expressing his delight at hearing 'some good news at last'. He exhorted those present to 'keep going' as the data showed what a difference could be made by our efforts. This was a surprising volte-face from this GP, who whenever performance measurement was raised previously expressed the view that in Baxby deaths from CHD would inevitably increase rather than decline and that any GP intervention would take many years to bear fruit in terms of improved outcomes. The health visitor sitting next to me grinned and said, 'Isn't it marvellous?'

As I made my way towards the exit, the MD asked, with a mock serious tone, whether the talk had been exciting enough for me. Although I did not view any of the claims for progress made at the meeting as valid, because of the data upon which they were based, I had found the MD's talk to be a fine piece of showmanship. Rather than take issue with him on his interpretation of data (a conversation we had had many times before), I complimented him on his performance. The reaction of the audience served to increase my awareness of the need to, at times, provide propaganda to 'rally the troops'. What harm was there in making a liberal interpretation of the local CHD mortality figures, if the aim was nothing more sinister than boosting morale and encouraging clinicians to deliver evidence-based care?

Could the MD claim legitimacy for his actions on the grounds that the ends justified the means? The exaggerated claims made for the cardiac nurses confirmed their success and made it much less likely that the intervention would ever be evaluated. If the nurses were ineffective, then this might be an expensive way of boosting morale, not to mention what the opportunity cost of the nurse project might be. Additionally, if data were to be manipulated to serve a purpose, who would be the final arbiter of what constituted 'acceptable' grounds for resorting to such a tactic?

THE RAPID ACCESS CHEST PAIN CLINIC REVISITED

In June 1999 the meeting discussed the cardiologist's proposal for a rapid access chest pain clinic. He and I spent much of the meeting on a circular discussion in which I asked for information on the service currently provided and he offered to collect data on the new service if we would fund it. (At the July meeting, which the cardiologist could not attend, the PCG CE lamented his absence, joking that he had already written the minutes which consisted of a long discussion between the cardiologist and me with me demanding evidence and the cardiologist promising to provide it when we funded his service!)

There was enthusiasm for the service from all the GPs present. My opposition stemmed partly from the failure of the cardiologist to provide data on the current service, but it was also prompted by a desire to encourage the PCG to think critically about resource commitments, taking a wider view. I was being disingenuous in asking for information since it is not clear that any information the cardiologist could provide would resolve the issue of whether the costs of the service were justified in terms of benefits arising.

The GPs saw benefits from ruling out CHD in disease-free patients. However, they acknowledged that many such patients would continue to present with chest pain even after CHD had been ruled out. If the cardiologist could provide a percentage split of patients attending the clinic by discharge diagnosis, this would tell us little. What percentage of patients with CHD would indicate an appropriate use of resources?

The chest pain issue highlighted clearly the extent to which the GPs were reluctant to contradict the cardiologist. After the latter's departure for his afternoon clinic, a local GP agreed that we should look at the existing service before making any decision. He also suggested that he knew 'full well that a lot of these [frequently attending] patients haven't got angina' and that what they needed was a job and 'somewhere decent to live'. The public health specialist supported my comments on the need to provide data and other group members joined in. The chairman of the PCG pointed out that the trust had already received a generous waiting list allocation and the money for the echo service. The atmosphere had become a lot more light-hearted since the cardiologist's departure. When I asked why nobody else on the group would support me when I challenged him, the PCG CE explained that I was well suited to this role ('You do it so well').

FUNDING THE CHEST PAIN CLINIC – MEDICAL POWER AND RATIONAL DECISION-MAKING

The last meeting of the group I attended was in October 1999. The PCG CE informed the meeting that money had been made available for local development and the PCG board had agreed that this should be used for funding the chest pain clinic. He was vague on the subject of how much money had been allocated. The cardiologist asked the meeting which group of patients should be targeted and explained that once the target group had been defined, an estimate of patient numbers should be prepared. This would allow the trust to calculate the number of sessions required to provide rapid access for this group. As the minutes record, 'A further meeting will be held early next week to decide which group of patients should be targeted first, how often the clinic should be run and the costs.'

In contrast to the assumptions of the rational model, the PCG had, first, decided to fund the service. Subsequently, a decision would be made about which group of patients to target. This decision would influence the number of slots required and the PCG would then look at whether it could afford this number. Aside from the problems of identifying patient numbers and likely take-up, if the patient number calculation suggested unaffordable levels of service, the PCG would be forced to reduce the number of slots, thus increasing waiting times and hence undermining the rapid access rationale for the service. Of course, none of this was discussed in any detail. The GPs welcomed the opening of another avenue down which to send 'problem' patients, whereas now that agreement to fund the clinic was secured, the cardiologist was at pains to seek the views of the meeting in order to structure the service to the 'right' group of patients. The GPs present, who were more interested in the date from which the service would be available and the means of accessing it, did not appear to be interested in patient categorization.

There are parallels here with the statins discussions wherein each GP had their own ideas about what constituted high risk. Although they engaged in discussions and asked the cardiologist's opinion in relation to statins and the meaning of technical terms such as triglycerides, they were also very clear that 'guidelines' were not a substitute for clinical judgement. GPs were perfectly happy to make their own judgements about which patients to send to this clinic and did not seem concerned that each GP might adopt different referral criteria. Although the cardiologist had secured the money for the clinic, he appeared anxious to resolve referral criteria and pointed out that the disregard of Shoreville GPs of the referral criteria meant that clinic slots were not being used for patients who would benefit most. Indeed, treadmill exercise test slots had been booked for patients who were incapable of walking, because GPs had not completed referral documentation or adhered to protocols.

Whilst the cardiologist's expert status helped in his ability to influence the group, he was also dependent on group members for development funds. The duty of GPs to exercise clinical judgement combined with the work context in which what they do is largely not open to scrutiny or peer review means that they have huge discretion in the way they perform their work. In a sense, these wide-ranging powers may be limited at points where their work impacts on others and exposes their practices to scrutiny.

As 90 per cent of episodes begin and end in primary care, the opportunities for scrutiny are limited. The expansion of the GP role from that of provider to encompass commissioner responsibilities may mean that the power of GPs increases relative to that of hospital doctors. This was certainly perceived to be the effect of fundholding and naively presented by some commentators as a wholly beneficial outcome of the process. The practical implications of this may be that unexplained variations in access to treatment and referral behaviour are perpetuated by a system in which provider clinicians, anxious to accommodate a disparate group of practitioners, accept inappropriate referrals, rather than attempting to impose a central protocol on the GPs concerned. Part of the challenge for PCGs and PCTs will be to address such variations, but despite national standards and GP reaccreditation, this will be no easy task. In addition to the resource consequences of implementing standards, as the discussion of the group indicates, it will be difficult to challenge the accepted wisdom in relation to GPs' freedom to practise in whatever way they judge to be appropriate.

Whilst the GPs accepted the cardiologist's expert opinion up to a point, it is by no means certain that GP behaviour changed as a result of his advice. Anonymized comparative data on statins prescribing for the 6 months before and 9 months after the launch of the statins guideline showed a huge variation between practices before the launch, with a similar pattern observed in the period following guideline dissemination.

The continuation of wide variation in statins prescribing and poor uptake of new CHD services (see below) suggests that GPs continued to exercise clinical judgement, rather than follow central guidance. The other important factor to bear in mind is that the cardiologist's role in the group had been to resist attempts to construct a narrow statins guideline and propose candidates for service expansion to be funded, for the most part, from HA budgets. It is by no means certain that the GPs would agree with the cardiologist if he proposed additional workload or responsibilities for primary care or advocated service reductions. In other words, the temptation to cast him in the role of powerful doctor leading the group by the nose should be avoided. The cardiologist had his uses for the group in that he acted as an articulate exponent of service expansion and took on the MD on issues such as heart failure and performance indicators. Whilst GPs were not keen to challenge the cardiologist to his face, the ability to practise medicine based on their individual judgement meant that there was no incentive for GPs to do so. If they disagreed with him, rather than risking alienating him by arguing in public, they could nod agreement at meetings, whilst continuing their existing practice back at the surgery. The group's willingness to let the cardiologist and I debate the merits of proposals in the absence of resources in a seemingly endless round of meetings, supporting my view after he had departed, suggests that the relationship between them and the cardiologist was much less one-sided than it first appeared.

The meeting also received an update on the echocardiography

service. Of the 18 referrals received during March to September, 12 were from one practice. One of the GPs in this practice was a member of the group and he announced that each of his partners had a file of referral forms on their desk in a manner which implied that high take-up indicated good practice. This 'more is better attitude' is resonant of Detsky's findings on the value of pure information to clinicians. However, judging from the way the GPs had expressed concerns about treating 'problem' patients who, they were sure, did not have heart disease, support may be understood in terms of the ability to refer on such patients. The cardiologist expressed disappointment that only one of the patients required an ACE inhibitor. The minutes report his view that 'it may be more beneficial for diagnostic purposes if more severe patients were referred'. Once again, this raises the issue of how to measure success. If these patients were treated as having heart failure based on presenting symptoms, then incorrect diagnoses, inappropriate prescribing and labelling would follow. If these patients were not suspected of having heart failure but were referred merely to reassure the patient of what the GP already knew, then the implications of the cardiologist's advice was that this latter explanation represented sub-optimal use of resources. However, this may be viewed differently if examined from the perspective of the GPs or the patients.

TAKING MY LEAVE

A combination of sadness at leaving the group and the sight of the cardiologist asking the group for direction and looking increasingly uneasy at the responses provided disarmed me. I felt it would be churlish to ask why the service was being funded. In any case, I expected the response would be that money had become available. I was sure that any response would not contain reference to benefits, health gain or evidence-based medicine and it being my last meeting I was disinclined to bow out on a dissonant note. I left early due to other commitments and as I walked towards the exit one of the GPs grabbed my arm. Instead of the 'good luck in your new job' sentiments and smile I had expected, I was greeted with the words 'Will you be replaced?' and a look of concern. Driving to my next meeting, I puzzled over this reaction. Looking back over my work with the group there is very little that I contributed which made an impact on the decisions taken and even less which can be defined as health economics input. The only explanation I can find for the GPs' apparent impression of me as an asset is that this is another manifestation of the 'more is better' attitude exhibited by the local GPs. Just as conduits for channelling patients enable the GPs to keep patients moving through the system without having to accept defeat or stalemate, the economist can be relied upon to take on problems whose resolution is ultimately unimportant. In a world where life can feel like wading through treacle, the sense of movement and of action as progress rather than a means towards some specified end begins to make perfect sense.

7

TOWARDS UNDERSTANDING

INTRODUCTION

This book began as an inquiry into the nature of decision-making at local level in the NHS and specifically into the role of health economic evaluation in those decision processes. Chapter 1 posed the question 'What happens when we try to use health economic evaluation at local level in the NHS?' It has been suggested that any attempts to answer such a question will amount to no more than 'gossip'. What is worse, this gossip will be highly biased, being 'geographically, jurisdictionally, culturally or personally specific' (Culyer 1996: 1). Unlike gossip, however, the preceding case studies represent the results of years of systematic research. What conclusions can be drawn on the basis of these observations? The research sheds light on the constraints on the use of health economics at local level in one HA and one PCG, but it tells us so much more besides.

This study provides insights into decision-making processes and contexts, which have relevance outside of Poppleton and beyond health economics. The suggestion here is that attempts to use rational or technical solutions to resource-allocation dilemmas at local level in the public sector face substantial barriers which cannot be overcome by methodological refinements or the collection of greater volumes of data. Even where data exist, the limits on our cognitive capacities and resources make it difficult to appraise all available options. Much of what we know is contingent and partial, even if it is obtained from randomized, multinational and double-blind trials. As events at Poppleton illustrate, making choices about health-care resources involves conflicting values, and decision-makers face competing objectives which arise precisely because of a failure to reconcile these conflicts. As Weber (1978) pointed out all those years ago, values 'cannot be measured in terms of formal calculation' and formally rational 'calculable rules' may fly in the face of societal values. This suggests that those attempting to use health economic evaluation as the basis for making health-care decisions at a local level will face huge problems.

Critics of this argument will no doubt counter that the rational model of decision-making is an ideal type. Nobody adheres to the rational model in its entirety, so its use here is as a straw man to be pulled apart in support of a weak argument. Having access to health economic or scientific analyses provides the decision-maker with additional information which they would not otherwise have had available, even if ultimately the choice is based on political expediency. This, so the argument goes, improves the quality of decision-making. Indeed, it is naive not to recognize that rational, systematic methods such as health economic analyses are only ever going to be one input to the decision process (Ashmore *et al.* 1989). If this is the case, then what are the other inputs and what are their relative impacts? If 'rational' analyses are considered but then ignored, can we really say that it has added value? Can we use a combination of rational analysis and political expediency by giving decision-makers technical solutions to inject into their decision processes as and when they are able? It seems unlikely, as rationality is incompatible with other approaches to decision-making. Decisions reflect the results of rational analyses or they do not. Decision-makers may choose to adopt the solutions generated by rational analyses or they may not. If they elect to follow the latter course of action (as events at Poppleton illustrate, there may be all kinds of compelling reasons why they do this), their decision-making cannot be understood in terms of the rational ideal. Having a bit of rationality is like being a bit pregnant. So the notion that choices based on a mix of technical appraisal and a range of other factors, with the end result departing from the appraisal are 'partially rational' makes no sense.

That is not to say that decision-makers will always ignore solutions to policy dilemmas generated by rational systematic processes. On the contrary, they will use the results of such analyses to justify their actions wherever possible. For those making difficult choices rational analysis which accords with their personal preferences serves a dual function of legitimating their argument, whilst at the same time associating it with independent 'experts' and not, in the event of a poor outcome, the whim of the policymaker concerned.

The biggest problem with rationality is that, ultimately, following its prescriptions is just not rational. To see why this should be so we need to return to Poppleton. All HAs are different, but, at the time of the study, they each faced a similar set of constraints which served to limit the potential for the use of health economics in resource-allocation choices. All HAs were grappling with resource scarcity, facing multiple and competing objectives and had weak or non-existent legitimacy for engaging in explicit rationing. This meant that decision-makers developed coping strategies which relied on unsystematic and implicit resource allocation. These strategies varied across HAs and between individuals. These strategies may have subverted the stated aims of the state. In the case of health care, they led to inequalities in access to treatments and unexplained variations in treatment patterns. The important thing, however, is that they facilitated the expeditious processing of patients and allowed the maintenance of a precarious stability. This stability was based on the denial of explicit rationing and the illusion of an NHS which is truly dependable. In other words, what might to an outsider appear as a collection of 'irrational' decision-making processes:

- Why construct guidelines when you have no idea whether they will be implemented, have no good estimate of the cost of implementation, no additional resources and are not even clear on the aim of the guideline?
- Why refer patients to heart disease services when you know they don't have heart disease?
- Why oppose policies intended to reduce waiting times for cardiac surgery?

are actually essential features of the life-support system of the NHS at local level. Any attempts to replace these devices with decision-making based on rational systematic inquiry threaten the system's ability to deliver and serve to undermine its long-term survival.

'IRRATIONAL' DECISION-MAKING AT POPPLETON

It should be apparent from the evidence presented in this book that there are aspects of the decision-making process at Poppleton which can be understood in terms of the bounded rational, pluralistic or external control models described in Chapter 2. However, the picture of decision-making which emerges from the case studies is far removed from the prescriptions of the rational model in a number of ways, as the following illustrates.

Decision-makers are forced to pursue many objectives simultaneously

All HAs were required to balance budgets, commission care to meet need, avoid bad publicity and so on. They could not focus huge efforts on meeting a single objective whilst ignoring other goals, but neither could they tackle everything at once. In the context of conflicting values about priorities in health care, the government was deliberately vague about its expectations of HAs. This means that it was not easy for HAs to prioritize goals, which in turn led to attention being focused on issues which are immediate and visible.

Decision-makers do not always share common objectives

The unity of purpose at the heart of the rational model was not a feature of decision-making at Poppleton. Within the HA, there existed a whole series of tribes with their own cultures and objectives. Outside of the HA, groups of stakeholders may have pursued goals which were at odds with those of the MD and his team. So, for example, the HA managers were keen to restrict the use of cholesterol-lowering drugs, but this was opposed by GPs and hospital clinicians. The PCG members chose to prioritize heart failure, although this was actively opposed by the HA MD. Although the hospital cardiologist supported shorter patient waiting times for access to the tertiary centre's cardiac surgeon, the latter opposed this.

Even where HA and PCG managers were able to gain agreement to guidelines or contracts, they could not employ top-down management principles to enforce compliance, but were compelled instead to resort to negotiation, compromise and bargaining. These features suggest a pluralistic decision-making context. External control models have some resonance here too, as the context of HA decision-making was heavily influenced by the actions of other stakeholders. Thus, the HA MD's objective of reducing investment in tertiary care to reflect underperformance on the contract with the tertiary trust was thwarted by the NHSE's directive to agree contracts, regardless of this issue. Similarly, where stakeholders did share common objectives, these might not necessarily have related directly to the improvement of patient care. So, for example, when faced with multiple goals, central directives and limited room for manoeuvre, staff at the HA colluded with the NHS trust counterparts in the 'manufacturing' of statistics for the efficiency index to avoid the NHSE's critical gaze.

Decision-makers are not trying to maximize anything and may be unwilling to be explicit about their goals

Decision-makers cope by reacting to demands or problems, often without being explicit about their decision criteria. Health economic evaluation can incorporate multiple goals, but this would require decision-makers to make their values explicit. For example, in the case of cholesterol-lowering drugs, the MD would need to specify the extent to which he is prepared to forego efficiency (in terms of the health gain lost by not treating older patients) and equity to achieve his cost-containment objectives. Since the MD had no legitimacy for his discriminatory approach (although opinion polls suggest that he commanded public support for his views), he was unwilling to be explicit about such issues. Despite his opposition to the heart-failure service developments, the MD endorsed the service when asked to speak at a public meeting to launch the heart-failure guidelines. Similarly, the Baxby GPs were happy to support the introduction of echocardiography services, ostensibly to improve diagnosis of heart failure. However, their comments and the data on service usage suggest that their goal related to the expeditious processing of workload and to the desire to deflect problem patients. Whilst coronary stents were supported by the tertiary trust on the grounds of health gain, the references to the centre's international reputation made by trust clinicians suggest that there may have been other reasons for pursuing this argument. The extent to which these decision-makers would be willing to be explicit about this in any economic evaluation exercise, however, is debatable. Even if decision makers were willing to be explicit about their values, quantifying these sentiments in numerical terms is likely to be problematic. This relates partly to the process of articulating values and then to the difficult business of assigning numbers to them. In addition, the process of formulating 'calculable rules' without regard to individuals is likely to be problematic for

GPs whose practice is largely informed by the particulars of the individual patient in front of them.

Decision-making is reactive and problem-definition fluid

Much of the day-to-day work of HA staff and GPs was spent reacting to perceived problems. HAs and GPs faced many issues which related to resource scarcity, but as the garbage can decision-making model illustrates, several factors may contribute to the relabelling of an issue as a 'problem'. In the case of statins, the potential cost and increasing uptake focused the minds of HA managers and other stakeholders on this problem. The issue was given a further push by the SMAC guidelines, which were sent to all GPs. Ultimately, however, the 'problem' of statins proved not to be amenable to resolution and faded as other more pressing 'problems', such as emergency admissions and coronary stents, displaced them. The system-wide modelling process was not prompted by the identification of problem areas requiring immediate action. It may be better characterized as proactive, than reactive. Here the timescales were flexible and attempts were made to pursue a more systematic process, along the lines of the health economic rational planning approach. This exercise received much less attention than statins, because the day-to-day business of managing and delivering services and agreeing contracts continued without any of the parties involved in service delivery looking to the modelling work to assist them in their immediate concerns. In other words, the failure of a systematic and proactive approach is understandable within the context of reactive and unsystematic decision-making.

Action is less a means to an end, than an end in itself

With bounded rational and garbage can decision-making, problem identification creates a clamour for action, irrespective of whether this ameliorates the problem. Bounded rational models are characterized by a vagueness of stated intent to allow post hoc rationalization about their success. However, the vagueness of intent on the MD's part on the statins issue was a product of the seemingly impossible task of reconciling conflicting objectives and values rather than a fear of identifying too closely with a policy that might fail. The garbage can model has some resonance here. Recall from Chapter 2 that in this model 'beliefs and preferences appear to be the results of behaviour as much as they are determinants of it.

Motives and intentions are discovered post factum . . . there may be attitudes and beliefs without behavioural implications . . . there may be behaviour without any basis in individual preferences' (March and Olsen 1976: 15). Faced with multiple goals, competing objectives, no mechanism for prioritizing goals and uncertain cause and effect relationships, relating ends to means is problematic. In this context, for those who want to make a difference doing something appears to be better than doing nothing and may become an end in itself. This explains, for example, why guidelines are produced as a matter of routine, without regard to the objectives of such guidelines or the cost of implementing them.

GPs 'process' patients, but have little feel for the impact of their work on health outcomes. Baxby GPs often expressed the view that they were powerless to influence those factors, such as housing, employment and income, which impacted heavily on their patients' state of health. However, they continued to process patients as quickly as possible within the resources available. Similarly, the MD, frustrated with a working environment characterized by constraints on resources and the requirement to get things done through others, felt that action was important regardless of the outcome.

More is always better than less

Just as some action is better than no action, more services are better than fewer services, particularly where these additional services are highly visible. Chapter 6 described how Baxby PCG members prioritized the heart-failure development over the proposed chest pain service, acknowledging the lack of evidence available for the latter.

However, when faced with a 'take it or leave it' offer of resources for the chest pain service, the PCG CE wrote welcoming the offer, suggesting that it was 'of the highest priority'. Nurses in primary care providing advice to CHD patients, extra doctors in A and E and hospital chest pain clinics are visible symbols which allow HAs, GPs and hospital trusts to claim credit for action, regardless of whether or not these developments represent an effective or cost-effective use of resources. Little or no attempt is made to evaluate service developments. As the goals of such actions are often specified in rather vague or diffuse terms (for example 'making things better' or 'buying goodwill'), it is difficult, if not impossible, to assess the success or otherwise of developments which have been implemented. When additional resources are requested (such as the chest pain clinic or additional doctors in A and E), proponents do not seek to construct 'rational' arguments based on objective identification and consideration of alternative options. Instead, they merely argue for more resources (rationalization as rationality), on the grounds that more is better. Thus, when asked to suggest service developments *and* at the same time to identify the likely outcomes of these, the system-wide modelling group members are silent.

The views and values of decision-makers exist prior to problem-definition and 'rational' optional appraisal processes

Although decision-makers may aspire to rationality, 'rational' health economic analyses may be shelved where their results conflict with deeply held values of end users. This is graphically illustrated in the attitude of the MD and his team towards 'older' patients in relation to statin treatment. Similarly, having made up his mind that heart failure was a low priority area, the MD refused to alter his beliefs despite evidence which undermined his case. GPs, hospital cardiologists and cardiac surgeons all view service issues from their own perspective. Thus, they focus on the way in which service options will impact on their workload, rather than examining overall benefits to patients. Patterns of statin prescribing and discussion amongst GPs about risk factors and eligibility criteria for statins revealed a huge variation between GPs. This suggests that despite the guidelines, which aim to standardize prescribing practices, GPs were using their 'judgement', based on their own values and 'knowledge' about who should receive treatment. Many GPs have decided that access to echocardiography will provide a route along which to divert problem patients, regardless of the guidelines for the service. The fact that only one of the eighteen patients required an ACE inhibitor (as opposed to one in four expected based on following the guidelines) appears to support this view.

Opinions differed amongst GPs as to whether smokers should receive statin treatment. HA managers chose deeply held beliefs over clinical evidence and claimed public support for their actions. In Weberian terms, these examples illustrate the conflict arising between formally rational processes based on calculable rules and substantive rationality. Society supports the 'rule of rescue', which results in the investment of huge resources in an attempt to save critically ill patients who have almost no chance of survival. A clear conflict exists here between formal rules aimed at the maximization of health gain and societal values which eschew the notion of battlefield-style triage of patients, leaving those with almost no chance of survival to expire quietly. In this case the abandonment of formal rationality, which involves the calculation of costs and benefits of heroic interventions, is widely supported. However, other issues are less amenable to consensus, as illustrated by the differences of opinion amongst decision-makers in relation to smokers, older patients and so on. Weber's 'substantive rationality' embodies the notion of a clear set of social values. However, in the absence of a forum for eliciting community values in Poppleton (or indeed nationally), individuals are free to apply their own beliefs about what is best for society and, in the absence of local discussions to elicit community views, can claim public support for their actions.

Ambiguity is a central feature of decision-making

Ambiguity is different from uncertainty, as the latter can be reduced by the collection of data, but the former cannot. When a situation is described as 'ambiguous', a decision-maker is less confident that any one thing is true, or that the world can be partitioned into mutually exhaustive and exclusive states, or that information will resolve the lack of clarity (March 1994). So the HA MD recruited nurses to increase statin prescribing in primary care, but at the same time he was investigating ways of restricting prescribing, because of his desire to contain costs. This ambiguity is evident in the contribution of the cardiac surgeon to the system-wide modelling process. Whilst he wanted to 'do the best' for patients referred to him, he would rather not have had to operate on patients whose degree of morbidity increased their risk of operative mortality. As he decided on treatment for patients referred to him, he could withhold surgery from these patients, but this meant denying them a chance to prevent sudden cardiac death. For this reason, he would rather that these patients were not referred quickly so that he would not be placed in the position of having to make such difficult choices. Ambiguity arises because goals conflict. Forcing decision-makers to consider this conflict explicitly, for example by asking them to specify objectives as with the statins modelling exercise, creates decision paralysis. This runs the risk of cognitive dissonance, by exposing the gap between the rational ideal and the reality. Thus, where goals conflict, action is facilitated, and decision-makers are happiest, if goals are not considered. Hence, where ambiguity prevails, action becomes an end in itself.

Policy actors enjoy wide discretion and freedom from central control, yet perceive themselves as powerless

The medical model of health and illness is seen as a major source of medical dominance. By equating ill-health with individual pathology, a response to morbidity is formulated in terms of individual medical interventions. In other words, doctors define problems using the language of medicine, which means that solutions are conceptualized in these terms. The paradox is, however, that the ubiquity of the medical model, which represents a source of medical power, also serves as a reminder to individual doctors of their own powerlessness. So, on the one hand, GPs perform an important gatekeeper role in controlling demand for health services and, for the most part, the way they fulfil this task is left to their own discretion. They are free to allocate resources (their time, prescription drugs, hospital referrals and so on) to patients as they see fit. Pluralist theories of decision-making which emphasize an unequal distribution of power provide some understanding of events here. Medical power may derive in part from the abilities of doctors to solve problems under conditions of uncertainty. It is not uncertainty which gives power, however, but the ability to cope with this uncertainty (Hickson *et al.* 1971). In exchange for coping, clinicians, the legitimate decision-makers in the eyes of the public, are afforded freedom to make choices, without having to account, in detail, for their actions.

However, the volume of resources they have at their disposal is easily outstripped by the potential demands of patients. In addition, the range of available resources is narrow, since problems are conceptualized in terms of clinical solutions. As Baxby GPs recognized, factors such as unemployment, poor housing and poverty all contribute greatly to ill health. GPs are unable to tackle these non-medical factors, focusing instead on the manifestations of problems whose roots lie outside of the medical sphere of influence. In this sense, they feel powerless.

External control models of decision-making emphasize the importance of the external environment on organizational behaviour. It is clear that although HA directors enjoy wide discretion, they are severely constrained in the options available to them by their external environment. The MD was able to present advice on statins to treat 'younger patients' as medical fact rather than prejudice. His specialist knowledge was a potential source of power, but as the HA as a decision-making body was merely asked to note the problem, no actions followed from this. HAs are unable to disinvest from existing services for fear of a negative response from the public and the government. The phrase 'there's no such thing as bad publicity' could not be more wrong in the NHS context. This acts as a huge constraint on the HAs' ability to influence their environment and ensures that the subject of disinvestment never reaches the HA agenda.

Health services represent only a small influence on the health of local populations. HA decision-makers involved in negotiating small numbers of extra cases at the margin, in the context of an uncertain, network environment, understandably may feel powerless to make an impact in any significant fashion. Yet despite their limited ability to influence their environment, HAs are held accountable for performance on a whole range of indicators. Building up trusting relationships with those outside the HA is seen as important, because it lends legitimacy to the actions of HA managers facing resource-allocation processes. The tangible returns from HA investments are often uncertain, but by allocating resources to the projects of trusted stakeholders, HA managers can claim support for their decisions. At the same time, this process is seen as buying goodwill which can be mobilized to bolster the weak or non-existent power base of HA decision-makers. The time and resources invested in building and maintaining trusting relationships illustrate just how little power the HA has at its disposal and how much it needs to rely on other organizations to make things happen.

'Knowledge' is contingent and subjective

Data paucity and the unavailability of information generally have been identified as barriers to the use of health economics (Williams 2000). The implication is that by collecting more and better data the problem will be reduced. Even where we have data from RCTs, however, this knowledge is always partial and contingent, although we tend to forget this. For example who would have predicted in 1998 that the pharmaceutical company Bayer would be forced to withdraw its statin Cerivastatin in 2001 following the revelation of

31 deaths in the US from the same condition in patients taking the drug (Charatan 2001)? In other words, there is always the possibility that RCT findings may be challenged or overturned by subsequent RCTs or events in the real world outside of the RCT environment.

In Poppleton much of the local information required for conducting the economic evaluations was not routinely available. However, obtaining estimates of clinical efficacy was less of a problem, in some respects, due to the large volume of published evidence from multi-centre randomized trials. Despite this, clinicians displayed a consistent preference for a case-based understanding of evidence rather than subordinating their judgement to the results of formally rational randomized trials.

Whilst these actions may be criticized as departing from rationality, it should be recognized that RCT results reflect aggregate and not individual patients. In addition, as RCTs reflect rarefied environments inhabited by patients younger and healthier than the target population and typified by unrepresentative practice, the extent to which results can be extrapolated wholesale to other settings is questionable. In Poppleton, GPs chose to interpret the evidence in the light of their experience rather than to apply it wholesale. In addition, they expressed a clear preference for treating patients with statins regardless of age, despite the fact that there was no evidence base for treating patients over 70. What counts as knowledge, evidence or information is dependent on the perspective of the beholder. The danger is that clinicians, as reflective practitioners, will interpret evidence differently and may ignore the issue of evidence altogether when it is expedient to do so. This raises the question of whether it is always 'rational' to follow evidence to the letter, as illustrated by the example of patients with raised cholesterol requiring a cholesterol reduction of over 40 per cent (described in Chapter 6). Of the statins available only atorvastatin would produce the desired effect, but the published evidence of efficacy was not obtained from a large multicentre RCT. If local experience suggests that atorvastatin can achieve a 40 per cent reduction in cholesterol levels, and individual GPs can monitor the effect on their patients, should this be ignored because the results do not come from a large multicentre RCT? Should the cardiologist (Chapter 5), whose injection therapy procedure enables patients to have a vastly improved quality of life, refrain from this practice since it has no evidence base? What is the rational course of action in each of these cases?

The implications for 'rational' decision-making

What all this means in practice is that 'rational' health economic approaches to resource allocation are unlikely to be adopted widely at the local level in the NHS. Faced with multiple and competing objectives, HA and PCG managers and GPs develop coping strategies the evolution of which is prompted precisely because of an unwillingness and an inability to engage in the sort of systematic and explicit decision-making processes which lie at the heart of health economics.

At Poppleton decision-makers resembled Lipsky's street level bureaucrats. They 'attempt to do a good job in some way [but] the job, however, is, in a sense, impossible to do in ideal terms'. 'How,' asks Lipsky, 'is the job to be accomplished with inadequate resources, few controls, indeterminate objectives and discouraging circumstances?' (Lipsky 1980: 82). One tactic is to 'modify their concept of their jobs, so as to lower or otherwise restrict their objectives and thus reduce the gap between available resources and achieving objectives'. Lipsky's work focuses on those involved in direct client contact, but this modification process is faced by HA decision-makers on an almost constant basis. '[A]ny recognition that performance is less than adequate is likely to make these bureaucrats seek and find the explanation someplace other than in their own inadequacy' (1980: 82). This may explain the constant resort to criticizing other departments and the NHSE in particular. For Lipsky, street-level bureaucrats are interested in processing work consistent with their own preferences, whereas managers are interested in achieving results consistent with agency objectives. This assumes constancy, clarity and consistency of objectives amongst the managerial stratum which is likely to be lacking in most HAs. HA managers are not involved in front-line service delivery. However, the notion that some of these managers are like Lipsky's street-level workers struggling to do the best they can, defined in terms of their own preferences is helpful in understanding the realities of HA life. If this is the case, then attempts to use health economic solutions which require explicit and systematic approaches will do little to change the outcome of decision processes. They will serve merely to make decision-makers more uncomfortable and more aware of the gap between their service ideal and reality.

For HA managers, the impact of their actions is uncertain. HAs charged with assessing need and commissioning care to meet that need have little control over the supply and demand of care. Their staff engage in the production of policy documents, but the extent to which these impact on patients is questionable. They disseminate guidelines, but have no control over the prescribing practices of local GPs. They contract for additional elective activity at the margins, but often this is dictated by the length of waiting lists and they have no choice in the matter. They have little or no control over demand for services, particularly in the context of emergency care. Government statements which promise that 'in the new NHS patients will be treated on the basis of need and need alone' (Department of Health 1997: 2.13) serve to further limit the range of options open to HAs. In practice, coping strategies at HA level may result in the production of different decisions by different HAs faced with similar problems. Given that HAs have such limited options available and such limited impact on their environment, the extent of variation between HAs with regard to the health impact of their actions is unlikely[1] to be as wide as that generated as a result of the coping strategies of individual GPs.

The 'street-level' working environment of GPs means that they are engaged in expeditious processing of patients who consult them. GPs have an immediate impact as they allocate resources and, in so doing, they make policy. They 'hold the keys to a dimension of citizenship' (Lipsky 1980: 4). This policy may be very different, however, from that contained in HA guidelines or Department of Health circulars. As each GP's coping strategy is different, the policy which is delivered will not be uniform. Indeed, the result will be to produce inequalities in care. Thus, the service delivered by GPs runs contrary to the declared aim of the government, which is to eradicate inequalities and to standardize patterns of care.

Paradoxically, these coping strategies are essential to the long-term survival of the system. They allow GPs to manage the gap between the service ideal and the resources available. In the context of resource scarcity and rising consumer expectations, GPs ration care and, importantly, they do so implicitly. Attempts at 'rational' decision-making which highlight cost-effective use of resources and aim to coerce GPs to process patients according to standard rules threaten to undermine the precarious stability of the system. Health economic approaches which identify optimal solutions, usually in terms of health gain, are of little use if no additional resources are available and explicit rationing is not permitted. A commitment to 'rational' systematic tools such as health economic analyses requires clear objectives to be specified and is likely to undermine the ability of decision-makers to apply coping mechanisms based on implicit rationing. Such a commitment rules out the 'quick fix', but the potential for inaction is enormous, as is the likely level of mental discomfort for policy actors engaged in such processes. By specifying parameters explicitly, health economic analysis provides a reminder for these actors of the gap between an idealized notion of their role in the health-policy process and what is achievable within the real-world constraints. Exposing the gap between the service ideal and reality by asking decision-makers to adopt systematic and explicit approaches in the context of weak or non-existent legitimacy, therefore, will produce decision paralysis, when what is required is precisely the opposite: the expeditious processing of the workload to maintain the illusion of an NHS which is both modern and dependable.

In Poppleton decision-making was reactive, action became an end in itself and more resources were always preferred to less. These features arose from the need there to manage the gap between resource scarcity and the service ideal. The requirement to cope with this gap is not unique to Poppleton, but has a more general application across the public sector generally. It seems likely, therefore, that the sorts of coping strategies in evidence in Poppleton are being used in other health-service organizations and more widely by those involved in the delivery of public services generally. The result of this will be to generate variations in access to services and to undermine attempts to standardize service provision. Whilst these outcomes run contrary to the equity goals set for the system by the state, they maintain its ability to deliver services. 'Rational' analyses, in failing to take this into account, provide solutions which are both partial and flawed. The consequences of adopting such solutions would be to close down the system's life-support system. In this sense, the pursuit of rationality is itself irrational.

THE CHANGING POLICY CONTEXT AND THE PROSPECTS FOR RATIONAL DECISION-MAKING IN THE NEW NHS

The research was undertaken at a time of enormous change in the NHS and these changes are part of a radical programme of reform in relation to the organizational and political context of local health commissioning which is still in progress (Department of Health 1997, 2000).

First, a whole raft of measures aimed at making GPs more accountable for their actions has been introduced. The thrust of policy has been to align clinical and budgetary responsibility in primary care, with PCGs now being replaced by PCTs. These organizations bring together commissioning and primary-care development with the provision of community health services. The expansion of the Personal Medical Services scheme, which pays GPs a salary on the basis of meeting set quality standards, instead of working to a standard national contract, means that salaried GPs will come to form a growing number of family doctors. As much of the freedom enjoyed by GPs derives from their status as independent contractors, these reforms can be seen as a move to bring them inside the NHS, at the same time making them subject to greater top-down controls over their actions. The government expects that salaried GPs will comprise the majority of GPs by 2004, by which time a revised national contract reflecting an emphasis on quality and improved outcomes will be introduced for all GPs (Department of Health 2000).

Second, a number of initiatives are being pursued which are designed to encourage clinicians to improve quality and reduce variations in access to care by following standardized approaches to care. The National Institute for Clinical Excellence (NICE) has produced guidance in relation to the dissemination of new technologies and PCGs are expected to follow this guidance. NSFs for a range of service areas outline minimum standards of care and contain clear timetables for their implementation with those who provide and commission care being expected to demonstrate progress on key NSF milestones. These initiatives can be seen as an attempt to impose bureaucratic calculable rules to resolve the problems of inequalities in access to care. Some commentators have identified this trend towards 'rational', top-down, 'scientific' solutions or 'scientific-bureaucratic medicine' in both the UK and the US (Harrison *et al.* 2002). However, the inadequacy of the evidence base for many interventions means that far from being independently generated 'technical' solutions, the guidelines are in some cases the result of a professional consensus based on judgement, rather than RCTs, but presented as evidence-based medicine nevertheless.

A third change relates to Labour's supposed 'third way', which involved neither a 'return to the old centralized command and control systems of the 1970s' nor 'a continuation of the divisive internal market system of the 1990s'. In order to pursue its aim of renewing the NHS as a 'genuinely national service with fair access to consistently high quality, prompt and accessible services right across the country' (Department of Health 1997: 2.4), the government appears to be reverting to the old centralized command and control systems, from which it was at pains to distance itself in *The New NHS: Modern, Dependable*. Previous administrations relied on discretionary 'guidance', which allowed HAs some flexibility in terms of strategies required to balance books. However, New Labour's move towards a more directive approach limits room for manoeuvre at local level. Implementation of standards will be overseen and performance measured according to a range of indicators, with poor results provoking intervention from the centre. This marks a break with previous arrangements whereby poor or nonexistent implementation ensured peaceful coexistence for the rhetoric of quality and the reality of scarce resources. Although 'local doctors and nurses who are in the best position to know what patients need will be in the driving seat in shaping services' (Department of Health 1997: 2.4), their ability to shape services will be severely constrained by the requirements placed on them to meet top-down, non-negotiable directives from limited resources.

Rising public expectations have been a feature of the health service landscape in the UK in recent decades. However, rather than tackling these rising expectations, the government's approach has been to raise them further. In an effort to 'rebuild public confidence in the NHS as a public service, accountable to patients, open to the public and shaped by their views', the new NHS promises that patients will be treated on the basis of need and need alone (Department of Health 1997: 2.13). Government policy documents designed to promote public confidence steer clear of talk of priority-setting. Instead, performance guarantees are provided which serve only to increase expectations still further.

A superficial reading of these changes might suggest greater scope for the application of rational priority-setting techniques, particularly as the language of economics is conspicuous in the policy documents announcing these changes. Barriers to the use of health economics identified by health economists prior to the current reforms included the inflexible NHS finance regime, the asymmetry of information between purchasers and providers of care and the lack of evidence on which to base commissioning decisions. By 2004, PCTs and new 'Care Trusts' (which will be able to commission and deliver primary and community care for older people and other client groups) will control 75 per cent of NHS funding.

The extension of the salaried GP scheme means that trust managers will have greater control over GPs than their counterparts at Poppleton ever did. PCTs will commission and provide care, and evidence gaps will be plugged by NICE which provides guidance on the cost-effectiveness of new drugs and technologies. Changes to the finance regime mean that savings in one part of the PCT budget can be used to fund developments elsewhere in the system. However, the issue of conflicting values at the heart of the debate on health-care resource allocation remains unresolved. The existence of multiple and competing goals, which are not amenable to explicit prioritization will remain a feature of local decision-making.

The requirements to eradicate postcode prescribing, promote local flexibility, meet higher standards of care, improve outcomes and balance budgets seems likely to perpetuate the need to develop strategies to avoid conflict. How, for example, is a PCT to respond to a decision by NICE to endorse a new drug or a NSF requirement to provide optimal treatment for a group of patients if explicit rationing is outlawed and additional resources are not available? What seems certain is that the preoccupation of health economists with methodological refinements, designed to increase the use of 'rational' methods is misguided. Where values conflict, such conflict cannot be resolved by an appeal to scientific enquiry or the formulation of calculable rules. In other words, the barriers to the use of health economics in practice are not amenable to speedy resolution by resort to 'rational' methods as they concern relationships of power, legitimacy and puzzlement at the heart of NHS decision-making.

NOTE

1 There are some exceptions to this, for example in the areas of tattoo removal and of infertility treatment, where some HAs have sought to ration explicitly on the grounds that the contribution to health is doubtful or at best diffuse.

REFERENCES

Allison, G. (1971) *Essence of Decision. Explaining the Cuban Missile Crisis*. Boston: Little, Brown and Company.

Ashmore, M., Mulkay, M. and Pinch, T. (1989) *Health and Efficiency*. Milton Keynes: Open University Press.

Audit Commission (1994) *Aspects of Managing Community and Hospital Services*. London: HMSO.

Bachrach, P. and Baratz, M. (1963) Decisions and nondecisions: an analytical framework, *American Political Science Review*, 57: 641–51.

Bachrach, P. and Baratz, M. (1970) *Power and Poverty, Theory and Practice*. New York: Oxford University Press.

Barnes, M., Harrison, S., Mort, M., Shardlow, P. and Wistow, G. (1999) The new management of community care: user groups, citizenship and co-production, in G. Stoker (ed.) *The New Management of British Local Governance*. Basingstoke: Macmillan.

Becker, H. and Geer, B. (1960) Participant observation: the analysis of qualitative field data, in R. Adams and J. Preiss (eds) *Human Organization Research: Field Relations and Techniques*. Homewood Illinois: Dorsey Press.

Becker, H., Geer, B., Hughes, E.C. and Strauss, A.L. (1961) *Boys in White: Student Culture in Medical School*. Chicago: University of Chicago Press.

Brambleby, P. (1995) A survivor's guide to programme budgeting, *Health Policy*, 33: 127–45.

Braybrooke, D. and Lindblom, C. (1963) *A Strategy of Decision*. New York: The Free Press.

Carley, M. (1981) *Rational Techniques in Policy Analysis*. London: Heinemann Educational.

Carr-Hill, R., Sheldon, T., Smith, P. *et al.* (1994) Allocating resources to health authorities: development of method for small area analysis of use of inpatient services, *British Medical Journal*, 309: 1046–9.

Cawson, A. and Saunders, P. (1983) Corporatism, competitive politics and class struggle, in R. King (ed.) *Capital and Politics*. London: Routledge and Kegan Paul.

Charatan, F. (2001) Bayer decides to withdraw cholesterol-lowering drug, *British Medical Journal*, 323: 359.

Churchman, C. (1958) *Challenge to Reason*. New York: McGraw-Hill.

Cleland, J. and Swedberg, K. (1996) Carvedilol for heart failure, with care, *The Lancet*, 347: 1199–201.

Cohen, D. (1994) Marginal analysis in practice: an alternative to needs assessment for contracting health care, *British Medical Journal*, 309: 781–5.

Cohen, D. (1995) Messages from Mid Glamorgan: a multi-programme experiment with marginal analysis, *Health Policy*, 33: 147–55.

Cohen, M., March, J. and Olsen, J. (1972) A garbage can model of organizational choice, *Adminstrative Science Quarterly*, 17(1): 1–25.

Craig, N., Parkin, D. and Gerard, K. (1995) Clearing the fog on the Tyne: programme budgeting in Newcastle and North Tyneside Health Authority, *Health Policy*, 33: 107–25.

Culyer, A. (1996) The impact of health economics on public policy, *Conferencia Inaugural do 5 Encontro Nacional de Economia da Saude*. Lisbon Associacao Portuguesa de Economia da Saude.

Culyer, A. (1997) Maximizing the health of the whole community. The case for, *British Medical Journal*, 314: 667–9.

Dahl, R. (1957) The concept of power, *Behavioural Science*, 2: 201–5.

Dargie, H. and McMurray, J. (1994) Diagnosis and management of heart failure, *British Medical Journal*, 308: 321–8.

Department of Health (1989) *Working for Patients*, Cmnd 555. London: HMSO.

Department of Health (1992) *The Health of the Nation: A Strategy for Health in England*. London: HMSO.

Department of Health (1995) *Public Health, The National Health Service and Social Care. Statement of Responsibilities and Accountabilities*. London: HMSO.

Department of Health (1997) *The New NHS: Modern, Dependable*. London: The Stationery Office.

Department of Health (1998a) *The New NHS Modern and Dependable: A National Framework for Assessing Performance. Consultation Document*. London: The Stationery Office.

Department of Health (1998b) *Our Healthier Nation: A Contract for Health*. London: The Stationery Office.

Department of Health (2000) *The NHS Plan*. London: The Stationery Office.

Detsky, A.D., Redelmeier, D. and Abrams, H.B. (1987) What's wrong with decision analysis? Can the left brain influence the right?, *Journal of Chronic Disease*, 40(9): 831–6.

Dolan, P., Cookson, R. and Ferguson, B. (1999) Effect of discussion and deliberation on the public's view of priority setting in health care: focus group study, *British Medical Journal*, 318: 916–19.

Donaldson, C. (1995) Economics, public health and health care purchasing: reinventing the wheel?, *Health Policy*, 33: 79–90.

Donaldson, C. and Farrar, S. (1993) Needs assessment: developing an economic approach, *Health Policy*, 25: 95–108.

Donaldson, L., Kirkup, W., Craig, N. and Parkin, D. (1994) Lanterns in the jungle: is the NHS driven by the wrong kind of efficiency?, *Public Health*, 108(1): 3–9.

Drummond, M., Cooke, J. and Walley, T. (1996) *Economic Evaluation in Health Care Decision Making: Evidence from the UK, Discussion Paper 148*. York: University of York.

Drummond, M., Cooke, J. and Walley, T. (1997) Economic evaluation under managed competition: evidence from the UK, *Social Science and Medicine*, 45(4): 583–95.

Duthie, T., Trueman, P., Chancellor, J. and Diez, L. (1999) Research into the use of health economics in decision making in the United Kingdom – Phase II. Is health economics 'for good or evil?', *Health Policy*, 46: 143–57.

Elmore, R. (1978) Organizational models of social program implementation, *Public Policy*, 26: 185–228.

Evans, R. (1990) The dog in the night-time, in T. Andersen and G. Mooney (eds) *The Challenges of Medical Practice Variations*. Basingstoke: Macmillan.

Ferguson, B. and Baker, M. (1997) Shifting finance out of acute hospitals, *Journal of Health Services Research and Policy*, 3(1): 2–4.

Flynn, R., Williams, G. and Pickard, S. (1996) *Markets and Networks*. Buckingham: Open University Press.

Flyvbjerg, B. (1998) *Rationality and Power*. Chicago: The University of Chicago Press.

Fox, A. (1974) *Beyond Contract*. London: Faber and Faber.

Fukayama, F. (1995) *Trust*. New York: The Free Press.

Gambetta, D. (1988) Can we trust trust?, in D. Gambetta (ed.) *Trust: Making and Breaking Co-operative Relations*. Oxford: Basil Blackwell.

Gans, H. (1982) The participant observer as a human being: observations on the personal aspects of field work, in R. Burgess (ed.) *Field Research: A Sourcebook and Field Manual*. London: George Allen & Unwin.

Giddens, A. (1991) *The Consequences of Modernity*. London: Polity Press.

Gold, R. (1958) Roles in sociological field observations, *Social Forces*, 36: 217–23.

Granovetter, M. (1985) Economic action and social structure: the problem of embeddedness, *American Journal of Sociology*, 91(3): 481–510.

Gravelle, H. and Rees, R. (1992) *Microeconomics*. London: Longman.

Green, C. (1998) Marginal analysis: experiences in Rotherham, SCHARR unpublished working paper.

Gunn, L. (1978) Why is implementation so difficult?, *Management Services in Government*, 33(4): 169–76.

Harrison, S. (1981) The politics of health manpower, in A. Long and G. Mercer (eds) *Manpower Planning in the National Health Service*. Farnborough: Gower Press.

Harrison, S. (1985) Perspectives on implementation, in A. Long and S. Harrison (eds) *Health Services Performance*. London: Croom Helm.

Harrison, S. (1996) *Northern and Yorkshire Regional Health Authority Purchasing Intelligence Project: An Evaluation Study*. Leeds: NHSE (Northern and Yorkshire) and Nuffield Institute for Health, University of Leeds.

Harrison, S. (1998a) The Politics of evidence-based medicine in the United Kingdom, *Policy and Politics*, 26(1): 15–31.

Harrison, S. (1998b) Evidence-based medicine in the National Health Service: towards the history of a policy, in R. Skelton and V. Williamson (eds) *Fifty Years of the National Health Service*. Sussex: University of Brighton.

Harrison, S., Hunter, D. and Pollitt, C. (1990) *The Dynamics of British Health Policy*. London: Unwin Hyman.

Harrison, S., Hunter, D., Marnoch, G. and Pollitt, C. (1992) *Just Managing: Power and Culture in the National Health Service*. Basingstoke: Macmillan.

Harrison, S., Moran, M. and Wood, B. (2002) Policy emergence and policy convergence: the case of 'scientific-bureaucratic' medicine, *British Journal of Politics and International Relations*, Vol. 4.

Harrop, M. (1992) *Power and Policy in Liberal Democracies*. Cambridge: Cambridge University Press.

Hart, J., Rhodes, G. and McMurray, J. (1993) The cost-effectiveness of enalapril in the treatment of chronic heart failure, *British Journal of Medical Economics*, 6: 91–8.

Heclo, H. (1975) Social politics and policy impacts, in M. Holden and D. Dresang (eds) *What Government Does*. Beverly Hills: Sage.

Henderson, L.R. and Scott, A. (2001) The costs of caring for stroke patients in a GP-led community hospital: an application of programme budgeting and marginal analysis, *Health and Social Care in the Community*, 9(4): 244–54.

Henshall, C. and Drummond, M. (1992) *Economic Appraisal in the British National Health Service: Implications of Recent Developments*, paper prepared for an EC Workshop on the Role of Economic Appraisal in Developing Policy for Health Technology, Iráklion Crete.

Hickson, D.J., Hinings, C.R., Lee, C.A., Schneck, R.E. and Pennings, J.M. (1971) A strategic contingencies' theory of intraorganizational power, *Administrative Science Quarterly*, 16: 216–29.

Hill, M. (1997) *The Policy Process in the Modern State*. New York: Prentice Hall/Harvester Wheatsheaf.

Hoffman, C. and von der Schulenburg, J. (2000) The influence of economic evaluation studies on decision making. A European survey, *Health Policy*, 52(3): 179–92.

Hunter, D. (1980) Coping with uncertainty: decisions and resources within health authorities, *Sociology of Health and Illness*, 1(1): 41–66.

Hunter, D. (1991) Pain of going public, *Health Service Journal*, 29 August.

Hurst, J. (1998) The impact of health economics on health policy in England and the impact of health policy on health economics 1972–1997, *Health Economics*, 7: S47–S62, Suppl 1.

Jabes, J. (1978) *Individual Processes in Organizational Behaviour*. Arlington Heights, IL: AHM Publishing Corporation.

Johannesson, M. and Jonsson, B. (1997) Cost-effectiveness of Simvastatin treatment to lower cholesterol levels in patients with coronary heart disease, *New England Journal of Medicine*, 336(5): 332–6.

Kingdon, J. (1994) *Agendas, Alternatives and Public Policies*. New York: Harper Collins.

Klein, R. (1995) *The New Politics of the National Health Service*. London: Longman.

Klein, R. (1999) Grating expectations, *The Guardian*, October 20: 8–9.

Klein, R. (2000) *The New Politics of the National Health Service*. New York: Prentice Hall.

Klein, R., Day, P. and Redmayne, S. (1996) *Managing Scarcity*. Buckingham: Open University Press.

Levine, J., Musheno, M. and Palumbo, D. (1975) The limits of rational choice in evaluating criminal justice policy, quoted in Carley, M. (1981) *Rational Techniques in Policy Analysis*. London: Heinemann Educational.

Lindblom, C. (1959) The science of muddling through, *Public Administration Review*, 19: 78–88.

Lindblom, C. (1979) Still muddling, not yet through, *Public Administration Review*, 39(6): 517–25.

Lindblom, C. and Woodhouse, E.J. (1993) *The Policy-making Process*. Englewood Cliffs, NJ: Prentice-Hall.

Lipsky, M. (1980) *Street-level Bureaucracy*. New York: Russell Sage.

Lockett, T., Raftery, J. and Richards, J. (1995) The strengths and limitations of programme budgeting, in F.R. Honigsbaum, J. Richards and T. Lockett (eds) *Priority Setting in Action*. Oxford: Radcliffe Medical Press.

Lukes, S. (1974) *Power: A Radical View*. Basingstoke: Macmillan.

Madden, L., Hussey, R., Mooney, G. and Church, E. (1995) Public-health and economics in tandem – program budgeting, marginal analysis and priority setting in practice, *Health Policy*, 33:(2) 161–8.

March, J. (1994) *A Primer on Decision Making*. New York: The Free Press.

March, J. and Olsen, J. (1976) *Ambiguity and Choice in Organizations*. Oslo: Universitetsforlaget.

Maynard, A. (1996) Lean, mean rationing machine, *Health Service Journal*, 1 February: 21.

McNamee, P. and Godber, E. (1995) *Experiences of using health economics in commissioning,* paper presented to Health Economics Study Group meeting.

Metcalfe, L. and Richards, S. (1990) *Improving Public Management.* London: Sage.

Miller, L. and Vale, P. (1997) *A synthesis of two independent surveys of purchaser views on the use of Programme Budgeting and Marginal Analysis. Evidence of the need for national guidance?,* paper presented at Health Economics Study Group meeting.

Mort, M., Harrison, S. and Wistow, G. (1996) The user card: picking through the organizational undergrowth in health and social care, *Contemporary Political Studies,* Vol. 2: 1133–40.

Mulkay, M., Ashmore, M. and Pinch, T. (1991) Dependency and despair: health economics and the health-care system, in J. Hutton, S. Hutton, T. Pinch and A. Shiell (eds) *Dependency to Enterprise.* London: Routledge.

Murphy, E., Dingwall, R., Greatbatch, D., Parker, S. and Watson, P. (1998) Qualitative research methods in health technology assessment: a review of the literature, *Health Technology Assessment Report,* 2(16).

NHSE (1998a) *Health Authority Revenue Allocations 1999/2000.* Leeds: Department of Health.

NHSE (1998b) *National Service Framework on Coronary Heart Disease Emerging Findings Report.* Leeds, Department of Health.

NHSE (1999a) *The NHS Performance Assessment Framework.* Leeds: Department of Health.

NHSE (1999b) *Faster Access to Modern Treatment: How NICE Appraisal Will Work.* Leeds: Department of Health.

Niskanen, W. (1971) *Bureaucracy and Representative Government.* Chicago: Aldine-Atherton.

Offe, C. (1984) *Contradictions of the Welfare State.* London: Hutchinson.

Olsen, J. (1976) Choice in organized anarchy, in J. March and J. Olsen (eds) *Ambiguity and Choice in Organizations.* Bergen: Universitetsforlaget.

Pfeffer, J. (1981) *Power in Organizations.* Boston (Mass): Pitman.

Pfeffer, J. and Salancik, G. (1978) *The External Control of Organizations: A Resource Dependence Perspective.* New York: Harper and Row.

Pharaoh, P. and Hollingworth, W. (1996) Cost-effectiveness of lowering cholesterol concentration with statins in patients with and without pre-existing coronary heart disease: life table method applied to health authority population, *British Medical Journal,* 312: 1443–8.

Poses, R., Cebul, R. and Wigton, R.S. (1995) You can lead a horse to water – improving physicians' knowledge of probabilities may not affect their decisions, *Medical Decision Making,* 15: 65–75.

Posnett, J. and Street, A. (1996) Programme budgeting and marginal analysis: an approach in need of refinement, *Journal of Health Services Research and Policy,* 1(3): 147–53.

Raftery, J., Robinson, R., Mulligan, J. and Forrest, S. (1996) Contracting in the NHS quasi-market, *Health Economics,* 5(4): 353–62.

Ranade, W. (1997) *A Future for the NHS? Health Care for the Millennium.* London: Longman.

Ratcliffe, J., Donaldson, C. and Macphee, S. (1996) Programme budgeting and marginal analysis: a case study of maternity services, *Journal of Public Health Medicine*, 18(2): 175–82.

Rhodes, R. (1995) *The New Governance: Governing without Government.* The State of Britain, Seminar 2, ESRC/RSA.

Rhodes, R. (1997) *Understanding governance: Policy Networks, Governance, Reflexivity and Accountability.* Buckingham: Open University Press.

Rhodes, R. (1999) Foreword, in G. Stoker (ed.) *The New Management of Community Care: User Groups, Citizenship and Co-Production.* Basingstoke: Macmillan.

Ritzer, G. and Walczak, D. (1988) Rationalization and deprofessionalisation of physicians, *Social Forces*, 67: 1–22.

Ruta, D., Donaldson, C. and Gilray, I. (1996) Economics, public health and health care purchasing: the Tayside experience of programme budgeting and marginal analysis, *Journal of Health Services Research and Policy*, 1(4): 185–93.

Sackett, D., Rosenberg, W., Gray, J.A.M., Haynes, R.B. and Richardson, W.S. (1996) Evidence-based medicine: what it is and what it isn't, *British Medical Journal*, 312: 71–2.

Sacks, F.M., Pfeffer, M.A. and Moye, L.A. (1996) The effect of Pravastatin on coronary events after myocardial infarction in patients with average cholesterol levels, *New England Journal of Medicine*, 335(14): 1001–9.

Salaman, G. (1978) *Work Organizations: Resistance and Control.* London: Longman.

Sanders, C., Egger, M., Donovan, J., Tallon, D. and Frankel, S. (1998) Reporting on quality of life in randomized controlled trials. A bibliographic study, *British Medical Journal*, 317: 1191–4.

Scandinavian Simvastatin Survival Study Group (1994) Baseline serum cholesterol and treatment effect in the Scandinavian simvastatin survival study (4S), *The Lancet*, 344: 1383–9.

Schatzman, L. and Strauss, A. (1973) *Field Research: Strategies for a Natural Sociology.* Englewood Cliffs, NJ: Prentice Hall.

Schmitter, P. (1974) Still the century of corporatism?, *Review of Politics*, 36: 85–131.

Scobie, S., Basnett, I. and McCartney, P. (1995) Can general practice data be used for needs assessment and health-care planning in an inner-London district?, *Journal of Public Health Medicine*, 17(4): 475–83.

Scott, A., Currie, N. and Donaldson, C. (1998) Evaluating innovation in general practice: a pragmatic framework using programme budgeting and marginal analysis, *Family Practice*, 15(3): 216–22.

Shepherd, J., Cobbe, S.M. and Ford, I. (1995) Prevention of coronary heart disease with pravastatin in men with hypercholesterolemia, *New England Journal of Medicine*, 333: 1301–7.

Simon, H. (1945) *Administrative Behaviour.* New York: Free Press.

Smith, G. and May, D. (1980) The artificial debate between rationalist and incrementalist models of decision making, *Policy and Politics*, 8(2): 147–61.

Smith, M. (1993) *Pressure Power and Policy: State, Autonomy and Policy Networks in Britain and the United States*. Hemel Hempstead: Harvester Wheatsheaf.

SOLVD Investigators (1991) Effect of enalapril on survival in patients with reduced left ventricular ejection fractions and congestive failure, *New England Journal of Medicine*, 325: 293–302.

SOLVD Investigators (1992) Effect of enalapril on mortality and the development of heart failure in asymptomatic patients with reduced left ventricular ejection fractions and congestive failure, *New England Journal of Medicine*, 327: 685–91.

Standing Medical Advisory Committee (SMAC) (1997) *The Use of Statins*. London: The Department of Health.

Stevens, A. and Gillam, S. (1998) Needs assessment: from theory to practice, *British Medical Journal*, 316: 1448–52.

Stocking, B. (1995) Why research findings are not used by commissions and what can be done about it, *Journal of Public Health Medicine*, 17(4): 380–2.

Stoykova, B., Drummond, M., Hoffman, C., Nixon, J. and Glanville, J. (2000) *The usefulness and limitations of published economic evaluations for NHS decision-making*, paper presented at the Health Economists Study Group meeting Nottingham, July.

Street, A., Posnett, J. and Davis, P. (1995) *Marginal analysis of dementia services*, Consortium report 2002a. York Health Economics Consortium, University of York.

Sutherland, S. (1992) *Irrationality*. London: Penguin.

Tanenbaum, S. (1994) Knowing and acting in medical practice: outcomes research, *Journal of Health Politics, Policy and Law*, 19(1): 27–44.

Twaddle, S. and Walker, A. (1995) Programme budgeting and marginal analysis: application within programmes to assist purchasing in Greater Glasgow Health Board, *Health Policy*, 33: 91–105.

Van Hout, B., Weilink, G. and Bounsel, G.J. (1993) Effects of ACE inhibitors in heart failure in the Netherlands. A pharmacoeconomic model, *Pharmacoeconomics*, 3: 387–97.

Walley, T., Barton, S., Cooke, J. and Drummond, M. (1997) Economic evaluations of drug therapy: attitudes of primary care prescribing advisers in Great Britain, *Health Policy*, 41(1997): 61–72.

Weber, M. (1947) *The Theory of Social and Economic Organization*. Trans Henderson, A.M., Parsons, T. New York: Free Press.

Weber, M. (1978) *Economy and Society*. Los Angeles: University of California Press.

Wheeldon, N., MacDonald, T., Flucker, C.J. *et al.* (1993) Echocardiography in chronic heart failure in the community, *Quarterly Journal of Medicine*, 86(1): 17–23.

White, M. (1999) Professing a need to keep taking the tablets, *Health Services Journal*, 109(5667): 17.

Williams, A. (2000) Setting priorities: what is holding us back – inadequate information or inadequate institutions?, in A. Coulter and C. Ham (eds) *The Global Challenge of Healthcare Rationing*. Buckingham: Open University Press.

Wolcott, H. (1995) Making a study more ethnographic, in V. Maanen (ed.) *Representation in Ethnography*. Beverly Hills: Sage.

INDEX

accountability
  of GPs, 46–7, 167
  of HAs, 44–6
  and relationships of low and
    high trust, 47–53
ACE (angiotensin-converting
    enzyme) inhibitors, and
    heart failure management,
    132, 133, 135, 139, 140, 150,
    159
AF (atrial fibrillation) guidelines,
    141
age of patients
  and decisions on statin
    treatment, 85, 86–7, 90, 126,
    129
  and heart failure management
    plans, 135
agenda setting, 40
Allison, G., 12, 13
ambiguity
  in decision-making, 160–1
    garbage-can model of, 16–17,
      21, 24
AMI (acute myocardial infarction)
    patients, 69
Ashurst NHS Trust, and Baxby
    PCG, 123, 125
aspirin, and CHD patients, 90, 96,
    113

Bachrach, P., 21
Bagust, Adrian, 101–2, 103, 105,
    111
Baratz, M., 21
Barnes, M., 72
Baxby PCG, 123–51
  developing a statins guideline,
    123–32
    and affordability, 127–8, 131–2
    and age of patients, 126,
      129–30
    choice of statin, 126–7
    and hyperlipidaemia
      management, 123–4
    and nurses, 131
    and patient management,
      128–9
    and patient risk factors, 124–6,
      131
    and SMAC guidelines, 110, 129
    and target groups, 127
  echocardiography services,
    132–3, 134, 141, 144, 149–50,
    156
  GPs and decision-making, 158,
    161
  heart failure management plan
    for, 132–41
    and ACE inhibitors, 132, 133,
      135–7, 139, 140, 150, 159

Baxby PCG – *continued*
  and AF guidelines, 141
  and age of patients, 135
  and beta-blockers, 140
  conflicting views on, 134–6
  and decision-making, 158
  July group meeting, 136–9
  launching the heart-failure
    guidelines, 144–6
  November meeting, 139–41
  October group meeting, 139
  locality manager, 122, 123
  rapid access chest pain clinic,
    142–4, 146–50
  funding, 147–50
BCS (British Cardiac Society), 59
beta-blockers
  and CHD patients, 113
  and heart failure management at
    Baxby PCG, 140
Bevan, Aneurin, 116
bounded rational decision-making,
  11–13, 19, 157
  and health economics, 159–60
  at Poppleton HA, 155
Brambleby, P., 33, 38
British Medical Association, 14
budgets
  introduction of unified, 63
  Poppleton HA, 43–4, 64
    GMS, 118
  and statins, 92
bureaucracy
  formal rationality, 9–10
  and New Labour, 64–7
  street-level bureaucrats, 25, 164

CABGs (Coronary Artery Bypass
  Grafts), 96, 98, 100, 115,
  117, 119
calculative specificity of
  reciprocation, 48–9
CARE (Cholesterol and Recurrent

Events) trial, older patients
  and statins, 126
Care Trusts, 168
Carley, M., 8–9
causality, and garbage-can
  decision-making, 16
ceteris paribus assumption, and
  economic evaluation, 31
CHD (coronary heart disease), 4
  and Baxby PCG
    developing a statins guideline,
      123–32
    heart failure management
      plan, 132–41, 144–6, 158
    rapid access chest pain clinic,
      142–4, 146–50, 147–50
  and HA performance
    measurement, 56, 57, 58
  NSF for, 65
  in Poppleton HA, 57, 67–76
    and pain relief for intractable
      angina, 112
    and stakeholder involvement,
      70–1, 75, 102–10
    and statin treatment, 77–93,
      94–5
    tertiary cardiology services,
      49–50, 74, 95–7, 98,
      113–17
    and the York CHD model,
      101–21
  tracking of patients, 53
chest pain clinics, 111–12, 134,
  142–4, 146–50
  and decision-making, 158, 159
CHI (Commission for Health
  Improvement), 64
choice opportunities, and
  garbage-can
  decision-making, 17
Cholesterol and Recurrent Events,
  see CARE (Cholesterol and
  Recurrent Events) trial

citizenship, and street-level
   bureaucrats, 25
clinical governance, 64
clinical trials, and health economic
   evaluations at local level, 29
Cochrane Collaboration, 42
Cohen, D., 37, 38
Cohen, M., 16, 18
command and control NHS model,
   and New Labour, 62, 66,
   168
Commission for Health
   Improvement (CHI), 64
commissioning health care, 41–2,
   59
community nurses, and Primary
   Care Groups (PCGs), 3–4
compromise, and pluralistic
   models of decision-making,
   13
coping strategies
   and decision-making, 165–6
   and HA performance
      measurement, 56
Coronary Artery Bypass Grafts,
   see CABGs (Coronary
   Artery Bypass Grafts)
coronary heart disease, *see* CHD
   (coronary heart disease)
coronary stents, 98
cost-effectiveness
   analysis of statins
      (cholesterol-lowering
      drugs), 76, 77–93
   cognitive problems of
      cost-effectiveness studies,
      30
   commissioning health care, 59
   and the efficiency index, 53
   and health economics, 41–2
   and NICE, 64
   and NSFs, 65
Craig, N., 33

Dahl, Robert, 21
decision tree software, and CHD
   patients, 100–1
decision-making
   conflicting values and objectives
      in, 152–3
   and the 'do nothing' option, 78
   and health economics, 2–3, 4,
      152–69
      in practice at local level,
         26–31, 39
   and health-care purchasing, 41
   and knowledge, 61, 162–3
   literature on, 28, 31–40
   models of
      bounded rational, 11–13, 19,
         155, 157, 159–60
      external control, 14–16, 20,
         155, 161–2
      garbage can, 16–18, 20–1, 24,
         40, 157–8
      incremental, 19–20
      pluralistic, 13–14, 20, 155
      unitary, 11, 18–19
   and power relations, 14, 20, 21–2
   rational, 8–9, 153–4
      and the Baxby chest pain
         clinic, 147–50
      and health economics, 164–6
      in the new NHS, 166–9
   see also HAs (health
      authorities),
      decision-making
democracy, and rationality, 22
Detsky, A.D., 34, 150
diagnostic tests, and CHD patients,
   106–10
dietary modification, reducing
   cholesterol levels through,
   79–80, 91, 92
disease prevalence, and health
   economic evaluations at
   local level, 29

disjointed incrementalism, 12
Dobson, Frank, 116, 118
doctors
    and decision-making
        PBMA studies, 38
        pluralist theories of, 20
        power of, 23, 39
        rationality and
            implementation problems,
            33
    see also GPs (general
        practitioners)
drug therapy, cost effectiveness
    analyses of, 36, 39
Drummond, M., 30, 36, 39
Duthie, T., 34
dynamic and uncertain systems, at
    Poppleton HA, 71–3

ECGs, and CHD patients in
    Poppleton HA, 106, 109
echocardiography
    at Baxby PCG, 132–3, 134, 141,
        144, 149–50, 156
    at Poppleton HA, 106–7, 113,
        132–3
ECRs (extra contractual referrals),
    60
effectiveness
    in commissioning health care, 59
    see also cost-effectiveness
efficiency, New Labour on the
    NHS and, 62, 65
efficiency index, as a measure of
    HA performance, 53–5
Enlightenment, and rationality, 22,
    23
evidence-based medicine, 42, 167
    and guidelines for the use of
        statins, 77, 88, 89, 126–7
excellence, New Labour on the
    NHS and, 62
external control models of
    decision-making, 14–16, 20

at Poppleton HA, 155
and health economics, 161–2

field notes, 6
financial scandals in the NHS, 1
Flynn, R., 49
Flyvbjerg, B., 22–3, 24–5, 61
formal rationality, and New
    Labour, 64–7
Fox, A., 48–9, 50

Gans, Herbert, 5
garbage can model of
    decision-making, 16–18,
    20–1, 24, 40
    and health economics, 157–8
Giddens, A., 47–8, 51
Gold, R., 5
governance
    clinical governance system, 64
    and fragmented service agencies,
        33
    and HA accountability, 45
GPs (general practitioners)
    accountability, 46–7, 167
    and Baxby rapid access chest
        pain clinic, 142–3, 146–7,
        148–50
    and CHD patients, 107
    and decision-making, 156–7, 158,
        161, 165
        bounded rational, 159–60
        implementation, 34
        and knowledge, 163
        pluralist, 20
        power of, 25, 39
    fundholders, 41, 43–4
    and heart failure management at
        Baxby PCG, 133–4, 136–8
    'more is better' attitude of, 151
    in the new NHS, 167, 169
    prescribing behaviour, 118
    and Primary Care Groups
        (PCGs), 3–4, 63–4

and statins treatment, 78, 89, 124, 125, 128–9, 130, 131, 163
Granovetter, M., 47, 49
Green, C., 32, 39, 121
Griffiths reforms, 1, 23
Gunn, L., model of perfect implementation, 33

Harrison, S., 14, 19, 23, 32–3, 39
  on decision-making, 10–11, 39–40
HAs (health authorities), 1, 41–76
  accountability, 44–6
  commissioning health care, 59
  decision-making
    and bounded rationality, 19
    cognitive problems in, 30
    and common objectives, 155–6
    and financial resources, 35
    and managers, 25–6, 60–2, 164–5
    and PBMA studies, 36–7
    pluralist, 20
    power and rationality in, 23–6, 39
    and public choice theories, 14
    pursuing many objectives simultaneously, 155
    rationality and implementation, 34
    and uncertainty, 60–2
  and New Labour, 62–7
  performance measurement, 53–8
  purchasers, 41
    and relationships of trust, 49
  replacement by Strategic HAs, 46
  see also Poppleton HA
HAZs (Health Action Zones), 63
Health Action Zones (HAZs), 63
Health Economics Study Group (HESG), 2
health visitors, and heart failure management plans, 133

health-care purchasing reforms, 41
heart failure management plan, for Baxby PCG, 132–41, 144–6, 158
Heclo, H., 20, 39
HESG (Health Economics Study Group), 2
hospitals
  admissions of CHD patients, 68–70, 97–8, 100
  closure of local, 90
  emergency cardiac and respiratory admissions, 137
  information systems, 52–3
  management of emergency medical admissions, 55
  managers, 33
  patient discharges and the efficiency index, 54
  problems of releasing resources, 35–6
  reduction in admissions to, 71–2
  Salford and Trafford HA, 116–17
Hunter, D., 20, 37, 39–40
hyperlipidaemia, management of, and Baxby PCG, 123–4

implementation
  and rationality, 10, 29, 32–7
    bounded rational theories, 13
    external control models, 16
    and pluralistic models of decision-making, 14
  incremental models of decision-making, 12, 19–20
  infertility treatment, 169
  information deficits, and CHD at Poppleton HA, 73–5
  intentionality, and garbage-can decision-making, 16
  internal market in the NHS, and New Labour, 62–3

Kingdon, J., 18, 40
Klein, R., 37, 46, 66
knowledge, and decision-making, 61, 162–3

Lindblom, C., 12
Lipsky, M., 25, 164
local health commissioning, 166
local level, health economics in practice at, 26–31, 39
local responsibility, New Labour on the NHS and, 62
Lockett, T., 32
Lukes, Stephen, 21, 22, 23

MA (marginal analysis), 32, 33–4
    at Poppleton HA, 70
Machiavelli, N., 22, 23
management, symbolic role of, 15–16
managers
    HA
        and decision-making, 25–6, 60–2, 164–5
        'dominant personalities', 38
        and PBMA studies, 36–7
        hospital managers, 33
        tertiary trust research and development, 24, 74
March, J., 16, 17
marginal analyis, *see* MA (marginal analysis)
Marxist theories, and external control theory, 14–15
maximizing health, and HA objectives and performance monitoring, 57
MI (Myocardial infarction) patients
    guidelines on the use of statins for, 84–5
    and heart failure, 132
    at Poppleton HA, 68, 69, 73–4

Milburn, Alan, 118
Miller, L., 36, 37

National Institute for Clinical Excellence (NICE), 64, 66, 167, 169
National Service Framework on Coronary Heart Disease Emerging Findings Report, 140–1
national service frameworks *see* NSFs (national service frameworks)
neo-elitist theories of organization, 14
New Labour
    and formal rationality, 64–7
    and the NHS, 62–4, 166–9
The New NHS: Modern, Dependable (White Paper), 62, 63, 66, 140, 168
NHS Community Care Act (1990), 41
NHS Trusts
    commissioning health care from, 59
    and Strategic HAs, 46
NHSE (NHS Executive)
    and CHD at Poppleton HA, 114
    and clinical governance, 64
    and HA accountability, 44–6
    and HA performance measures, 55
NICE (National Institute for Clinical Excellence), 64, 66, 167, 169
Nottingham Health Profile, 87
NSFs (national service frameworks), 65, 140–1, 167, 169
    and Baxby heart-failure guidelines, 145

and Baxby rapid access chest
pain clinic, 143
nurses
cardiac, 61, 62, 71, 78, 94, 96,
106, 120, 123, 146
and cholesterol measurement,
131

observers, role in observational
research, 4–5
Olsen, J., 17
optimum care, and HA objectives
and performance
monitoring, 58
organizational process model of
decision-making, 12
Our Healthier Nation (White
Paper), 57

participants
in garbage-can decision-making,
17
in observational studies, 5–6
partnership, New Labour on the
NHS and, 62
PBMA (programme budgeting and
marginal analysis) studies,
26–9, 30–1, 121
and the 'do nothing' option, 78
and 'dominant personalities', 38
and implementation, 32, 35, 36–7
PCGs (Primary Care Groups), 3–4
and accountability, 46
creation of, 63–4
and financial resources, 35
purchasers, and relationships of
trust, 49
see also Baxby PCG
PCTs (Primary Care Trusts), 168–9
and accountability, 46, 167
and Strategic HAs, 46
performance measurement in
HAs, 53–8

Pfeffer, J. and Salancik, G.,
resource dependence
model, 15–16
pluralistic models of
decision-making, 13–14, 20
at Poppleton HA, 155
policy proposals, and garbage-can
decision-making, 18
Poppleton HA, 42–4
and accountability, 46
budgets, 43–4, 64, 92
CHD and health economics in,
57, 67–76, 94–121
capacity and waiting-time
issues, 117
cardiac nurses, 61, 62, 71, 78,
94, 96, 106, 120, 123, 146
chest pain clinic, 111–12, 134
and diagnostic tests, 106–10
dynamic and uncertain
systems, 71–3
and echocardiography, 106–7,
113, 132–3
effects of no changes, 118–19
information deficits, 73–5
and stakeholder involvement,
70–1, 75, 102–10
and statin treatment, 77–93,
94–5
system-wide modelling of
CHD services, 94–121
tertiary cardiology services,
49–50, 74, 95–7, 98, 100,
107–9, 113–17, 119
and the York CHD model,
101–21
commissioning health care, 59
decision-making
'irrational', 154–6
and knowledge, 163
rational, 153, 154
reactive, 166
and statin treatment, 86–93

Poppleton HA – *continued*
  and street-level bureaucrats,
    164
  under uncertainty, 60–2
  directors and chief executive, 42–3
  and the efficiency index, 54
  and puzzlement around
    objectives, 58
  and relations of trust, 49–51, 52
  see also Baxby PCG
Posnett, J., 31, 37
postcode prescribing, 65, 169
power relations
  and decision-making, 21–2
    pluralist theories of, 14, 20
  medical power and health
    economics, 39
    and the Baxby chest pain
      clinic, 147–50
  and rationality, 22–6
  and reactive management, 37
prescribing budgets, 43–4, 63
primary care
  and CHD patients at Poppleton
    HA, 97–9
  nurse project, 106, 112–13, 120
primary prevention, and statin
  treatment, 78, 85, 130
priority-setting techniques, and the
  new NHS, 168
privatization, and HA
  accountability, 45
problems, and garbage-can
  decision-making, 17–18
professional groups, powers of in
  policy-making, 14
professional values, conflicts with
  social values, 66–7
providers, commissioning health
  care from, 59
PTCA (Percutaneous
  Transluminal Coronary
  Angioplasty), 98, 100,
  114–15, 117, 119, 120

public choice theories, and
    pluralistic models of
    decision-making, 14
public confidence in the NHS, and
    New Labour, 62
public expectations, and the new
    NHS, 158
purchaser–provider split, 14, 48
purchasing, *see* health-care
    purchasing reforms
puzzlement
  and garbage-can
    decision-making, 20–1
  and HA decision-makers, 37, 39,
    40
  and HA objectives and
    performance measurement,
    58

QALY (Quality Adjusted Life
    Year), 34
quality of life
  data, 42
  and decision-making at
    Poppleton HA, 87
  and the York CHD model, 103
quasi-market in health care, 41
  and accountability, 47

rationality
  and bureaucracy, 9–10
  and cognitive problems, 29–31
  and decision-making, 8–9, 153–4
    in the new NHS, 166–9
  defining, 8–9
  and implementation, 10, 29, 32–7
  New Labour and formal
    rationality, 64–7
  and power, 22–6
  substantive, 10, 160
  see also decision-making
rationing health care, 42, 169
RCTs (randomized controlled
    trials)

knowledge and decision-making,
162–3
and rational decision-making in
the NHS, 167
and statins, 88, 93, 124, 127
reality, and garbage-can
decision-making, 16
research diary, 6
resource allocation
and relationships of trust, 50–1
studies of, 35, 40
resource dependence model, 15–16
Rhodes, R., 33
Riverview HA
heart-failure guidelines, 133,
134, 135, 139, 141
statins guidelines, 83–4, 87, 124,
125–6, 130, 131
Rotherham HA, PBMA work at,
32, 121
Royal Colleges, influence on
policy-making, 14

Salaman, G., 15
Salford and Trafford HA, 116–17
satisficing, and rationality, 31
Schmitter, P., 13
secondary care, and CHD patients
at Poppleton HA, 99, 100,
106–7, 108, 112, 120–1
secondary prevention, and statin
treatment, 78–9, 83, 84–5
Shoreville HA
heart failure guidelines, 133
rapid access chest pain clinic,
142, 148
statins guidelines, 124
Simon, H., on bounded rationality,
11–12
SMAC (Standing Medical
Advisory Committee)
guidelines on statins, 84–5, 88,
89–90, 91–2, 157
and Baxby PCG, 110, 129

social values, conflicts with
professional values, 66–7
solutions, and garbage-can
decision-making, 17
spinal patients, investment in, 87,
89
staff recruitment, regional finance
in the NHS, 1
stakeholder involvement
at Poppleton HA, 70–1
in decision-making, 155–6,
162
and statins, 78–81, 81–3
and the York CHD model,
102–10
statins (cholesterol-lowering
drugs)
and Baxby PCG, developing a
statins guideline, 123–32
cost-effectiveness analysis of, 76,
77–93
decision-making about, 156,
159–60, 163
Strategic HAs, 46
Street, A., 31, 37
street-level bureaucrats, 25
and decision-making at
Poppleton HA, 164
substantive rationality, 10, 160

tattoo removal, 169
tertiary cardiology services, at
Poppleton HA, 49–50, 74,
95–7, 98, 100, 107–9, 113–17,
119
tertiary trust research and
development (R and D)
managers, 24, 74
trust, low-trust and high-trust
relationships, 47–53
Twaddle, S., 30

uncertain systems, at Poppleton
HA, 71–3

uncertainty
  decision-making under, 60–2
  and the prescription of statins,
    80
unitary models of decision-making,
    11, 18–19

Vale, P., 36, 37

waiting list targets, failure to meet,
    55
Walker, A., 30

Walley, T., 36
Weber, Max, 9–10, 65, 153, 159, 160
White, M., 66
Wolcott, H., 7
Woodhouse, E.J., 12
Working for Patients (NHS White
    Paper), 14, 41, 52

York CHD model, 101–21
York University, Centre for
    Reviews and Dissemination,
    42

HEALTH CARE REFORM
LEARNING FROM INTERNATIONAL EXPERIENCE

Chris Ham (ed.)

> If you want a broad introduction to international health care reform, written by some of the best health policy analysts alive today, then this is it.
>
> Chris Heginbotham

- What policies have been adopted to reform health care in Europe and North America?
- Which policies have worked and which have failed?
- What new initiatives are emerging onto the health policy agenda?

This book provides an up-to-date review and analysis of health care reform in five countries: Germany, Sweden, the Netherlands, the United Kingdom and the United States. It reviews the experiences of introducing competition into the health service as well as policies to strengthen management and change methods of paying hospitals and doctors. The experience of each country is described by experts from the countries concerned. In this lucid introduction, Chris Ham sets out the context of reform, and in the conclusion identifies the emerging lessons.

The book provides an authoritative introduction to health care reform in Europe and North America at a time of increasing political and public interest in this field. It has been designed for students of social policy and the full range of health service practitioners on courses of professional training.

Contents
The background – The United States – The United Kingdom – Sweden – The Netherlands – Germany – Lessons and conclusions – Index.

Contributors
Reinhard Busse, Chris Ham, Bradford Kirkman-Liff, Clas Rehnberg, Freidrich Wilhelm Schwartz and Wynand van de Ven.

160 pp   0 335 19889 9 (Paperback)   0 335 19890 2 (Hardback)

THE PURCHASING OF HEALTH CARE BY PRIMARY CARE ORGANIZATIONS
AN EVALUATION AND GUIDE TO FUTURE POLICY

Nicholas Mays, Sally Wyke, Gill Malbon and Nick Goodwin (eds)

Governments in a number of Western countries are attempting to improve the efficiency, appropriateness and equity of their health systems. One of the main ways of doing this is to devolve purchasing responsibility from national and regional to more local agencies based in primary care. These primary care organizations are allocated budgets that span both primary and secondary services. This book draws on an extensive government-funded evaluation of the UK primary care led total purchasing experiment to shed light on important questions raised by these policies. In particular, it attempts to answer these questions.

- Can general practitioner led primary care organizations successfully use an ability to purchase health services to achieve either more efficient or better health care for their patients?
- What are the ingredients of more or less successful primary care purchasing organizations?
- What lessons can be drawn from the experience of such a large and complex evaluation?

Contents

Health service development: what can be learned from the UK total purchasing experiment? – Designing the evaluation of the total purchasing experiment: problems and solutions – Developing primary care organizations – What did total purchasing pilots achieve? – How was change achieved? – Purchasing maternity care, mental health services and community care for older people – Managing emergency hospital activity – The management and transaction costs of total purchasing – Budget setting and its influence on the achievements of total purchasing pilots – Managing budgets and risk – Holding total purchasing pilots to account – Evaluating complex policies: what have we learned from total purchasing? – The total purchasing experiment: interpreting the evidence – The total purchasing experiment: a guide to future policy development? – References – Index.

352 pp   0 335 20900 9 (Paperback)   0 335 20901 7 (Hardback)

REFORMING MARKETS IN HEALTH CARE
AN ECONOMIC PERSPECTIVE

Peter C. Smith (ed.)

There has been an international move towards the creation of explicit markets in health care, in which the purchase of care is separated from provision. While the creation of such markets has undeniably led to improvements in certain aspects of health care, it has also raised important issues that have yet to be resolved – for example, is an escalation of management costs an inevitable consequence of the introduction of a market in health care? What sort of information is needed to make the market function efficiently? Can a market-based system be compatible with society's objectives relating to equity and solidarity? The UK government is introducing reforms to the internal health care market in the UK National Health Service which seek to address concerns such as these, and this book comprises a series of commentaries on their plans from a group of leading health economists. Authors examine the contribution of economics to the debate on the reforms, while seeking to make the analysis accessible to a general audience.

Reforming Markets in Health Care is recommended reading for students and researchers of health policy and health economics, as well as health professionals and policy makers at all levels in the health services.

Contents
Reforming health care markets – The cornerstone of Labour's 'new NHS': Reforming primary care – Towards a locally-based resource allocation – Longer-term agreements for health care services: What will they achieve? – Shaping up to improve health: The strategic leadership role of the new health authority – Economics and public policy – research and development as a public good – The performance framework: Taking account of economic behaviour – Performance indicators for managing primary care: The confounding problem – Reference costs and the pursuit of efficiency – A NICE start? Economic analysis within evidence-based clinical practice guidelines – Clinical governance: Striking a balance between checking and trusting – The new NHS: A principal-agent viewpoint – Index.

320 pp   0 335 20461 9 (Paperback)   0 335 20462 7 (Hardback)